OUT OF THE
VIETNAM VORTEX

OUT OF THE
VIETNAM
VORTEX

a
study
of poets
and poetry
against the war

by JAMES F. MERSMANN

THE UNIVERSITY PRESS OF KANSAS
Lawrence/Manhattan/Wichita

© Copyright 1974 by the University Press of Kansas
Printed in the United States of America
Designed by Fritz Reiber

Library of Congress Cataloging in Publication Data

Mersmann, James F.   1938–
    Out of the Vietnam vortex.

    Bibliography: p.
    1. Protest poetry, American—20th century—History and criticism. 2. Vietnamese Conflict, 1961–   —Literature and the war. I. Title.
PS309.P7M4   811'.05   73–17366
ISBN 0-7006-0113-9

Where permissible, quotations have been suitably credited in notes at the back of the book or inserted parenthetically in the text rather than listed on the copyright page. As required by some publishers, other credit lines are here listed.

W. H. Auden. *The Collected Poems of W. H. Auden.* Copyright © 1940 and renewed 1968 by W. H. Auden. Reprinted by permission of Random House, Inc.
From *The Light Around the Body* by Robert Bly. Copyright © 1967 by Robert Bly. By permission of Harper & Row, Publishers.
Reprinted from *Silence in the Snowy Fields,* Wesleyan University Press, 1962. Copyright © 1962 by Robert Bly. Reprinted by permission of the author.
The Teeth-Mother Naked at Last, by Robert Bly. Copyright © 1970 by Robert Bly. Reprinted by permission of City Lights Books.
Reprinted by permission of Dodd, Mead & Company, Inc., from *The Collected Poems of Rupert Brooke.* Copyright 1915 by Dodd, Mead & Company. Copyright renewed 1943 by Edward Marsh.
Revolutionary Letters, by Diane Di Prima. Copyright © 1971 by Diane Di Prima. Reprinted by permission of City Lights Books.
Robert Duncan. *Bending the Bow.* Copyright 1963, 1964, 1965, 1966, 1967, 1968 by Robert Duncan. Reprinted by permission of New Directions Publishing Corporation.
Lawrence Ferlinghetti, *The Secret Meaning of Things.* Copyright 1967 by Lawrence Ferlinghetti. Reprinted by permission of New Directions Publishing Corporation.
Reality Sandwiches, by Allen Ginsberg. Copyright © by Allen Ginsberg. Reprinted by permission of City Lights Books.
Planet News, by Allen Ginsberg. Copyright © 1968 by Allen Ginsberg. Reprinted by permission of City Lights Books.
Howl and Other Poems, by Allen Ginsberg. Copyright © 1956, 1959 by Allen Ginsberg. Reprinted by permission of City Lights Books.
Selection from Goethe's *Faust*, translated by Louis MacNeice, reprinted by permission of Oxford University Press.

iv

Dedicated to Karolyn
and our children
Dianne, Tim,
Jeff, and
Susan

PREFACE

The following study is a thematic analysis of the poetry written during the 1960s in protest of the American war in Vietnam. It focuses primarily on the works of Allen Ginsberg, Denise Levertov, Robert Bly, and Robert Duncan, and relates their work to the anti-war poems of other poets collected in the several anthologies growing out of the protest movement.

Unlike many thematic treatments of poetry from World War I and World War II, this study largely avoids paraphrased summaries of poems grouped by themes, and turns instead to integrated discussions of the full canons of four chosen poets, relating their protest poems to their poetics and other work in order to discover the common techniques, attitudes, and images that have shaped the poetic outpourings against the war. This approach offers the added advantages of seeing the "war poems" in their proper context, a context that can reveal (1) whether the war protest is a legitimate and natural outgrowth of the writer's world-view and poetic, (2) whether the experience of the war has altered a poet's beliefs and practices, (3) whether common themes and attitudes toward war and the culture are tied to similar biographies and philosophic tempers or arise equally well from different backgrounds, (4) whether a poet's protest is grounded in opportunism (protest being the fashion) or whether he is deeply committed, and (5) whether—as has so often been asserted—the protest poetry is generally inferior to the more detached and "objective" work of the same poets.

Beyond these considerations, the study hopes to raise numerous questions, many of which it can hope only partly to answer. Did the protest of the sixties grow out of the particular nature of *this* war? out of a changing attitude toward *war itself?* out of a changing consciousness that affects *all areas* of life? Has the changing direction of poetic theory affected, or has it been affected by, our attitudes toward war? Are both related to larger changes? What is the real value of the poetic imagination in matters of war or cultural survival? Is there an imagination large enough to shape a world without war?

Such questions as these necessarily imply at least a partial comparison of the poetry on Vietnam with the poetries of the two world wars. The first chapter, therefore, offers a brief overview of the poetries of two world wars, their assumptions, techniques, and themes.

The next four chapters turn to separate essays on the work of the four poets who have been among the most active against the war, and who offer a representative array of talents, "schools," backgrounds, and value systems. Allen Ginsberg is, of course, the acknowledged patriarch of the Beat Generation of poets. Denise Levertov, though she has sometimes been associated by critics with the Beats and the Black Mountain poets, does not rightly belong with either, and produces her own distinctive "poetry of the immediate." Robert Bly has been the most energetic "protestant" poet of the "new imagination," working with the deep or emotive image drawn untamed from the subconscious. Robert Duncan ranks with Charles Olson and ahead of Robert Creeley among those Black Mountain poets who trade in "composition by field." In religious orientations, Ginsberg is drawn to the religions of the East; Levertov has Jewish origins and Anglican loyalties; Bly operates out of what may at first seem a "secular-ethical" base; and Robert Duncan omnivorously takes all religion for his province. Respectively, they attempt in poetry to produce a "transcript of consciousness"; to say "Thou" to all persons and things; to mine the surreal riches just below the consciousness; and to allow the poem its own erratic imperatives. Geographic, economic, and social origins are similarly wide ranging. Where common themes emerge from these poets, then, we may with some confidence suppose that those themes reveal much about the general spirit and consciousness of our age.

Chapter six verifies the importance and representative nature of some of the common themes by finding them echoed and repeated in the poems of other poets against the war.

A final brief chapter summarizes the study's findings and suggests some probable conclusions.

ACKNOWLEDGMENTS

I wish to express my special thanks to Sister Mary Faith Schuster, O.S.B., my former colleague and incomparable friend, who was years ago my first and greatest undergraduate teacher of English. Her great soul and love of literature and people first awakened in me a kindred spirit and determined the direction of my life (I would otherwise perhaps have ended as chemist or accountant). She continues to teach and inspire me, still.

I am especially grateful to Professor Edward Grier of the University of Kansas for his helpful advice, and for the generosity and enthusiasm with which he encouraged this work. Special thanks also to Professors Victor Contoski and Michael Johnson for their generous help in reading and commenting on the text.

I wish to thank my friends and former colleagues at Benedictine College (where I taught while the book was in progress) for the quality of their association, for their good will and kindness. Especially meaningful has been the integrity and friendship of Mrs. Faye Lacy, Dr. Robert Brannan, Sr. Joan Offenberger, Dr. Frank Carpinelli, and Sr. Mary Faith Schuster.

I owe special gratitude to Mrs. Yvonne Willingham of the University Press of Kansas for her skillful and generous help in seeing the book through the press; to Miss Alexandra Mason and staff at the Kenneth Spencer Research Library for their assistance and patience; to Sr. Mary Noel Walter, former President of Benedictine College, for her vision in affording me the opportunity to work on the book; to my wife, Karolyn, for many hours of typing and for keeping life sane and whole; to my parents, Fred and Regina Mersmann, for life and for simple anchors in reality; to my children, brothers, sisters, and friends for making life worth caring and writing about.

Especially warm thanks go to the poets included in this study who have graciously cooperated with interviews and correspondence; and to all the poets against the war for their humanity and their concern for life and peace.

CONTENTS

New politics, new literatures and religions,
new inventions and arts.
These! my voice announcing—I will sleep no more,
but arise;
You oceans that have been calm within me! how I feel
you, fathomless, stirring, preparing
unprecedented waves and storms.

Walt Whitman, "Starting from Paumanok"

1 POETRY, POLITICS, AND PAST WARS

*Blake knew [that men lived by Law and Judgment
instead of Mercy] because Reason is so much easier than
Imagination. "An eye for an eye and a tooth for a tooth"
appeals to the reasoning faculty. It is a perfectly
logical statement of justice; but great is the imagination and
large the understanding of those who, without cant,
love their enemies and bless those that curse them.
Reasonably, this is impossible. It is the work of the
Imagination; the supreme work.*

Max Plowman, *An Introduction to the Study of Blake*

In *Peace with Honour*, a book inspired by the dark memory of the First World War and the gathering threat of the Second, A. A. Milne argues that modern war "as a new thought" would be "completely unthinkable." We accept war only because it has always been a part of our world and because we are unable to conceive a world without it. But, he insists, war is a human convention and not an inherent feature of the universe: "tell the innocent visitor from another world that two people were killed in Sarajevo, and that the best that Europe could do about it was to kill eleven million more."[1] We, like Milne, would like to believe war is not an ineluctable condition of man's existence; but the long evidence of history, as well as the present bellicose readiness to use violence at every level of life, demands that we indeed have an agile imagina-

3

tion. Civil and world leaders, rather obviously, have not been able
to imagine other ways of coping with the world's problems. Where
then, if anywhere, are we to find the imagination to transcend the
habit of war?

If war is a failure of the imagination—and William Blake
thought all failures were failures of the imagination—then there
are more than aesthetic reasons for giving serious study to the poetry
of war. Perhaps only here, if our traditional assumptions about
poets and poetry are correct, will be found the vision that can lead
to a world without war. What is the poetic imagination that speaks
about war and in protest of war? Has it changed? Are the changes
attributable to changes in war, changes in poetics, or changes in
consciousness? Is the poetic imagination able to offer believable
visions and alternatives to the present world in which war is inevitable?

Attitudes toward war, like most other attitudes, grow out of
a complex tangle of assumptions and dispositions, and no one is
likely to pinpoint precisely how the forces shaping the poetic reactions to Vietnam differ from those shaping the poetry of the world
wars. There are of course some differences so obvious as to seem
almost to disqualify comparisons: the most important poetry of
World War I came from British soldier-poets, while the Vietnam
protest comes from American civilians; in both world wars England
and America alike could imagine themselves heroic participants
in a war they did not choose but could not avoid, whereas in South-
east Asia, America has not been able to conceal a very different
profile. And yet, in surveying the poetry of the three wars, one
senses that the changes go deeper, are more truly *radical*, than can
be accounted for by these and other political circumstances.

Though the burden of this study is to explore the Vietnam War
poetry rather than compare war poetries, that exploration gains
significance when seen against the backdrop of previous modern
war poetry. The surveys that follow are necessarily brief.

I

If we look at the poetry of World War I, we find that it is
chiefly of three kinds—naïvely heroic-romantic, starkly realistic, or

radically socialistic—and that it was written respectively by English and American civilians and raw recruits, soldier-poets with battle experience, and left-wing American poets who saw only a "capitalist war" against which the workers of the world needed to unite.

i

The familiar tradition of war poetry prior to 1914 had been, of course, the heroic-romantic, and that manner suited well the spirit of empire and hearty muscularity proffered by Rudyard Kipling and W. E. Henley in the decades just before the war. And before the Oscar Wilde scandal turned the public away from the "Decadents" to the "healthy poets" and the innocuous velleities of the "Georgians," the English public had been able to find sustenance for the "British spirit" of empire in Decadent poetry, too. "After all 'decadence' can be regarded as 'a form of imperialism of the spirit, ambitious, arrogant, aggressive, waving the flag of human power over an ever wider and wider territory.' "[2]

The flavor of imperialism—not a conscious and ugly empire building or quest for territorial expansion, but a set of assumptions about one's self, one's country, and one's universe—is heavy in the early poetry of World War I. It is, for example, implicit in "The Soldier" by Rupert Brooke, a poem that deserves full quotation here for the several revelations it makes about the naïve-heroic:

If I should die, think only this of me:
    That there's some corner of a foreign field
That is for ever England. There shall be
    In that rich earth a richer dust concealed;
A dust whom England bore, shaped, made aware,
    Gave, once, her flowers to love, her ways to roam,
A body of England's breathing English air,
    Washed by the rivers blest by the suns of home.
And think, this heart, all evil shed away,
    A pulse in the eternal mind, no less
    Gives somewhere back the thoughts by England given;
Her sights and sounds; dreams happy as her day;
    And laughter, learnt of friends; and gentleness,
    In hearts at peace, under an English heaven.[3]

This famous, or perhaps now infamous, sonnet carries an adulatory patriotism such as few citizens anywhere today are capable of feeling for their fatherlands. Eyes have been opened too wide. It is not that such patriotism is or ever was evil (indeed, it is in many ways beautiful and praiseworthy), but rather that it was necessarily somewhat less than full-sighted, and therefore easily lured into foolishness or perverted toward evil ends.

In Brooke's vision of the enriched "corner of a foreign field" and the "English heaven," one detects, at some distance, some of the same presumptions that lie behind Kipling's "white man's burden." The poem is confident of an after-life and a reality where all things are ultimately just and orderly—a world that is, after all is said and done, the best of possible worlds. Implicit, but unmistakably present, is the assumption that England is on the side of God, and that in going to war, a holy war, she will be doing God's work. The sentiments of "The Soldier"—the glory of the fatherland, the fatherland as the scourge of God, the promise of eternal justice and reward, and the belief in the beauty of death—these permeate the poetry written and read by the English and American public during the war.

It would be easy, given the temper of the present time, to be unjustly harsh and disdainful of Brooke and others who wrote poetry of a similar feather. But it is important to remember that they too, like the best poets of today, were sensitive and generous men facing a great issue and trying to make honest poetic and personal sense of it. If from our present vantage point we see and believe them to have been wrong, it need in no way belittle them as persons or as poets. The ignorances of our own times will one day also be painfully clear to those who look back upon them. But though Brooke's attitudes and language were beautiful when he wrote them, and may be beautiful still, we are surely right in viewing their beauty as we might a plate of beautifully prepared but uncertain mushrooms.

That the skill and language of much of the popular verse of the First World War is far inferior to Brooke's is to be expected; and except for Brooke's poems, poetry in this vein has been largely ignored by critics. And it should be—except to notice what has not been sufficiently emphasized: the largeness of the gulf between the popular concept of war and war's reality, and the way in which the "habit of poetry" perpetuated and increased that gap. That the people were without Audie Murphy movies and television news-specials can only partly account for the public ignorance and sentimentality that so infuriated the soldier-poets in the trenches. Another part must be attributed to the habit of "redeeming" through the purifying language of poetry all that threatened to be disturbing or disorderly. Rather than admit estrangement from nature, one wrote a poem to nature; rather than fear death, one wrote a poem extolling it; rather than doubt popular eschatologies, one wrote a poem giving oneself fully to the faith. The language, the poetic diction, was itself a shield from the knowledge one sought to avoid. Only in this light can one account for the classical and medieval martial imagery of popular verse: chariots, warriors, swords, chargers, knights, maidens, thanes, and trumpets. Poetry of the kind gathered in *War Verse* and *A Treasury of War Poetry: British and American Poems of the World War 1914–1919* not only springs from an unreality but seeks to maintain and create the unreal.[4] It is as if any troublesome aspect of life needed only the saving grace of poetry to lift it to its eternal and beautiful significance in the perspective of the Hegelian grand design. Faith in the grand pattern, the consoling assumptions of a benevolent universe and a heroic righteousness, had to be maintained intact, and all else tailored and barbered to coincide. Certainly it was not a conscious dishonesty on anyone's part, but rather a "habit of poetry" that no longer very well fit the changing reality that poetry faced, or avoided facing, in the twentieth century. The very forms and conventions of poetry may well have helped delay a growth of consciousness, and shielded for a time the public and personal psyche from the meaning of modern war. For if the war was at all a psychic threat, that awareness never found its way to the surface of the poetry. The heroic complacencies of these poems, one feels, must surely be greater than those that the writers actually enjoyed.

Under the saccharine surfaces of the poetry romanticizing war, there seems also to have been a fascination with violence, and a boredom and revulsion that deserves to be called "anti-life." In

England especially, as Bernard Bergonzi has pointed out, all was not blue sky and English heaven. The forces of violence had been growing for fifteen years, and the fascinations of war and bloodshed were evident in Kipling's "The Islanders" (1902), G. K. Chesterton's *Napoleon of Notting Hill* (1904), H. H. Munro's *When William Came* (1913), the novels of H. G. Wells, Ezra Pound's "Altaforte," and in other literary productions of the time. Plagued by social and political ferment, strikes, suffragettes, and Irish discontent, liberal England was "riddled with self-doubt and preoccupied with violence" and berated by Kipling and Saki for its pacific lethargy. "It is not hard to see why the country should have found in the outbreak of the war, that apparent thunderbolt from a cloudless sky, something very like an act both of fulfillment and deliverance."[5] Such a context helps explain Rupert Brooke's "Peace":

> Now, God be thanked Who has matched us with His hour,
>   And caught our youth, and wakened us from sleeping,
> With hand made sure, clear eye, and sharpened power,
>   To turn, as swimmers into cleanness leaping,
> Glad from a world grown old and cold and weary,
>   Leave the sick hearts that honor could not move,
> And half-men, and their dirty songs and dreary,
>   And all the little emptiness of love!
>
> (*Collected Poems*, p. 101)

Brooke and his contemporaries were leaving physical health for physical danger, but saw in war an escape from psychic danger to psychic health. Life, as Brooke portrays it here, is indeed a sad and empty affair that one would readily trade in favor of a grand cause. But he seems to have no hint of the perception that the killing demanded by war in any way sullies the "cleanness" of his idea of war or the activity of his wakened soul.

The writer who so easily writes that war has no ills because "the worst friend and enemy is but Death," and "naught [is] broken save this body" has not seen the death and broken bodies witnessed by Edmund Blunden, Robert Graves, Charles Sorley, Wilfred Owens, Isaac Rosenberg, Siegfried Sassoon, and others who spent endless days in fields and trenches.

ii

The poetry of the soldier-poets has much in common, though it ranges from the "undertones" of war to the starkest graphicality. Though the poems sometimes achieve a stoic resignation, they are more characteristically angry and bitter complaints informed by a profound pity. For Owen, the "poetry was in the pity"; for Sassoon, it was in his resentment of the blind smugness of "scarlet majors," rotund businessmen, and starry-eyed housewives of England.

Whether inspired by pity, anger, or attempts to find war's significance, the poetry of the English soldier-poets is primarily a *poetry of the physical eye*. It is a visual poetry in that its sight is detailed, sharp-edged, and clear, and generally without the melting of lines and distinctions that come with a more interiorized, subjective poetry. To be sure, it calls upon all the five senses, but the lasting impression on the reader is the one etched into the visual memory. It is a masculine poetry, free of self-pity, free of self-doubt, brutal, crisp, courageous, compassionate. The emotions are deep, but the poet's feelings do not destroy his psychic stability, mine his spirit with guilt, or threaten his sense of a world that is ultimately rational and orderly. By seeking a starkly realistic honesty, the poet could best disabuse the public of its misconceptions and reveal the true pity of war without contaminating the truth with maudlin sentimentalities. War, if presented honestly, spoke for itself.

> The place was rotten with dead; green clumsy legs
> High-booted, sprawled and grovelled along the saps
> And trunks, face downward in the sucking mud,
> Wallowed like trodden sand-bags loosely filled;
> And naked, sodden buttocks, mats of hair,
> Bulged, clotted heads, slept in the plastering slime.
> And then the rain began—the jolly old rain!
> (Siegfried Sassoon, "Counter-Attack")[6]

> If in some smothering dreams, you too could pace
> Behind the wagon that we flung him in,
> And watch the white eyes writhing in his face,
> His hanging face, like a devil's sick of sin;

If you could hear, at every jolt, the blood
Come gargling from the froth-corrupted lungs
(Wilfred Owen, "Dulce et Decorum Est")[7]

To-day I found in Mametz Wood
A certain cure for lust of blood:
Where, propped against a shattered trunk
In a great mess of things unclean,
Sat a dead Boche; he scowled and stunk
With clothes and face a sodden green,
Big-bellied, spectacled, crop-haired,
Dribbling black blood from nose and beard.
(Robert Graves, "A Dead Boche")[8]

The trench poets had their eyes on the object. They did not attempt to put war in any historical perspective: the immediate reality was enough. War was ugly, inglorious, and stupid, and not at all like the heroic idea. Yet the poetry never pretends to imagine a world without it, nor did the poets generally experience the war as a spiritual threat. Perhaps worry about the spiritual effects of war is a luxury reserved for those who are stateside or at least behind the lines; but this poetry is nevertheless remarkably free of any agonizing about the nature of man. The pity and agony is rather that men are wounded and maimed and tormented, and not at all that men wound, and maim, and torment. The pity is that these young men who ought to be enjoying love and nature and English girls are instead cold, hungry, and slimed with mud. The soldier-poets had grown beyond the romantic assumptions about war to a realization that war brought mutilation and death and was a purposeless interruption of life.

Only well after the war were World War I poets able to move yet further and see the war as a blight or infection upon the earth:

What then, was war? No mere discord of flags
But an *infection* of the common sky
That sagged ominously upon the earth
Even when the season was the airiest May.
(Robert Graves, "Recalling War")[9]

But even if Graves and a few others were able to see war as a disease and therefore perhaps outside the healthy order of the universe, they nevertheless found it a familiar and inevitable presence. And, more importantly, even if war could be seen as a sore on the body of the universe, it had not yet chafed any existential sore on the forehead or soul of the individual. Instead, those oppressed by the lowering sky "thrust out boastful tongue, clenched fist and valiant yard."

iii

Very little poetry came from the pens of American combatants, largely because they saw action so briefly, and perhaps because they had experienced the war and its "heroic" dimensions from a distance (in the news and especially in civilian poetry) for several years prior to America's entry. Though much good American prose and fiction eventually spiraled from the war, the quality of American war poetry, civilian or soldier, was not high: "although thousands of minor American authors felt moved to write about the First World War, none was transformed by the conflict into a true poet. More important writers, of course, composed a few war pieces, but none produced a major poem."[10] The two most popular soldier-poets at the time were Joyce Kilmer and Alan Seeger, whose poetic reputations have now fallen below zero and whose poetry is now held up for derision, denied even the grace of oblivion. The civilian poetry prior to 1917 had high praise for England's "heroic dead," even though it leaned heavily toward America's staying out of the war. After America's entry, however, patriotic poetry flourished in a plethora of assertions that "Life is not lovelier than death may be."[11] These poems, too, assumed an eternal justice, a heavenly banquet of heroes in store for the fallen dead, and an evil enemy whose extirpation was the will of God.

But America, like England, had its internal unrest in the war decade, and not all of its civilian poets wore glasses tinted with the same hue. Anarchists and socialists saw the war as a battle of autocratic, greedy governments for power and wealth, and versified their propaganda against the insanity of fighting for bosses, emperors, and kings. Carl Sandburg was one of the more notable "poets of the people." His "Wars" seems prophetic of the spirit of the war protest of the 1960s.

> In the old wars Kings quarreling and thousands of men following
> In the new wars Kings quarreling and millions of men following
> In the wars to come Kings kicked under the dust and millions
>   of men following great causes not yet dreamed out
>   in the heads of men.[12]

Whether or not the war was presented as heroic or horrible, the poetry of World War I commonly accepted war as unavoidable, or readily pointed the blame to specific persons or classes of persons. The anger was directed at the smugness of individuals or the workings of an economic system.* The poetic voice did not turn in upon itself, collapse in despair at an absurd universe, or question assumptions and systems beyond an elementary level. Moreover, the verse for the most part adhered to rhymes and traditional meters, though it is interesting that "an avoidance of traditional techniques was particularly true of the left-wing authors."[13] (The relation between open and changing forms and revolutionary contents will be of continuing concern to this study.)

II

The poets of World War II differed from those of World War I, first of all, because they had the earlier poetry to build on. Not only did experience of the First World War end any possibility of the heroic-romantic war poem, but the realistic poetry of that war made it unnecessary to write further poems showing the grimness and pity of war. Not only would it be difficult to surpass Sassoon's picture in "Counter-Attack" for sheer physical horror, but also

---

* William R. Brown says of Sassoon: "Sassoon does not blame these people for anything more than their insensitivity; he does not blame them for causing the war or even for permitting the kind of world to exist in which war is inevitable." "American Soldier Poets of the Second World War" (Ph.D. dissertation, University of Michigan, 1965), p. 441. Indeed, Sassoon was himself a "fox-hunting man" and thoroughly accepted the social and economic status quo in England.

most people by 1940 were already more reluctant to boast *dulce et decorum est pro patria mori*. That poetry had been done, done well, and did not need to be done again. Furthermore, most of the poets of the later war did not often see the gruesome sights the earlier British poets had seen. World War II was fought on many fronts, with more mobility, more complex weaponry and logistics, and larger support systems. Many men served at sea, far behind the lines, in air or artillery squadrons, and saw the war only from some distance. The poetry likewise viewed the war with a greater distance and moved toward the more abstract and philosophical. Not any longer a poetry of the physical eye, it was ruminative and speculative, perhaps a poetry of the "mind."

"Redemption of disorder" was in this poetry still a primary function, however. Richard Fein sees in the five major voices of the Second World War—Karl Shapiro, John Ciardi, Randall Jarrell, Richard Eberhart, and Robert Lowell—a "poetry which while it recognizes the nature of war in the twentieth century also strives for an intelligent and artistic description and redemption of such disorder and inhumanity."[14] Of Lowell and Eberhart specifically: they "attempt to somehow override the sheer violence of the war with some knowledge that would make of the war more than meaningless destruction, yet that would not flinch from perceiving all the horror that war is."[15] (In contrast the Vietnam War poetry asserts that war is nothing but meaningless destruction.)

The very fact that poetry could continue to be a part of a country at war many chose to see as a justification of the national honor. Norman Cousins noticed, with what now seems strange naïveté, that Winston Churchill and Franklin Roosevelt quoted poetry in their speeches, but Adolf Hitler did not—poetry being the vehicle of light and truth, only those on the side of light and truth found it compatible with their purposes.[16] David Daiches similarly saw a green light for war poetry in England and America because they were on the right side:

> The artist is in a position where he can freely accept it as a part
> of his experience and include it without self-consciousness or
> inhibition among the materials on which he draws in creation.

This is not to say that war becomes under any circumstances welcome to the artist, anymore than to any other citizen; but he is now in a position where he can hate it as war, not as something which makes for dishonesty in art. It is surely neither sentimental nor naive to say that the poet in Germany or Japan today cannot accept the war and be honest as an artist, while the poet in Britain and America can. There can be no doubt in anyone's mind as to the nature and necessity of the struggle in which America is now fully engaged. The poet, therefore, can perform his function freely; there is no conflict between his duties as a citizen and as an artist. If his vision is timeless, it will also be timely, for all honest perception is today on our side.[17]

Poetry need not attack war or the enemy, but only show that man could endure with honor and dignity in spite of war. Kenneth Burke advised, "Let war be put forward as a *cultural* way of life, as one channel of effort *in which people can be profoundly human*, and you induce in the reader the fullest possible response to war, precisely such a response as might lead one to appreciate the preferable ways of peace."[18]

Because the war had to be fought, poets and public alike generally felt that there were some compensations in growth, courage, and manhood to be won from it. They approached the war wearily, not from the hardships of battle but from the awareness of the age-old and inescapable story of war. Painfully aware of two world wars occurring within twenty years, and a history cancerous with war, they accepted that it had always been so, would always be so—and that it was all very sad. The situation tastes of Jean Paul Sartre, Albert Camus, and *Waiting for Godot*. Quiet, stoic endurance, no heroics, a job to be done. War was part of the nature of things. Captain Donald Stauffer's letter to Oscar Williams sounded the representative note:

In the Olympian hierarchy, Mars and Apollo were not opposed deities, like Ormazd and Ahriman; they were independent spiritual forces whose sway and power men recognized and rightly respected.

It is as useless to consider that war and poetry are the same thing as to consider that they are unalterable opposites. If we must avoid the dilemma of choosing one or the other, we must also resist the temptation to identify them. Only by accepting them both as important parts of human experience and by trying to relate them may we do justice to the two forces and to our own intelligence.

I do not wish to try to establish a case for either war or poetry at the expense of the other, nor even a case for war *and* poetry. Human nature being what it is in its weaknesses, strengths, and desires, both war and poetry will continue to subsist very well without benefit of defense or argument. I should like to consider their close and mysterious relationship, and the strange fact that different though the two are, intimate contact of the one with the other seems to bring out the finest qualities both in war and in poetry. They are mutually sustaining.[19]

Others, too, saw war firmly rooted in man's nature. Richard Eberhart believed, "War is another kind of show than the peace show, intractable, profoundly ingrained in man's nature. It is the evil standing up" (*War Poets*, p. 19). Herbert Creekmore's words carry both acceptance of war and faith in its virtuous by-products: "Today's poets will not want the catharsis of the military monument and the paean of courage, but rather that of man progressing. From them will emerge, I believe, a detached and reasonable compromise position: war *is* hell, but hell is sometimes expedient; and as we go through it, let's be men, not so called in bombast, sycophancy and intrigue, but by virtue of justice in our own hearts" (*War Poets*, p. 28). Man's tininess in relation to the enduring and universal fact of war found expression in Karl Shapiro's *V-Letter*: "We learn that war is an affection of the human spirit, without any particular reference to 'values.' In the totality of striving and suffering we come to see the great configuration abstractly, with oneself at the center reduced in size but not in meaning, like a V-letter."[20]

Resignation is the dominant temper of World War II poetry as it struggles to salvage meaning in camaraderie, quiet bravery, and dedication to duty. There is little energy, either angry, indignant, or satiric. The poets of the First World War could be angry in their disillusionment about war because they were not disillusioned about the world. But poets of the Second World War were thus disillusioned, and world disillusionment leaves scant room for anger. Only the idealist knows anger; the pessimist or cynic is incapable of it. The poetry of World War II was not cynical, for that would have implied a too ready acceptance of evil, but the poets had gone a good many paces beyond idealism. The dominant temper was caught in lines Shapiro wrote to his compatriot Selden Rodman: "Look Selden, let's not follow the gleam / It's dynamite now to try to dream." Not only did poets lack the energy for satire, but they could find no obvious targets for it.* Not only were issues too large and complex to affix blame but there was little blame to be fixed where war was seen as inherent in man's nature. If the keynote of World War I poetry was pity for suffering men, a keynote of World War II poetry was pity for suffering mankind.

In describing the British poetry of the Second World War, Stephen Goode speaks again and again of "bitter despairing poetry," the "meaninglessness and emptiness" of life, "unabashed nihilism," "the conviction of the complete evil of mankind," "emptiness of the earth," "the futility of life," and "profound cynicism."[21] I have already suggested that "cynicism" is not a wholly accurate word for this poetry, and on the whole Goode paints the picture a bit too darkly, I believe. Certainly there is a loss of hope and positive vision, but the tone is resignation and endurance, not cynicism. There are, to be sure, some cynical poems. The best-known American poem, "The Death of the Ball-Turret Gunner," may indeed deserve that adjective, but it is neither representative of Randall Jarrell nor of British and American poetry in general. Granted that the British poetry was, with good cause, darker than the American verse, Jarrell's other war poetry more nearly mirrored the general temper of the poetry of both countries. Jarrell was seldom so barbed as in the

---

* There was "virtually no serious satire, for in a war of this complexity and magnitude the targets were either too massive for an effective assault, or the poet was too overwhelmed by the number of targets that flashed into and out of his sights, merging too rapidly for an effective focus." Charles Andrews, "A Thematic Guide to Selected American Poetry about the Second World War" (Ph.D. dissertation, Western Reserve University, 1967), p. 8.

"Ball-Turret Gunner"; more frequently, as in "Losses," he was off-hand, casual, matter of fact—sometimes, even, shall we say, "yawning."

> In our new planes, with our new crews, we bombed
> The ranges by the desert or the shore,
> Fired at towed targets, waited for our scores—
> And turned into replacements and woke up
> One morning, over England, operational.[22]

The technique affords mild but effective irony, but for the most part does not question war, systems of government, or the structure of the universe; it focuses instead on the gap between the ugliness of war and the humanity of the men who learn to perform it matter-of-factly. His conclusion generally was that though one perhaps cannot deny that man is a wolf to man, this poet, at least, could not condemn the men around him: "Men wash their hands, in blood, as best they can: / I find no fault in this just man" ("Eighth Air Force," p. 143). The echo of Pontius Pilate suggests, of course, that Jarrell's speaker is avoiding the real issue, that he should either condemn the men for their crimes or for not refusing obedience to those who send them to kill and be killed. As a matter of fact, Pilate may be taken as an excellent symbol of the poets of the Second World War, men who resigned themselves to an evil they felt helpless to avert.

Jarrell's submission—"It happens as it does because it does" ("Siegfried," p. 149); "The wars we lose, the wars we win; / and the world is—what it has been" ("Range in the Desert," p. 176)—takes on different guises in different poets, but is seldom entirely absent. In John Ciardi a similar acceptance may be recognized behind the ironic and grim humor he directed at himself in "Elegy Just in Case":

> Here lies the sgt.'s mortal wreck
> Lily spiked and termite kissed,
> Spiders pendant from his neck
> And a beetle on his wrist.[23]

Robert Lowell also, by juxtaposing "Mary and Bellona," Christianity and war, and shaping his poems around religious Holydays

("Christmas Eve Under Hooker's Statute," "On the Eve of the Feast of the Immaculate Conception," "To Peter Taylor on the Feast of the Epiphany"), accepted war as a permanent cross upon which suffering man might work out his individual salvation.[24]

Though many poets echoed Selden Rodman's plea, "Tell me, and tell the rest of us who believe / Against all signs; that something can be done / To stop the meaningless cycle Marx foresaw,"[25] they could seldom escape the refrain of James Schevill's "Siege of Leningrad": "Life is a fugue repeating war. / Time is the calendar of scars."[26]

Confronted with onmipresent war, the soldier-poets from both sides of the ocean could and did take solace in camaraderie and an uncomplaining devotion to duty. The civilian poets, lacking this, and perhaps feeling an inevitable guilt about their own safety and comfort, sometimes turned their eyes inward to examine and confess their own complicity. Marianne Moore's "In Distrust of Merits," probably the finest poem to come out of the war, is exemplary:

> Hate-hardened heart, O heart of iron,
>   iron is iron till it is rust.
> There never was a war that was
>   not inward; I must
> fight till I have conquered in myself what
>   causes war, but I would not believe it.
>   I inwardly did nothing.
>   O Iscariot-like crime!
>   Beauty is everlasting
>   and dust is for a time.[27]

Moore understands the solution to war, but she, too, fears that "the world's an orphan's home," and that we shall perhaps "never have peace without sorrow."

The English civilians, especially the Oxford poets, still saw the "rebirth of humanity in love" as the only answer to war, but by the 1940s they had lost most of their faith that the revolution would ever occur. The loss of Spain to Franco had hit hard. Visions of community gave way to images of futility and hysteria, as in Louis MacNeice's "Autumn Journal VII":

And as I go out I see a windscreen-wiper
   In an empty car
Wiping away like mad and I feel astounded
   That things have gone so far.[28]

W. H. Auden himself, having just changed shores, could only lament "the low dishonest decade" that had begun with Japan's invasion of Manchuria in 1931. He knew certainly that "We must love one another or die," but he was not taking bets on which we would do. All hope was reduced to vestigial "ironic points of light," and one could do no more than pray to hold on to his own remnant of integrity:

Defenseless under the night
Our world in stupor lies;
Yet, dotted everywhere,
Ironic points of light
Flash out wherever the Just
Exchange their messages:
May I, composed like them
Of Eros and of dust,
Beleaguered by the same
Negation and despair,
Show an affirming flame.

                                     ("September 1, 1939")[29]

The shift of sensibility between the two world wars takes on a shape not unlike the behavior of young Hamlet. Upon first being initiated into previously unguessed evils, he is both energized with rage and obsessed with the specific unlovely images of rank weeds, enseamed beds, and his mother's lechery. With time to ruminate, and as more and more evil manifests itself, his initial anger is "sicklied o'er with the pale cast of thought," and he falls into a profound and ineffective melancholy. World War I poets, after they had given up the sugared sonnets of Wittenberg sophomores, wrote poetry obsessed with the specific horrors of war; World War II poets, having seen too much of evil, were enervated by a sense of universal blight. Both viewpoints assumed a larger unchanging reality, a human and universal nature beyond the understanding or control of man. The first group was outraged because that reality was not perfect; the second group was devastated by the thought that it was generally corrupt.

III

Much has happened since the poetry of World War II was written. The end of World War II itself, the events of August 6 and 9, 1945, carried cultural, philosophic, and spiritual implications that are not yet fully understood. Moreover, the United States has grown greatly as a world power and can no longer dream of itself as valiant underdog: the heroic David has become the terrible Goliath —and the Vietnam War has helped us experience this in a new way. Hardly less important have been the advent of television, increased urbanization and population, rising levels of education, the glamour and dashed hopes of the Kennedy era, the burst of political assassinations, the "Death of God" theology, the "new morality," moon exploration, and "mind-expanding" drugs, to name only a few.

Important social changes have been paralleled by equally significant shifts in the shapes and attentions of poetry in general. Certainly important among these are the changing ideas about the relationship between poetry and politics, the poem and the poet. The idea that neither a man's life nor his poetry can be divided into compartments is especially strong only in very recent years, though, of course, it was simply assumed in classical times without need of argument. The fragmentation of functions and personalities may have begun with the "dissociation of sensibilities" in the seventeenth century but it has increased greatly, for a number of reasons, in the last hundred years.

T. S. Eliot himself believed strongly in the distinction between the man and the poet, and between the poet and his work, and desired that these should keep their proper distance from one another. The poet was to be the catalyst, storing and transmuting experience but seeking always the negative capability, the objective correlative, and a proper aesthetic distance. During the Spanish

Civil War, Eliot could still argue (perhaps with some good sense) that it would be "better for poetry" if at least some of the poets abstained from involvement in the issues of that passion-fraught war. He, of course, planned to be one of the abstainers.* William Butler Yeats, too, had felt a wide gulf between the poet and the political exigencies of his day, and "On Being Asked for a War Poem" curtly refused to involve himself in the issues of the First World War:

> I think it better that in times like these
> A poet's mouth be silent, for in truth
> We have no gift to set a statesman right;
> He has had enough of meddling who can please
> A young girl in the indolence of her youth,
> Or an old man upon a winter's night.[30]

Yeats's attitude is no doubt related, though distantly, to that mentality that so angered Siegfried Sassoon—the mentality that assumed England could have its war and still have its "poetry" at the same time.

Poets of the thirties and the Spanish Civil War, in spite of their abundant political energies, were still cowed by the sense that politics and poetry really did not mix, and tormented themselves with questions about whether they were responding to the events and "rhetoric" as political men, or to the meaning and feeling of those events as poets.[31] On the American side, in the Preface to his *Reactionary Essays*, Allen Tate called for a divorce of poetry and politics and argued that "A political poetry, or a poetical politics, of whatever denomination is a society of two members living on each other's washing. They devour each other in the end. It is

---

* Only a few writers refused to take sides, and it is interesting that Ezra Pound, T. S. Eliot, and H. G. Wells were among them. Of 148 replies to questionnaires sent out by the editors of *Authors Take Sides*, 127 favored the Republic. Eliot's reply was: "I still feel convinced that it is best that at least a few men of letters should remain isolated, and take no part in these collective activities." Hugh D. Ford, *A Poet's War: British Poets and the Spanish Civil War* (Philadelphia: University of Pennsylvania Press, 1965), p. 88–89.

the heresy of spiritual cannibalism."[32] Similar arguments have persisted in academic circles throughout the Vietnam War.

But arguments against politics in poetry have also a political bias, and grow out of an analytic rather than synthetic, a disjunctive rather than unitive, mentality. In subtle ways, all poetry is unavoidably political in its very choice of form. Dante understood that he was recreating a cosmology in his *Comedy* by his use of *terza rima*, triads, and decads. John Dryden's and Alexander Pope's couplets, though less consciously, carry an important correspondence to their ideas of government and world order, just as Whitman's expansive catalogues and long breaths are inseparable from his democratic enthusiasms. The New Critics' insistence upon tension, conflict, paradox, and irony likewise contains a world view that has both political origins and implications. One may even learn to realize that the absence of certain content becomes itself a "content." In poetry, perhaps more than in any other communication, there is more than a modicum of truth to the idea that the medium is the message. A number of critics, most notably Leo Spitzer, the enthusiastic advocate of "linguistic criticism," have understood that "the style is the man"; there seems reason to believe that the style is even more specifically the man's biography, religion, philosophy, epistemology, and politics.

Perhaps neither "political poetry" nor "war poetry," alone, is a sufficient label for the poetry studied in the following chapters. The terms are, obviously, widely overlapping but non-synonymous: there are war poems without ostensible political content and intention, and political poems that appear to have little relation to war. (Generally, more of the poetry written about the world wars than about Vietnam is without wider political implications.) And yet, in another sense, there cannot be a war poem that is not political, nor a political poem without some pertinence to war. A good case may be made, too, for calling any poetry written during the active war years "war poetry," since the contamination of war is usually so pervasive it cannot be wholly ignored in poetic activity of any kind. Moreover, some poets argue that every poem is political, for its very existence implies something about how the world should be shaped and governed. It is easy, then, to understand the impatience of poets about questions of classification, and easy to share their distaste for reductive definitions.

In general, contemporary poets vehemently reject any thinking that assigns taboos and "proper" roles for poetry. Much of Allen Tate's argument in the *Reactionary Essays* would be acceptable to the poets of the sixties (primarily he dislikes poetry of "the practical will," since poetry should rightly *apprehend*, not program or promote) but his viewpoint is partly prompted, as past concepts of poetry so often have been, by the assumption of "a place for everything and everything in its place." A similar concern for proper things in proper places can be recognized behind the recent fears and complaints of critics within the academies about the stridency and "inferior quality" of the Vietnam protest poetry. In the protest poem the poet is "too emotionally involved" and fails to meet the standards of objectivity and neutrality that science, New Criticism, and value-neutral "academic freedom" have conditioned intellectuals to expect. It is not the war alone, however, that is to be blamed for the increasing breaches of objective proprieties (though it has accelerated them), for the rebellion has been growing steadily for twenty years, spurred by such apparently polar influences as Charles Olson's "Projective Verse" essay and Allen Ginsberg's "Howl."

Neutrality, objectivity, careful categories, and neat divisions are no longer sacred but are instead generally anathema to contemporary poets. Certainly the strong sense of dichotomy between politics and poetry has irretrievably crumbled away. For example, Galway Kinnell—surely one of the more soft-spoken of spokesmen —believes that all poetry is rightly political just as all poetry is religious because it attempts to break through, rend, or transcend the barriers and veils that separate men from one another and from the divine. (His "The Bear," for instance, dealing as it does with the violence of the hunt, seems to him as political as his Vietnam poem "Vapor Trail Reflected in the Frog Pond.")[33]

Distinctions between poetry and politics have been only part of the larger wall that has for years separated art from the life it was to mirror, criticize, and re-create. Writing at the end of the fifties, Barbara Gibbs and Francis Golffing could already sense "that poets are seeking, in one gut-bursting effort, to finally break through that 'fence' which has plagued them through the centuries and has become unbearable."[34]

As distances between the poem and the world have shortened, so has the gap between the poet and the poem. It has never been fully safe to assume that the "I" of a poem is the person of the poet, for the poet must be given the freedom of his large imagination and his ability to see and speak with others' eyes and voices. Yet the idea of *personae* that grew up in the time of early Pound and Eliot and bore its brittle fruit in the New Criticism has not been applied to the masks of Fra Lippo Lippi or Kliff Klingenhagen but has often been used instead to anesthetize the emotional umbilical between the life of the poem and the life of the poet, or to inoculate poetry against the disease of "interestedness." The poem was not to be read as a statement but as an artistic exploration of the possibilities of statement. The *personae* idea was then not so much a substitution of voices as it was, in a sense, a denial of any "voice" at all.

The revolt against just such an emasculated concept of poetry is very much a part of the revolt against Vietnam. An egregious example of how the two come together can be seen in Robert Bly's attack on the insensitivity and "American ambiguities" in James Dickey's *Buckdancer's Choice*, a book that critics generally acclaimed:

> We can only lay this blindness to one thing: a brainwashing of readers by the New Critics. Their academic jabber about "personae" has taken root. Instead of thinking about the content, they instantly say, "Oh, that isn't Dickey in the 'Firebombing' poem! That is a persona!" This is supposed to solve everything. ... There are no personas. The new critical ideas do not apply at all. Readers go on applying them anyway, in fear of the content they might have to face if they faced the poem as they face a human being.[35]

The turning away from "distancing" and "personae" can be seen in recent years generally in the abundance of confessional poetry, and in poetry's focus on immediate experience and the person; the abandonment of a poetic diction and regular rhythms in favor of spoken cadences has likewise reduced the inclination toward poetic masks.* In the protest poetry especially, where poems are intended as witness and testament and are often shaped for protest readings, the voice is nearly always the poet's own. If it is not the poet's, it is usually of the poet's idea of himself as he observes that second person of his trinity. Though discussion of such unions is best left to St. Thomas Aquinas, we are right in feeling that though the first and second person of this trinity are different, they are somehow also the same. In approaching anti-war poetry we seem generally on safe ground in assuming that the "I" of the poem is indeed the voice of the poet (except, of course, where it speaks with the accent of a Georgia cracker, or is given all the wrong lines). There are also instances, however, in which the "I" is only the locus or reification of the five senses at work in the poem, or the hole through which the wind of the imagination is allowed to blow.

IV

Certainly the poet's life would be more comfortable if he could ignore political situations. At the same moment they felt the necessity to speak, the poets against the Vietnam War also felt a certain helplessness and futility. At the Angry Arts Week activities in New York, January 29–February 5, 1967, Mitchell Goodman confessed, "I don't know why we're here—unless it is just to torment ourselves." At the related symposium on "The War, The Artist, His Work," Harold Rosenberg complained, " 'What can art do in politics? Nothing except say, "I'm against this war." But to expect that you can produce a result is a dumb idea.'...'you can't go about your business these days, *especially* if you're an artist. That

---

* Ed Dorn remarked that contemporary poets have turned to a "visceral" poetry of experience and have learned that before they try to go to the river for water, they have to learn to urinate in their own bucket. The way to a poetry that speaks with authority is through a poetry that understands the self and speaks with one's own voice. (Poetry Writing Seminar at the University of Kansas, Spring 1969.)

is a disaster. Nobody can go about any creative work without having this thing over their shoulders.'...'art cannot be itself without criticizing the world.' "[36]

The art that cannot be itself without criticizing the world is not the same art (nor the same world) as that in which there once was safety from disorder and chaos. Peter Whigham speaks for most contemporary poets in claiming:

> We do not seek safety in Art.
> We recognize Art as a serious business
> Art has "sociological concerns."[37]

For many of those who were not open to a poetry with "sociological concerns" before the mid-sixties, the Vietnam War brought about a conversion. Some were quicker to change than others. Perhaps those poets of the Black Mountain persuasion held on a bit longer to Charles Olson's idea that "the only object is a man, carved out of himself, so wrought he fills his given space, makes traceries sufficient of others' needs (here is social action, for the poet, anyway, his politics, his news)."[38] But the war "entered" Robert Duncan's poems anyway. Poets found that they could no longer "fill their space" without speaking out, and could not survive in silence either as poets or as men. Denise Levertov first held with Olson, but she later says of "Life at War," "I couldn't write anything *but* a political poem because this was what was on my mind night and day."[39] Of Yeats's poem and reaction she claims, "It isn't so much that we think we can set the statesman right as that, because we are verbal people, we have the obligation to be the spokesmen for humanity, and that it can't be left to the statesmen, whether they're honest statesmen or dishonest statesmen . . . ." That art can no longer be taken simply as one of the amenities of life, one statesman, President Johnson, abruptly discovered in the events surrounding the "White House Festival of the Arts," 14 June 1965. When Robert Lowell, in protest of American action in Vietnam, retracted his acceptance of the President's invitation to participate, "The roar in the Oval Office could be heard all the way into the East Wing."[40] Johnson's pain continued through the actual festival, whereat John Hersey read from *Hiroshima,* and Phyllis McGinley, extempore, chided Mrs. Johnson's failure to applaud him:

> And while the pot of culture's
>   bubblesome,
> Praise poets even when they're
>   troublesome.[41]

V

As we shall see in the following chapters, the new attitudes of poets and the new voice of poetry in matters of politics and war seem to be intimately connected with the shift toward a more open poetics. That shift itself seems to coincide with a general shift in the educated culture's *operative* philosophic temper away from the filtered-down but persisting assumptions of scholasticism and rationalism toward more existential values and a sense of an "open universe." "Open poetry" and "open forms," we may infer, are somehow importantly tied to an "open universe." There is little imagination for change in a universe or a human nature irrevocably locked in by *a priori* laws and limitation, a static and unchanging order. Only in an open universe can anything new be expected under the sun—and only in an open-ended human nature where "existence precedes essence" can man imagine himself rising above the ubiquitous scourge of war or discovering possibilities for a different, fuller, and more ecstatic life than he has known throughout history.

In years when the forces interested in maintaining the status quo and the old values have been in fearful reaction against the possibility of change, poetry has been energized by new forms, visions, and spiritual impulses. In the fifties Kenneth Rexroth pretended in characteristic hyperbole to see the arts and poetry already in open revolt:

> "For ten years after the Second War there was a convergence of interest—the Business Community, military imperialism, political reaction, the hysterical, tear and mud drenched guilt of the ex-Stalinist, ex-Trotskyite American intellectuals, the highly organ-

ized academic and literary employment agency of the Neoanti-reconstructionists—what might be called the meliorists of the White Citizens' League . . . . This ministry of all the talents formed a dense crust of custom over American cultural life—more of an ice pack. Ultimately the living water underneath just got so damn hot the ice pack has begun to melt, rot, break up and drift away into Arctic oblivion. This is all there is to it."[42]

The real revolution, however, did not come until the Gulf of Tonkin incident and America's large-scale entry into the Vietnam War. In poetry the revolt had been preparing for twenty years. Since the early fifties the precise petals of New Criticism's metallic flower had slowly begun to fall before the fire of "open composition." The revolutionist and visionary poets William Blake, D. H. Lawrence, and Walt Whitman, too much neglected and disdained in the forties, were coming into their own even in the academies; and the young were already turning away from Urizen toward the "wisdom of the blood" and the "one institution of the dear love of comrades." ("Dear D. H. Lawrence, Thanks for getting your foot in the door," writes one of my students.) Gary Snyder and the San Francisco poets had infected almost all poetry with an interest in the insights of the East, and Allen Ginsberg had opened wide the gates for attack on America and on Western values.

With the deepening of American involvement in Vietnam, the changing voice of American poetry made itself heard with a new insistence. "There are drums beating in the distance, America. / They beat with a new and different rhythm." "America, have you guessed it? Your new spirit is speaking to you."

> You [Walt Whitman] tried to speak to us once,
> About something you discovered in the June grass,
> Something precious and warm and pulsating,
> Beating with the beat which is wild with love,
> But we were too entranced by another vision,
> A hard, metallic vision with steel wings
> And copper rivets and gold edges . . .
> We didn't hear you.[43]

The new spirit—not new except in its ubiquity—is the Whitmanesque rebellion against rigidity, in favor of spontaneity, all-embracing love, and the apotheosis of a spiritualized American dream.

2

ALLEN GINSBERG: BREAKING OUT

Vivas to those who have fail'd!
("Song of Myself," Section 18)

*I will go to the bank by the wood and become
undisguised and naked.*
("Song of Myself," Section 2)
Whitman

There are many reasons why a study of the protest poetry of the sixties properly begins with Allen Ginsberg. Ginsberg is not the best, and surely not the most typical, poet of the decade, but the impulses that find exaggerated statement in his life and poetry are found in more muted tones in the writings of nearly every poet at work in this period; and though his poetry and poetic creed may still be at the periphery of general poetic practice, he seems to express the *Zeitgeist*, or that portion of the larger poetic spirit that is peculiar to this moment in history, unique to this time.

Many of the impulses that Ginsberg has elevated to the status of celebrated causes have perhaps been common to poets at all times, though they have never seemed so vital and endangered as in the 1960s. Poets have always gone to battle against the dull, the stiff, the constricted, the limited quotidian perception, the encroachments of death-in-life, and have always more or less opted for the spontaneous, the imaginative, the spiritual, the sensuous. But the battle has never been pressed too strenuously; there has always been room and time for circumspection, always a place for reasonable compromise and accommodation. And if the poet demanded certain freedoms for poetry, he was seldom so troublesome as to insist that these freedoms also extend immediately into all other realms of public and private life. The poet had been able to work with certain constraints and limitations of poetic form, and indeed even welcomed them and found them essential; and if the tyrannies of his social and political existence were greater than he could have tolerated in his artistic concerns, he was generally able to keep the two halves of his life separate and go on with his work. Only in very recent years has the dividing wall begun to be chipped away beyond the possibility of repair. Some have variously welcomed its demise and seen it as poetry's "emancipation," or warned of its dangers and abhorred it as a "contamination" of poetry. But few have worked so hard to crash through the paling as Allen Ginsberg. The energy that he has devoted to the annihilation of this barrier is only part of his larger effort to destroy division and restraints of every kind.

I

If the reader is to appreciate the integrity of Ginsberg's outcry against all forms of spiritual and psychological oppression, he needs first to appreciate how cruel Ginsberg's experience of those forces has been. If Ginsberg's poetic rantings are generally successful and convincing where others fail, it may be largely because he speaks from experience and has earned his right to shout. What John Ciardi has written of William Burroughs surely applies to Ginsberg: "Though many readers will find this writing revolting, the revulsion is from reality. Its passion has been suffered rather than theorized."[1] Unlike those whose protest is necessarily modish and insincere, Ginsberg knows his enemy firsthand; his stance has not been conceptually determined but has been experientially evolved; and he has sufficient cause to champion "our true personal feelings rather than the homogenized national TV feelings" and similar introjected values that tormented his early life.[2]

Anyone acquainted with "Kaddish" will understand something of Ginsberg's excruciating struggle, but even the voice of "Kaddish" is a voice that has survived and transcended the experiences; only in the early poems of *The Empty Mirror* do we find Ginsberg's struggle nakedly revealed in a voice too embattled to protest, too confused and guilt-ridden to shout.[3] If Ginsberg's mature poetry "communicates excitement like a voice yelling from inside a police car," this youthful poetry communicates the muted terror of a child lost in a city at night.[4]

Though it is not overtly political, anti-war, or social protest, the little *Empty Mirror* volume demands treatment here because (1) it establishes the autobiographical nature of Ginsberg's poetry and demands from us a different critical approach, (2) it records the origin and source of Ginsberg's rebellion, (3) it demonstrates that his poetry is essentially all "anti-war" poetry, and (4) it points to an important relation between the content and form of his writing.

Almost from the first page of *Empty Mirror* it becomes apparent that one cannot deal with these poems adequately by conventional standards alone; there is not much possibility of treating these verses as made-objects, aesthetically washed and distanced from the grime of their experience. Here is a man revealing himself in all his fear, naïveté, and desperate longing for normality and acceptance; "here, indeed, is an Israelite in whom there is no guile" but much terror and despair. Ginsberg the rebel, it becomes clear, was first Ginsberg the victim. This kind of personal and autobiographical poetry cannot be any more appropriately measured by the sextants and calipers of conventional criticism than skyscrapers can be measured by cupfuls. One may choose not to be interested in such poetry, but one cannot justly condemn it on grounds that are in fact quite extraneous to it. Such poetry begs to be read as impassioned poetic autobiography and perhaps requires not so much analysis as psychoanalysis. Approached in this way, these poems hardly seem deserving of Ciardi's general dismissal of Beat poetry— "Sorry boys: I find it zany without illumination, precious rather than personal, and just plain dull,"[5] or James Dickey's characterization as "of the familiar our-love-against-their-madness-and-money variety."[6] We must, if we care about humanity and are not entirely caught up in art, objects, abstractions, and arguments, find something interesting in the passions and doubts displayed in such poems. It is true that Ginsberg's poems are not so polished and permanent as to be interesting as finished figurines and sculpture; but they are interesting as flowing amoebas engulfing or fleeing the random particulate experience they encounter, or as naked, shaggy, fibrillating paramecia, shuddering with excitement or revulsion. They offer the soul, brain, guts, and jissum of the man with unique honesty—fully and boisterously in the later work, tentatively and sadly in these early poems. If it is true that it is the outward texture, the exoskeleton of the poem alone that makes it interesting centuries after the inspiration and the life of its content has passed, then Ginsberg's poems are merely timely and not enduring; they rarely give us experience fully digested and secreted as flesh-polished mother-of-pearl, but offer instead the raw experience, the exposed mussel. And yet in parts of "Howl," "Kaddish," and "Wichita Vortex Sutra" the passion is animated enough to have an endoskeleton of its own that may endure as an interesting object after its topical life has shriveled away. But it is always vitality and authenticity, not imposed order, that Ginsberg seeks in his poetic form as well as in his life.

The Empty Mirror records the beginning of Ginsberg's search for wholeness and authenticity. Like all quests for light, it begins in darkness. William Carlos Williams sees in this volume an almost Dantesque darkness. We may well go beyond Williams's hint and see the book as a descent into Ginsberg's private hell, as the play-by-play account of his neurasthenic wrestlings with the angels of self-pity, guilt, alienation, and despair. These poems record the dark night of the soul of a scatological St. John of the Cross; these, though they possess neither the faith nor energy of Gerard Manley Hopkins or John Donne, are Ginsberg's "terrible sonnets." It is from this base of suffering that Ginsberg survives to launch his life-long campaign against the mind-forged manacles that cause such agonies.

To readers acquainted only with Ginsberg's writings after "Howl," the *Empty Mirror* poems will come as a surprise. The first poem establishes the dominant themes and reveals a characteristic rhythm:

> I feel as if I am at a dead
> end and so I am finished.
> All spiritual facts I realize
> are true but I never escape
> the feeling of being closed in
> and the sordidness of self,
> the futility of all that I
> have seen and done and said.
> Maybe if I continued things
> would please me more but now
> I have no hope and I am tired.   (*Mirror*, p. 7)

These are confined measures like Williams's but they lack the organic energy and cadencing of Williams's own, and display something of the broken and halting tentativeness that Robert Creeley cultivates in his vestigial verbal squeezings. Contrasted with "Howl," these constricted lines, controlled and obedient to another man's rhythm, seem pathetic indeed. Apparently written before Ginsberg had his Blakean visions, this poem encapsulates many of the issues with which his entire life and poetic career have been concerned. There is here the painful gap between known spiritual facts and vitally experienced truth; the alienation and separateness; the inadequate and guilt-ridden self-image; the feeling of sordidness; the sensation that all things lack any ultimate significance; and the societally conditioned response—"Maybe if I continued things would please me more." At this point Ginsberg, like most men, seeks to overcome his separateness by conformity, and internalizes the guilt for his failure to be comfortably assimilated into the status quo.

Fearing insanity, suffering from aberrations both physical and mental, Ginsberg reveals the degree of his hopelessness:

> ... what a
> terrible future. I am twenty-three,
> year of the iron birthday,
> gate of darkness. I am ill,   ("Tonite," *Mirror*, p. 8)

How sick I am!
   that thought
always comes to me
   with horror.
Is it this strange
   for everybody?   ("Marijuana Notation," *Mirror*, p. 19)

This latter poem, and the volume generally, carries a wistful pathos reminiscent of Thomas Hardy's "Impercipient." In that poem Hardy, too, is an outsider, not because he willfully rejects the faith that is such a salve to others, but because he is incapable of feeling it, because instead of seeing "the glorious distant sea" he sees only "dark and windswept pine." "Why joys they've found I cannot find, / abides a mystery" not only to Hardy but to Ginsberg as well. Ginsberg is not an alien because he dislikes the world in which others have found comfort, but because he himself cannot partake of it, and suffers from an incapacity that he does not choose.

    There are infrequent moments of order and clarity in *The Empty Mirror* when assimilation into the world as it is seems to be at least a possibility, and Ginsberg is able to write a poem as hopeful as "A Desolation." This four-stanza poem, though it possesses a greater aesthetic distance and objectivity, is nevertheless still transparently an expression of Ginsberg's own reaching for "normalcy."

What have I done but
wander with my eyes
in the trees? So I
will build: wife,
family, and seek
for neighbors.

   Or I
perish of lonesomeness
or want of food or
lightning or the bear
(must tame the hart
and wear the bear.)   (*Mirror*, p. 27)

    Looking back on this twenty years later, one has to feel that it would have been tragic if Ginsberg had succeeded in taming the hart and wearing the bear. But his desire for a place in the universal wilderness where he might feel "awake and at home" is real, and still manifests itself in the sixties in such poems as "This Form of Life Needs Sex" and in his frequently professed desire to have children. In the late fifties, Diana Trilling (no doubt solipsistically and erroneously) saw Ginsberg's need for union and affection as a desire for "respectability" and acceptance by such "fathers" as Lionel and the Columbia English faculty.[7]

"A Desolation" is an anomaly in *The Empty Mirror*, and one suspects it came at a moment after hospital treatment had momentarily "re-conditioned" Ginsberg for life-suburbia-style. Such moments of heart-wrenching hopefulness do not stand up long against the onslaught of Ginsberg's unique psychological problems. The more characteristic note is a Hardyesque darkness and despair that lacks Hardy's strength. (Indeed, Hardy is on Ginsberg's mind in these years; perhaps Ginsberg sensed a kindred spirit and possible source of strength.) In these years life is for him "Oh God, how horrible!" returning at night to his attic on

> the old ghetto side
> of the street I tenement
>   in company with obscure
> Bartlebys and Judes,
>   cadaverous men,
> Shrouded men, soft white
> fleshed failures creeping
> in and out of rooms like
>   myself. Remembering
>
> ("Walking Home at Night," *Mirror*, p. 45)

Ginsberg was surrounded with failure, in his home, in Paterson, in Harlem, and in himself; and that word, "failure," remains omnipresent (along with "paranoia") in Ginsberg's later poetry and prose. Fear and failure are the weightiest burdens Ginsberg carried in these years when he thought of himself as "meat creephood." He "was lonely" and alienated and took all the guilt of it upon himself, not yet having the awareness or the freedom to point the finger at forces outside of himself.

But there are a few poems in this early volume that show that greater awareness and psychological freedom were beginning to develop. In many of the poems Ginsberg is simply talking to himself, sorting through things, implicitly or explicitly formulating precepts by which to endure. Occasionally he achieves an objectivity free of guilty self-laceration and captures his own and modern man's predicament, the predicament against which he later devotes all his energies.

> Man lives like the unhappy
> whore on River Street who
> in her Eternity gets only
>
> a couple of bucks and a lot
> of snide remarks in return
> for seeking physical love
>
> the best way she knows how,
> never really heard of a glad
> job or joyous marriage or
>
> a difference in the heart:
> or thinks it isn't for her,
> which is her worst misery.
>
> ("The Terms in Which I Think of Reality," *Mirror*, p. 29)

The ubiquitous "I" of Ginsberg's poems is temporarily absent here, but surely the whore's "worst misery" is precisely his own at this time. One comes away from these poems with a new appreciation of the confusion, loneliness, and trauma that Ginsberg experienced; and the term "lacklove," which recurs again and again in his later poetry, takes on significance. Displayed here is a unique ingenuousness and a unique struggle, and unless one is concerned with art only as art, he can hardly avoid finding the *Empty Mirror* poems interesting and moving. They are not merely honest, but skillfully honest. In the Preface, Williams says of them, "the poem is not suspect, the craft is flawless"; they are "prose but prose among whose words the terror of their truth has been discovered" (p. 6). (The latter compliment is one that perhaps applies also to the best of Ginsberg's later poetry.) What is pertinent to this study is that these poems reveal the young poet living in the social world where Williams and Wallace Stevens were at home, writing of that experience in its acceptable measured rhythms, and feeling miserable and alien to both the life and the poetic form. Neither grows organically out of the self; and, more tragically, there is as yet no self to sustain any such growth. Both are received, borrowed, imposed, obeyed—both contain the poet but are not contained by him.

II

The Empty Mirror is the one volume of Ginsberg's poems that is not "anti-war." It is the volume in which he is busy discovering the enemy. Subsequent poetry is a war against the Moloch not named but experienced in *The Empty Mirror*. In *Empty Mirror* he is not on the outside describing and criticizing but on the inside agonizing. To speak for him in his later idiom (an idiom he is incapable of at this time): "Moloch! Eater of men! Miserable in the bowels of Moloch!"

Actual physical war, in Vietnam or elsewhere, Ginsberg in time comes to see as only one, though the most visible and ostensibly horrible, of the inevitable activities of a Moloch whose essence is "lacklove." To critics who in 1965 and 1966 were suddenly confronted by his explanation of Vietnam as "lacklove" ("Who Be Kind To") or as Carry Nation's smashing of saloons ("Wichita Vortex Sutra"), Ginsberg's political outlook may seem facile indeed, and deserving of dismissal as "a composite of ready-made-radical-isms-good-for-a-cheer."[8] But Ginsberg did not come to his political or aesthetic radicalisms, nor they to him, ready-made. They evolved painfully over the twenty-nine years before 1955 and are still evolving. The transition from *The Empty Mirror* to the breakthrough in "Howl" was itself gradual and difficult, and possible at all only through exhaustion and defeat. During these years Ginsberg went through a succession of analysts—Reichians, Freudians, and Sullivanians—and spent eight months in a mental hospital. When he was not on the couch or in the sanitarium he was struggling to fit into the "real world" as he still then conceived it, working at a long procession of jobs, including copyboy and market-research analyst. In a letter to Neal Cassaday in 1953, written after he had lost another job, he writes: "Needless to say I am as usual all hung up in every way on the wrong kicks—now I don't know what I'll do about a job again in the long run—maybe I should become a social bum . . . or look and still make the social effort to adjust, etc. And I still at this old age am torn between various kinds of sexual impulses which I don't, can't satisfy."[9] It is obvious that he has here not yet solved the question of whose values and expectations are to be primary in his life.

One of the "wrong kicks" that Ginsberg had just discovered at the time of the letter was Zen painting, and from that, an introduction to Zen philosophy and religious insights. He shares his excitement with Cassaday in animated and guileless language. The paintings lead him to D. T. Susuki's *Introduction to Zen Buddhism* and the immediate result is the poem "Sakyamuni Coming Out from the Mountain." In it one detects Ginsberg identifying with the Buddha, the sufferer, the man who has given up desire and realized his smallness before the Absolute World.

> [Sakyamuni] who sought Heaven
>   under a mountain of stone,
>   sat thinking
>   till he realized
>   the land of blessedness exists
>   in the imagination—
>   the flash come:
>   empty mirror—
> how painful to be born again
>   wearing a fine beard,
>   reentering the world
> a bitter wreck of a sage:
>   earth before him his only path.
>   We can see his soul,
>   he knows nothing
>   like a god:
>   shaken

meek wretch—
     humility is beatness
          before the absolute World.[10]

Here is a new vista opening for Ginsberg, a new avenue of
adjustment, a new stance to take with regard to the "separation"
he experiences. The poem above shows that he understands and
identifies with a "beatness" that need not be guilty, but which is
common to spiritual men. It is the opening of a new and alternative
reality, the beginning of his *experiences* of the "spiritual facts" he
had known were true but didn't feel in *The Empty Mirror*. Part of
his new insight is not unlike that of Socrates in "The Apology" and
"Phaedo" where he claims that *the only wisdom is to know that
one is not wise* and to accept that truth. It is significant that the
line and rhythm are still essentially those of Williams's poetry, but
the format has opened up and the poem now has "air" in it; the
smallness is no longer constricted and congested as in the poems of
The Empty Mirror. The momentary serenity achieved by such a
significant spiritual discovery can achieve permanence only after
years of discipline and cultivation, and writing one poem in the
flush of discovery does not really change how a poet relates to himself and to the world. This poem, nevertheless, marks a beginning
and is an important milestone along the road toward "Howl" and
beyond.

The Sakyamuni poem also shows a growth in the ability to get
a larger view into a poem, a perspective that sees more of the world
and has more universal application. Many of Ginsberg's later poems
are perhaps unforgivably narcissistic and solipsistic, but at least there
are moments when he succeeds in capturing the world at a glance,
or in catching truth that applies not to one but to all men. Of the
Mirror poems Williams had said, "This young Jewish boy, already
not so young anymore, has recognized something that had escaped
most of the modern age, he has found that man is lost in the world
of his own head" (Preface). Those poems do indeed show that he
is lost in that world, but not that he really understands this fact.
A man seldom knows where he is lost while he is lost. But with
the discovery of Zen, Ginsberg, unlike Archimedes, finds a new

place to stand to assess and move his world. In doing so he finds it is "amazing to realize how truly we create our own world—delight and romance out of our own hearts. As if youth's sweetness, once gone, can be re-created in another elder form of activity and delight through the realization that the feeling we have for existence is up to us to choose. One choice I made before was the empty mirror. Now I will make a brighter and fuller. Amen" (Letter to Cassaday).

The empty mirror was not really a free choice, however; it had been conditioned from without, and the mirror was empty because the self was atrophied. What this and bits of other poems reveal is that Ginsberg is slowly coming to Coleridge's awareness that "we receive but what we give," and that modern man has nothing to give because all his values are external and introjected rather than native and organic. No doubt this emphasis on the person, the true self under the mask of social ego-self, was increased by Zen's insistence on the primacy of personal experience and all knowledge coming from within. As Ginsberg begins to look to sanctity and the powers of the self, he begins to experience and speak of the conflict between the inner and outer man in terms of real warfare. For all his innocence and innate humanity in choosing a "brighter and fuller" world, reality is not so responsive to man's subjective decisions, and demands an active and prolonged fight against all that is dim and narrow. The world we choose must first do battle with the world that is.

The one poem of *The Empty Mirror* where the verse form points toward the later cataloguing and bardic breath of "Howl" is also the one poem that threatens open rebellion against the system; and it is here that Ginsberg first speaks of this contention as war. Almost unconsciously, it seems, Ginsberg begins to perceive the market-place world as a war zone where ignorant armies clash by day and where one risks mortal psychic wounds in quest of "success" and material gain:

> old clerks in their asylums of fat, the slobs and dumbells
> > of the ego with money and power
> to hire and fire and make and break and fart and justify
> > their reality of wrath

and rumor of wrath to wrath-weary man,
what war I enter and for what a prize! the dead prick of
    commonplace obsession

("Paterson," Mirror, p. 39)

Implicit here is the assumption that the same dispositional complex
or "wrath" that brings physical mutilation on the battlefield is also
the source of the psychic scars and existential wounds of competitive
American society. This disposition has in fact shaped its own
"reality," and within the terms of that reality the disposition itself
is the inevitable and rationally defensible one. But the reality is
one of fear, lunacy, and joylessness; it is built on artificiality, death,
and impotence. The last image indicates how inextricably bound
together are Ginsberg's perceptions in political, psychological, and
sexual matters.

As out of place as the conjunction of Longinus and Ginsberg
may seem, one cannot help feeling that here as in "Howl" the
metaphors are spontaneous and spring naturally from genuine passion, and that "the proper time for using metaphors is when the
passions roll like a torrent and sweep a multitude of them down
their resistless flood" *(On the Sublime)*. One suspects that few poets
share the special experiences and revulsions necessary to find a more
expressive metaphor than the "asylums of fat." It is against these
loveless relationships and this moribund sexuality that Ginsberg
later celebrates his "college of the body."

In a number of other poems written after *The Empty Mirror*
but before the outburst of "Howl," Ginsberg reveals a growing
awareness of the soul of America as the sleeping giant who dreams
of war, or as a battleground in which people daily fight a war
against their real desires in order to "get ahead" and meet external
expectations. The burdens of this daily self-rape seem more painful
to this poet than to most men. His reactions are not conceptual and
objective, but highly subjective; they are not facile condemnations,
but painfully experienced struggles. In "Paterson," Ginsberg had
given himself to howling hyperbole in expressing his revulsion
against the market-place world, and had claimed he would "rather
crawl on my naked belly over the tincans of Cincinnati; / rather

drag a rotten railroad tie to a Golgotha in the Rockies" than to face daily the "department store supervisory employees." Such rejections of this world increase in number after 1953, as do the instances of martial imagery. In "My Alba" Ginsberg decries the lost years he has spent in offices where he, too, "deceived multitudes / in vast conspiracies / deodorant battleships" (*Reality*, p. 7). This last image is startlingly strange, and yet it brings together elements from the opposite extremes of deceit and artificiality and makes their connection seem inevitable. Between the sophisticated prudery of the office and the cold power of the battleship, Ginsberg senses a huge conspiracy that stifles life, that hates and seeks to destroy the living flesh.

In the years between 1948 and 1955 Ginsberg is never really sure of the validity of this perception. He is not sure which is reality and which is illusion, whether it is he or the world that is crazy. Like the angel-headed hipsters of "Howl," he suspects he is "only mad" "when Baltimore gleams in supernatural ecstasy," and though his daily experience is becoming increasingly anarchic and scandalous by conventional standards, he is not at all confident that his actions are not evil aberrations. For the most part these are years of terrible conflict when his natural inclinations lead him into situations that bring condemnation from the establishment. After befriending the hapless Herbert Huncke and subsequently being involved in the tangle of Huncke's thieveries, Ginsberg does not know how to understand the reactions of his father, professors, and psychiatrists. It was, he explains,

> an archetypal situation where a kid gets busted and a lot of middle-class values are offended and the whole family gets excited and says, "Why does it have to be *our* son? Why does he *do* these things?" And where the lawyer is paternal and helpful but is like saying, "Abandon everybody! Abandon these terrible people." And where the youthful offender, like me, becomes very confused and unsure of himself and doesn't know what he's doing and feels like he must have made some terrific cosmic *error*.[11]

Thus, in spite of his overtly rebellious actions, he paid for his failure to live up to the imposed values with serious inner torment.

Though already in 1953 he could write the "Green Automobile" to Neal Cassaday (the "Dean Moriarity" of Jack Kerouac's *On the Road*) and idealize their Denver escapades as a war against all the limitations to ecstasy and joy, he was yet far from certain of their mission to be

> ... real heroes now
> in a war between our cocks and time:
> let's be the angels of the world's desire
>   and take the world to bed with us before we die.
>
> (Reality, p. 15)

The "Green Automobile" celebrates or over-celebrates what has been called the "juvenile camaraderie" of Jack Kerouac's picaresque Beat bible. The lines attempt a dithyrambic justification of Dionysiac youthful abandon, but lack mature conviction. The insight may be real enough—that life parades for most people under a false banner of reality—but there seems little potential for amelioration by

>   driving drunk on boulevards
> where armies march and still parade
> staggering under the invisible
>   banner of Reality—   (*Reality*, p. 13)

More pertinent is the reappearance of the military language. This poem also speaks of smashing sweet bottles of muscatel "on Diesels in allegiance" creating "ageless monuments to love" and "memorials built out of our own bodies"; all of which echo the pageantry of ship-launchings and VJ-Day demagoguery. Apparently his mother's and society's specific and general insanity during World War II left impressions that shape the images with which Ginsberg experiences reality.

In the poem "Siesta in Xbalba," written during Ginsberg's Cuba and Yucatan expedition in 1954, there is a more calculated focus on the warlike insensitivity of our culture. In staying among the ruins of Yucatan among weathering images of man's quest of the divine, Ginsberg feels nostalgia for

> the classic stations
> of the earth,
> the ancient continent
> I have not seen

and is painfully mindful of

> the few years
> of memory left
> before the ultimate night
> of war   (*Reality*, p. 30)

In a mood not unlike "Dover Beach," Ginsberg (who later rejects history as for the most part irrelevant) seems to associate Europe and the Yucatan ruins with spirituality and grandeur much as Henry James might. In speaking of the ultimate night of war he is not speaking only of the possible nuclear holocaust, but of the deadening effect of the culture to which he must return, and which in a few years will have dulled his present sensitivity and closed him in to the ultimate darkness and false reality of the Denver boulevards. The experience of the ruins and the trip outside the United States gave him new perspectives and temporary respite from nagging self-incriminations. In lines of admirable discipline and economy he condemns America and identifies in himself an anterior urge associated with the spirituality of Europe and the Mayan ruins:

> There is a god
> dying in America
> already created
> in the imagination of men
> made palpable
> for adoration:
> there is an inner
> anterior image
> of divinity
> beckoning me out
> to pilgrimage.
> O future, unimaginable God.   (*Reality*, p. 33)

These lines are prophetic and hopeful, showing a faith that he will succeed somehow in discovering this God. He has behind him already the Blake visions and his experimentations with hallucinogenic yage, but here it seems the God he seeks is more grand and substantial than any he has yet known.

The trip seems to have given him new strength and confidence, and he shucks off momentarily the self-disgust that colors his early poems. The last lines of Part II of "Siesta in Xbalba" catch the Whitmanesque confidence and stride as no other of his poems have to this time. One glimpses here that the healthy muscularity of Whitman has replaced the emasculated inadequacies and hyperbolic celebrations of the body.

> —Returning
> armed with New Testament,
> critic of horse and mule,
> tanned and bearded
> satisfying Whitman, concerned
> with a few Traditions,
> metrical, mystical, manly
> . . . and certain characteristic flaws
> —enough! (*Reality*, p. 38)

The traditions that now concern him are of a higher kind; they no longer box him in but lead him out to a new pilgrimage. At this point he not only endures and survives the "characteristic flaws" and sources of alienation he shares with Whitman—but carries them lightly as a knapsack that makes the hike only more satisfying. Enough, it is good. He has the strength to face the future. But what he faces is an America oblivious to the meaning of Yucatan, a country that has cheapened its God for purposes of easy adoration, reduced Him to something confined to churches and to the golden rule so expedient for capitalism (the "fair play" competitive business ethic that replaces communion and love). It has built a justice of retribution and fear that persecutes the spirit Ginsberg momentarily enjoys:

> The nation over the border
> grinds its arms and dreams
> of war: I see

the fiery blue clash
of metal wheels
clanking in the industries
of night, and
detonation of infernal bombs

. . . and the silent downtown
of the States
in watery dusk submersion.   (*Reality*, p. 39)

Such lines would seem to possess enough discipline and texture to
please Cleanth Brooks, and yet the richness and cohesion of images
seems unpremeditated. Without pushing the incipient metaphors
too far, Ginsberg suggests the nightmare giant grinding its teeth
in the watery dusk of its dream of reality. In some of the poems of
this interim period, Ginsberg is at his best because he is discovering,
finding order, and almost living up to Denise Levertov's ideal of
making "poems of an inner harmony in utter contrast to the chaos
in which they exist." In them he is at moments free from either
a debilitating anxiety or a political cause to promote.

Had Ginsberg returned to the East Coast after his Cuba and
Yucatan expedition, his poetic development might have been different—he might have been able to compromise with the straight
world and embrace it in a growing Whitmanesque capacity to love
and accept the evil along with the good. But he himself sensed that
his move across the country was the end of one season of his life
and the beginning of another.[12] The escape from Paterson was not
abrupt, however; during his first two years on the West Coast he
was plagued with doubts and tormented by the conflict between
his desires and the demands of society. He held various jobs for
brief periods and generally chafed under the restraints and demands
of steady employment. In his poetry of 1954 and 1955, and in
numerous comments to interviewers in later years, Ginsberg reveals
these to have been years in which he felt a sense of failure and un-
easiness about not having made the expected "healthy adjustments."

In a sense, Ginsberg was trying to serve two masters, Moloch
and Dionysus: the daytime god of market research, propriety, conformity, and success was in sore conflict with the nighttime ecstatic

god of jazz, drugs, and poetry. The former made too many demands, and the latter seems not to have been compensatingly fulfilling, for the poetry indicates life was wasting away without the tenderness, consolation, and union that Ginsberg sought. No doubt each world tainted and undermined the validity of the other.

The forces of Moloch and Dionysus are thus frequently counterposed in poems, with war and orgiastic sexuality acting as the respective synecdoche of each. This hyperbolic juxtaposition of war and sexuality had occurred already in "Paterson," but gets heaviest use during and after the mid-fifties. It is perhaps indirectly present even in the obscene instructions he gives America for use of its atom bomb at the beginning of "America." Normally it is more explicit. The most striking image and compressed paradigm of this juxtaposition occurs in "To an Old Poet in Peru," where Ginsberg speaks of "the joy of armies naked / fucking on the battlefield" (*Reality*, p. 81). Whether or not such an image may be offensive to some poetry readers, its effectiveness cannot be questioned. The uninhibited, orgiastic abandon is the extreme opposite of the orderly, uniformed, strategically calculated killing of the flesh. Though orgies are not primarily procreative in purpose, orgy is here the sign of life, fertility, and creation as opposed to the death, sterility, and destructiveness of war. Here, at a breath, is the genesis and the nemesis, the two polar forces of existence, caught at the apocalyptic moment of life-victory when swords are traded for fleshy ploughshares. And the opposition is more inclusive than love and war. A whole complex of polarities collides around this primary opposition in Ginsberg's poetry, and in life and poetry everywhere: freedom-restraint, compassion-anger, selflessness-selfishness, content-form, genius-art, imagination-reason, spirit-matter, true-Self–ego-Self, openness-defensiveness, spontaneity-control, subjectivity-objectivity. The list could be made very long, but the opposition chiefly has to do with conflicts of freedom and restraint, spontaneity and control, emotion and reason.

Surprisingly, Ginsberg's special way of juxtaposing war and sex was anticipated at the time of World War I by none other than the surprising Amy Lowell. The war/sex or war/love conflict is, of course, as old as myth and literature, but Lowell's "Patterns" carries new implications and perceptions that are interestingly similar to those of Ginsberg. Like Ginsberg, Amy Lowell senses that war is a "pattern" closely related to other patterns that constrict, stiffen, and stifle life. Her passion, too, "wars against the stiff brocade." The brocade hides and denies "the softness of a woman bathing in a marble basin" and is, along with the lover's heavy boots and rough thick uniform, in conflict with the water, the cool lime tree, the blessing of sunlight, the expression of love and passion. In her imagination the buttons of his waistcoat bruise her body; and the unfeeling and "patterned" death letter (growing out of the same system) bruises her soul. The man that would have released her from the "button, hook, and lace" is dead in another "pattern called a war. / Christ! What are patterns for?" It is especially important that a broad spectrum of concerns are contained here between opposite and antagonistic extremes: the life and tenderness of love and sexual union, and the death and rigidity of war.

At the time of "Patterns," faith in the logical, orderly Western manner was beginning to falter; and Lowell believed innovations in poetic form were directly related to this change of life-styles. She says of the "new manner" of poetry after 1914 that it "is not a dress assumed at will, it is the result of a changed attitude towards life," and that it "is an inevitable change, reflecting the evolution of life."[13] Ginsberg's expansion of Lowell's attitude toward pattern and imposed static order seems also an evolutional progression and part of a changing approach to life. Ginsberg's life and work are an expansion of the impulse struggling toward expression in "Patterns," an expression made easier for him by the general spirit of his time and his own contact with Eastern religions, drugs, and psychotherapy.

III

In "Howl" Ginsberg shucks off the stiff brocade of inhibitions that his culture imposed on him. It is a therapeutic disburdening and breaking free, and the freedom shows itself in the form as well as the content of the poem. It comes at the same moment in Ginsberg's history that he breaks thoroughly away from traditional life-styles and behavior. The break grows out of Ginsberg's sessions with a psychiatrist who, he says, "gave me the authority, so to speak, to be myself." After long explorations of Ginsberg's discontent, the psychiatrist had asked Ginsberg, " 'What would you like to do? What is your desire really?' " What Ginsberg would really like to do was never to go to work again, to give himself totally to exploring perceptions and visions, "to keep living with someone—maybe even a man—and explore relationships." But Ginsberg's captivity is evident insofar as he could not express this to his therapist without considerable apologetic prefaces (" 'Doctor, I don't think you're going to find this very healthy and clear' "). When the doctor's response was " 'Well, why don't you?' " Ginsberg was astounded—what would the American Psychoanalytic Association say about *that* kind of advice! He hadn't followed his desires because his life-long experience and his past psychoanalysis had made him feel "that kind of screwy thinking wasn't exactly contributing toward my general development."[14]

What Ginsberg had long "really wanted to do" is apparent in his poetry. His felt need for love and tenderness might be interpreted as almost pathological, but it may be that his long history of psychotherapy simply made him more aware of the need and less inhibited about expressing it. Sometimes the need and the desire is expressed in the most sensitive and gentle terms, at other times in a language that makes it impossible for most readers to understand that what is sought is spiritual as well as erotic love. Ginsberg painfully experiences his "separateness," feels he is "no one" and is cut off from human affection. Flying across the United States on a business trip in 1954, his thoughts were:

Better I make
a thornful pilgrimage on theory
feet to suffer the total
isolation of the bum,
than this hipster
business family journey
—crossing U.S. at night—

in a sudden glimpse
me being no one in the air
nothing but clouds in the moonlight
with humans fucking
underneath   (*Reality*, p. 46)

After his permission "to be himself," Ginsberg embraces "the total isolation of the bum," arranges (for purposes of unemployment insurance) to be fired from his job, moves into a small apartment with Peter Orlovsky, and one long weekend, with no other anesthetic than amphetamines and peyote, gives birth to "Howl."

"Howl" is the moment of breakthrough, the violent externalization of the ulcerous guilt of Ginsberg's discontent. Poetry is act, not object; but the more genuine the act, the more fully shaped is the object that is left behind. Poetic acts may be precise or passionate, careful or carefree—the clothes they leave behind will be their own, and differences in kind need not be differences in quality. "Howl" is not "The Red Wheelbarrow," but neither poem wears borrowed or ill-fitting clothes. "Howl" is a shaggy poem, the explosive purgation of what has been too long held in; the blast of words and feelings that have long been hoarded. (See Edmund Wilson's "Morose Ben Jonson" on the linguistic habits of the anal erotic.[15]) To criticize "Howl" for its lack of control, or as Cleanth Brooks does, for its lack of balance and tension, is to criticize it for being the very thing it claims to be. It is the breakout from control, the escape from tension. To use something like a Zen paradox, its control is lack of control, its tension tensionless.

More so than most readers have realized, "Howl" is a vehement anti-war poem. It is anti-war in its specific statements and in its stance towards "control." The poem describes, blames, purges, and transcends the world of relative consciousness, the It-World as described by Martin Buber in his *I and Thou* classic, the world of things, of walls, and doors, and inhibitions, and discriminations. The title page of "Howl" carries below the author's name these lines of Whitman: "Unscrew the locks from the doors! / Unscrew the doors themselves from their jambs!" The stops are also loosed from the tongue and the throat, and Ginsberg's own long Melvillean-Hebraic-Bardic breath asserts its native rights over the borrowed forms of William Carlos Williams. Influenced by the prose of Jack Kerouac and the new freedom to be himself, Ginsberg claims to have written "Howl" thinking that it would not be published (what would his father think of the experiences it describes?). Ginsberg, recalling his first passionate reading of "Howl" before a receptive crowd in San Francisco, tells us that Kerouac exclaimed, " 'Ginsberg, this poem "Howl" will make you famous in San Francisco,' but Rexroth said, 'No, this poem will make you famous from bridge to bridge,' which sounded like hyperbole, but I guess it did."[16]

"Howl" cannot be imitated. One can never learn by art to write such a poem. It is a historical document, the record of the individual and the moment in time when a century's build-up of pressure erupts and vents itself. Kenneth Rexroth's explanation of the Beat phenomena (quoted in chapter 1, p. 27–28) may be an oversimplification, but it seems true that in Ginsberg's case the living water underneath the dense crust and ice pack "just got so damn hot" that it burst through. "Howl" is the primary example of modern poetry's "gut-bursting effort" to finally break through the fence between poetry and life. For those who assume that the fence is inviolable, and that poetry should be consciously made and invented, it may seem that "Howl" is "pathetically dependent on a concurrent movement of literary opinion, on the *Zeitgeist* as familiar ally," and that it "simply puts its fingers between its teeth and whistles up all its friends."[17] But the history behind the poet and the poem would seem to make it more than only that. It is not merely dependent upon the *Zeitgeist* but is itself one of the larger eruptions of a growing spirit reaching back to the French Revolution, maturing in Kierkegaard, and spreading in the present lust for Eastern paradox in place of Aristotelian logic. There are rigid aristocracies and hierarchies to be overthrown in philosophy, theology, psychology, epistemology, and poetics as well as in governments. (Wits may be quick to point out that Ginsberg's revolution in form has been followed by a Reign of Terror by a multitude of poetic Robespierres.)

A look at the specific images of "Howl" reveals that behind the professed and apparent spontaneity there is a well-defined and consistent position. Our interest at this moment concerns only those explicit references to war and the implicit attitudes towards "patterns." It is readily clear that Ginsberg has no specific war in mind except the inevitable one that must come again and again to the culture he describes; and it is clear that he sees the daily experience of living in that ambience as a war against the spirit. The first section of "Howl" is almost totally description of the sufferings of the hipsters, and only a few glimpses of the forces that are responsible. The first of these instances associates academia with war. The madmen of "Howl" are those "who passed through universities with radiant cool eyes hallucinating / Arkansas and Blake-light tragedy among the scholars of war."[18] The scholars of war are a part of a university-Pentagon alliance that does indeed "study" war and its machinery, but more importantly, Blake might describe them as scholars of war in that they are servants and captives of Urizen rather than imagination. They are busy building the "mind-forged manacles" that destroy the radiant cool eyes, defeat and annihilate the angelic nature of the mystic with the cold sterile steel and iron of cause and effect and syllogism. (Blake's "London" suggests that man's desire to manacle and "charter" results in all manner of evil: harlotry, infant abuse, adult fear, religious persecution, soldier's sighs, and blood running down palace walls.) Further light on the "scholars of war" may be found in Ginsberg's analysis of the ideas and teachers he encountered at Columbia. John Crowe Ransom and Allen Tate were "like the supreme literary touchstones. Joyce and Lawrence were the property of funny modernist cats like William York Tindall, who were considered eccentric by the rest of the faculty." Almost no Whitman was taught and, like Shelley, Whitman "was considered like a creep." Even though William Carlos Williams lived but thirteen miles away, he was largely an "unknown factor." Pound was taught only as "a freak-out."

> In economics, they had like Louis Hacker teaching the triumph
> of capitalism. In history, it was Jacques Barzun, who was just
> teaching politeness. Anthropology was more or less dead. And
> the French Department was filled by old, sour-tempered profes-

sors whose idea of contemporary French literature was a few reactionary novels written about 1910. And there was a total lack of any sublime teaching. A lack of teachers with praxis for the delicate religious areas that we were approaching *intellectually* in all those seminars on Plotinus and Plato but never really entering.[19]

Exaggerated as this no doubt is, it indicates that the real objection is that ideas were handled as learned lumber rather than living and affective truths. The failure of imagination had made education the dull tool of the status quo and the remote past. Greater than the physical evils to which such learning led was the psychological damage it did; the scholars of war stifled the spirit of truth with its letter.

War is twice associated in "Howl" with asylums and jails in negative catalogues of suicide cases:

> a lost battalion of platonic conversationalists jumping down
> the stoops off fire escapes off windowsills off Empire State
> out of the moon,
> yaketayakking screaming vomiting whispering facts and
> memories and anecdotes and eyeball kicks and shocks of
> hospitals and jails and wars, (p. 10)

(and again)

> who created great suicidal dramas on the apartment cliff-banks
> of the Hudson under the wartime blue floodlight of
> the moon & their heads shall be crowned with
> laurel in oblivion, (p. 13)

More significant and revelatory of Ginsberg's association of our values and habits with the furniture of war is the following:

> who were burned alive in their innocent flannel suits on
> Madison Avenue amid blasts of leaden verse & the tanked-up
> clatter of the iron regiments of fashion & the nitroglycerine
> shrieks of the fairies of advertising & the mustard gas
> of sinister intelligent editors, or were run down
> by the drunken taxicabs of Absolute Reality, (p. 14)

Here "blasts," "leaden," "tanked-up," "iron-regiments," "nitroglycerine," and "mustard gas" combine the noise and machinery of war with the domestic activity of Madison Avenue. This apparently smooth and suave, well-oiled machine of polish and manner comes through to Ginsberg with all the noise and clumsiness of the *Wehrmacht*. The words spontaneously chosen also indicate a stiffness, a heaviness, a sameness, a restriction, and a grating. It is a clatter, a room full of hard objects, scraping and impinging metallically on one another. This constellation of forces tends to arrogate to itself the Absolute Reality, making all visionary or spiritual possibilities seem aberrant and foolish.

The metallic and physical verse-paragraph above contrasts sharply with one following six breaths later. Here we see the madmen as visionaries

> Who fell on their knees in hopeless cathedrals praying for
> each other's salvation and light and breasts, until the soul
> illuminated its hair for a second, (p. 14)

While Madison Avenue shuts out all possibilities of spirit, it also ironically drives people broken and hopeless to the life of the spirit. "Your machinery is too much for me. / You made me want to be a saint" ("America," p. 31). That is essentially the history of the Beat generation as Ginsberg would like to have it told. The proliferation of Christian imagery implies that the hipster is the Christ caught in a rock-bound, pharisaical society, seeking freedom and fluidity of spirit, and being crushed and crucified by law, custom, and system. America—that is, the real buried soul of America, the America of Walt Whitman—is also the Christ, suffocated by the Moloch built over its skin, crying out from the depths of its defeated soul, the desperate "eli eli lamma lamma sabacthani." A similar theme runs through much poetry of the sixties; Robert Duncan goes so far as to call the whole youth movement the "sublime crêche."*

---

* Duncan is thinking as well, perhaps especially, of the "underground" in each of us where the last vestiges of hope and integrity reside; but in the macrocosm of American society this underground is the "Underground." See "Earth's Winter Song" in his *Bending the Bow* (New York: New Directions, 1968), p. 94.

It is in Part I that "Howl" finds its core; here is the swivel where defeat is total and turns to victory. William Carlos Williams warns in his Preface to "Howl," "Hold back the edges of your gowns, ladies, we are going through hell." Indeed, "Howl," with the "Footnote to Howl" functioning as "Part Four" forms a complete divine comedy, with Part I as the dark wood where one descends to face the frozen blackness before ascending to purgation in compassion, and going beyond to a transcendent affirmation where all things lose their distinctions in light. In Part II comes that moment when the journeyer who has been climbing down Satan's body arrives at the anus and the center of gravity, and mysteriously must turn feet for head and begin climbing upward without changing direction. William Carlos Williams saw "Howl" as a poem of defeat, and yet a poem of the transcendence of defeat; it is within the mystery of Dante's image that Williams's idea is valid—defeat penetrated deeply enough *is* victory. Within the reality of the poem, it is by facing Moloch and saying his name that Moloch's power is destroyed.

Is the attack on Moloch a collection of radicalisms-good-for-a-cheer? Or is it the passionate cry of the tortured soul that is at the bottom of the black sack, the point of breakthrough where the darkness turns to light? Radicalisms-good-for-a-cheer are held in the mind; these cries are visceral, not cerebral. They are the cry of the deeper self against the encrustations of the shallower self, against the boa constrictor of the It-World illusion that swallows up the Thou-World of spirit. Experientially the tragic spirit of "Howl" matches Henri Bergson's comic spirit in the struggle against inflexibility, stiffness, and artificiality.

Moloch is the hard crust that the weaker moments of the soul have laid over the more vital spirit. It is the "machinery" of Matthew Arnold, the "mind-manacles" of Blake, the *"avidya"* of Zen, the *"maya"* of Hinduism. Moloch is the retributive justice that has taken place of a mercy that has failed, the competition, solitude, and fear that has replaced the cooperation, union, and love of the free spirit. The Moloch section does not criticize an administration, a particular national spirit, a foreign policy; but grapples head-on with the Western mentality as it finds its epitome and concentration in the most Western country, the country where the Western frontier ended and the tide of Western mind has begun to back up upon itself.

The most remarkable aspect of the Moloch section is the clutter and crowd of its images, their hugeness and heaviness. They combine in a bruising profusion of cement, tombs, banks, dynamos, buildings, jailhouses, armies, bombs, robots, pavements, tons, industries. In this great smash of objects the spirit has been crushed to nothing, and in the idiom of Moloch, the "whole boatload of sensitive bullshit" has at last been washed down the American river. But that river was once a river of hope, a tide of a different kind, full of visions, hopes, omens, ecstasies, and "Whitmanic" democratic love; the boatload was once precious cargo rather than refuse to be flushed away.

A number of concentrated images and assertions establish without question the relationship of war to "patterns," "charters," and the demands of the analytical and logical mind. Blakean implications are everywhere. As Ginsberg draws it, the twentieth century is the dotage of the once vigorous enlightenment of the seventeenth and eighteenth centuries, the prurient and senile old man suffering from the hardened arteries of the intellect. Now that there is little further room for beneficial exploration, the values that were so necessary to man as he pushed back the frontiers of science and the New World have turned to rend their master and suck his soul-blood. Modern man's rational emphasis has, like the nose of Pinocchio, gone on growing beyond its optimum size and use. In this case the aberration is not liable to correction by the Bergsonian spirit of comedy that ridicules all that is not properly flexible and ready to change; in this case only the spirit of tragedy can apply the knife to a growth that has gone beyond the limits of humor. Much of the corrective surgery attempted in the first half of this century was done with the scalpel of comedy—that, it seems, is really the dominant spirit of E. E. Cummings's *The Enormous Room* or John Dos Passos's *Nineteen-Nineteen*—but the monstrousness of the problem, especially since the Gulf of Tonkin incident, has prompted poets to reach for the meat-cleaver of tragedy or the frail and reckless hatchet of political harangue.

The Moloch section provokes questions about how thoroughly Ginsberg had read into and understood the spirit of Zen Buddhism, with its strong prejudice against relative consciousness and the *"avidya"* of the everyday world. Surely the bias of Part II is the bias of Zen, but it is also a disposition that Ginsberg would have picked up from Blake and Lawrence, and especially from Whitman, who speaks of "knowing things first hand" and who refused to make the discriminations so essential to the hierarchies of Western culture:

> Not till the sun excludes you do I exclude you,
> Not till the waters refuse to glisten and the leaves
>   refuse to rustle for you, do my words refuse to
>   glisten and rustle for you.
>
> ("To a Common Prostitute," *Complete Poetry*, p. 273)

Whitman's statement is strikingly main-line Zen. The uncluttered, unencumbered mind and soul reflect all things without making judgments of relative worth. If a flower comes to the mirror of pure consciousness, a flower is reflected; if a stone comes to the mirror, the stone is reflected. The pure consciousness always says a rose is a rose is a rose, never a rose is redder than a tulip; always a prostitute is a prostitute; never a prostitute is less noble than the Queen of England; or never a prostitute is someone to be scorned. In embracing this relationship with the world around him, Whitman likened himself to the things of nature who also accept indiscriminately all things as they are; the leaves and the waters do not decide that certain objects are worthy of consideration and others of scorn. In this sense and not in any pantheistic sense, Zen Buddhists understand the *koan*, "Where is the Buddha? The Cypress tree in the court." In a way, the leaves and the water "love" all things equally, and there is none of Ginsberg's "lacklove" in the realm of nature. And thus it is *in the demands of discrimination* that Ginsberg finds the vortex of "lacklove," which is the soul of Moloch and the cause of pain to sensitive souls who seek to give and receive love. Without it they are driven to perversions, brutalities, fears, and spiritual death.

It is characteristic of Moloch and the logical method to deal

with the forms and shapes of ideas; by its very nature it must deal
in "things" rather than essences and spirits. As a basic premise it
assumes that a thing cannot both be and not be at the same time.
Zen denies this and asserts (it is perhaps the only assertion pure Zen
will ever agree to make) that the highest wisdom is known not by
Aristotelian categorical logic but by paradoxical logic and intuition.
The highest reality is not a thinkable god, but is the Void or God
that lives in the core of the paradox. Moloch cannot touch that
reality, cannot deal with its shape because it has no shape, and
therefore Moloch flushes such nonsense down the river. Such an
understanding causes Ginsberg to see that Moloch's "buildings are
judgement!" The usual interpretation of this line is that our buildings are architecturally cold and ugly and are thus a symptom of
our soulful malaise; but more importantly, they are not only the
judgment upon Moloch but are the very reification of judgment
itself. They are monolithic, inflexible, lifeless, blind; their eyes are
a thousand blind windows that reflect only the material specter of
things; they multiply in quantity what they lack in quality and
acuity. The eyes of judgment are like the eyes of the building.
Judgment deals with externals, demands retributive penalties, external conformity, overt obeisance. It does not see, hear, or respect
anything but itself.

> Moloch whose mind is pure machinery! Moloch whose
>   blood is running money! Moloch whose fingers are ten
>   armies! Moloch whose breast is a cannibal dynamo!
>   Moloch whose ear is a smoking tomb!   (p. 17)

Moloch's touch is incapable of caress and knows only punishment and force; it has no heart for compassion, no intuition and
imagination capable of vision. It would be wrong to think that
Ginsberg is describing only a particular American culture; he is
attacking the radix or soul of which our culture is but the body.
In that sense Ginsberg is indeed a *radical* poet and thinker. His
particular radicalism is not by any means original (it is essentially
Christ's battle with the Pharisees, Siddhartha's struggle with Vedic
Brahmanas, Tolstoy's struggle with Russian orthodoxy, Lear's strug-

gle with Goneril and Regan), but it is unique in its passion and in its grounding in Ginsberg's own personal suffering.

Moloch "enters the soul early," and most men make the necessary sacrifices to accommodate the invader. Only those with peculiar "flaws" are unable to do so. Through this inability, gap, or flaw flows the "light streaming out of the sky!" Thus in defeat victory is found, and thus in the insane asylum Ginsberg finds sanity. It is not an artistically conceived choice that sets "Howl: Part III" in Rockland Hospital, but neither is it an accident. Ginsberg's personal history has dictated this progression, but the same Tao operates in Ginsberg's life as in his art. It is fitting that the purgatorio (after passing over the body of Moloch stiffly wedged in the frozen pit of Mind) should begin in a setting totally estranged from mind and *avidya* sanity, in the asylum where mind has failed. In the death of Mind (whether in Ginsberg's history or this art work), Compassion is born and expurgation begun.

Virgil had to warn Dante in the pit of hell to restrain the hatred he felt for those imprisoned there—he was being corrupted by the corruption he saw. Ginsberg's strong hatred of Moloch in Part II may be of the same order. But the cure of "aloneness" found in being "with" Carl Solomon in Part III promotes different feelings toward the U.S.

I'm with you in Rockland
>   where we hug and kiss the United States under our bedsheets
>   the United States that coughs all night and won't
>   let us sleep

I'm with you in Rockland
>   where we wake up electrified out of the coma by our own
>   souls' airplanes roaring over the roof they've come to drop
>   angelic bombs the hospital illuminates itself   imaginary
>   walls collapse   O skinny legions run outside   O starry-
>   spangled shock of mercy the eternal war is here
>   O victory forget your underwear we're free   (p. 20)

Significant here again is the juxtaposition of erotic and martial imagery, but most striking is the changed stance toward the United States. The United States, with its bad case of Mind, is a bad and sickly lay; but it is nevertheless cared for, and not rejected despite its consumptive coughing. In this realm the bombs and armies of Moloch are replaced by the soul's airplanes and angelic bombs that destroy the walls that were after all "imaginary" in the first place. That war of the deeper soul and mind against the barriers and limitations fabricated by the shallower mind or ego-consciousness is an eternal war, but a war of joy rather than blood: "O victory forget your underwear we're free." Such cries are apt to strike us as puerile. Certainly they alienate many readers and make it difficult to take Ginsberg seriously as a prophet or thinker. And yet with a little thought one sees that just such abandon is the only ammunition to be used in a war against an enemy who demands that all things be "mature" and "sensible." Real war has always been the "mature" and "reasonable" response to the particular circumstances that precipitate it; the other response, so "irrational" and "immature" that it has never been attempted.

In the "Footnote to Howl" Ginsberg proclaims transcendence and wholeness. It is the Paradiso of the piece; and in the tradition of the mystics, Zen, and the spirit of Whitman, Ginsberg here succeeds even in affirming negation.

> Holy time in eternity holy eternity in time holy the clocks in
> space holy the fourth dimension holy the fifth International
> holy the Angel in Moloch! (p. 21)

In the Zen perception the highest reality transcends the duality of good and evil, existence and nonexistence, affirmation and negation, and is itself affirmative. The higher Void is the genus that subsumes the species. (In a way, it even makes compatible the bombs of Moloch and the angelic bombs of the lunatics in Rockland.)

No one has yet written the explication of "Howl" to put alongside Cleanth Brooks's "*The Waste Land*: An Analysis." And yet if such a study were to be done along the lines suggested here, it may well prove "Howl" to be equally worthy of a detailed analysis of rhythms and images. Certainly this poem was not written by a "catalyst" nor with a scholarly, precise consciousness; yet if one were to analyze carefully what has, so to speak, swum up from the bowels of this poet, one might find—I wince at the thought of the firing squad—that "Howl" is in the best sense as intellectual (intelligent) as *The Waste Land*. In the idiom of Zen, the mind of no-mind is a higher mind than mind. In the idiom of D. H. Lawrence, the wisdom of the blood is not the lower wisdom of animals but the higher wisdom of the human. In the idiom of Blake, lust is not the impulse of the blood but the mind-perverted direction of innate responses. In Ginsberg's idiom we throw bombs because we are afraid to take off our underwear. Few people listened to Blake or Lawrence: the young are listening to Ginsberg.

Ginsberg's idiom is not always so vulnerable as the line just quoted above. But there are such lines, and they prompt critics to complain that Ginsberg's poetry is "mixed" in quality and lacking in "discrimination"—it is as if he believes one image is as good as another. Ginsberg and Zen would, of course, argue that images indeed are one as good as another if they are all deep and natural responses to the experienced truth. Only the biased perspective of the relative consciousness wants to make judgments about them; the mind that wants to handle and compare them as things concerns itself with questions of superiority and inferiority. (The integrated self desires only to feel and respond to them as forces.) The mind does so under "the myth of objective consciousness,"[20] but its judgments are not really so much determined by what is out there as by the shape and smudge of the mirror, the perceptual disposition and mind-set of the viewer. The proof lies in the *reductio ad absurdum*: is it really more innate in the Tao or ingrained in the nature of the universe to speak of "setting one's own lands in order" (*The Waste Land*) or to speak of abandoning one's underwear? At what point in time did it become so?

It is commonly expected that a study of a poet or a poem culminates in a critical judgment of a qualitative kind; yet surely with Ginsberg one ought to avoid what Northrop Frye has called the "debauchery of judiciousness." A poet and a poetry that draw inspiration from the battle against Moloch, the heavy judger, may perhaps be granted the boon of our nonjudgment. They deserve attention and description, but are not illuminated by qualitative tags. This poetry purposely seeks to throw away, violate, and make such standards inoperative. It is perhaps formless, but it may be formless as a living amoeba compared to an inanimate clam shell; it is perhaps mixed, but it may be mixed as a rich stew compared to purer but plainer broth. It may be without art, but it is also without artificiality and carries its own natural inscape.

IV

Ginsberg traveled to Cambodia and Vietnam in 1963 at a time when American involvement was still slight. The sense of menace that Ginsberg felt from the military presence there at that time reveals a prophetic perception of what was to come. The experience resulted in a long poem centering around the image of banyan roots slowly engulfing the temples of Ankor Wat. In a manner reminiscent of his thoughts on America while he was at the Mayan ruins, he here seeks the ancient spirituality that slow time seems to be eroding beyond reach. The 1968 Fulcrum Press edition of *Ankor Wat* is graced with excellent photographs by Alexandra Lawrence.[21] The first of these, the frontispiece, is a banyan-strangled statue of Avalokitesvera, the Buddha of Mercy. The giant head, with its multiple faces gazing in four directions, is nearly hidden under a profusion of snaking and twisting roots. The benevolent Buddha is very nearly transformed by the tenacious growth into a Medusa's head. Other pictures show the octopus tentacles of the banyan crawling over palace and temple roofs and walls, closing it in what seems an inexorable death grip. Ginsberg seems to have read his own fate in these

> Slithering hitherward paranoia
> Banyans trailing
> high muscled tree crawled
> over the roof its big
> long snakey toes spread
> down the lintel's red
> cradle-root
> elephantine bigness

He seems to be in an unusually agitated and unhappy state in these poems, troubled by the military presence in Indo-China, the negative advice he had received from Indian gurus about his desire for children, and a multitude of other disappointments. He felt all his fine shouting in poems such as "Howl" was somehow false, and he lacked strength to fight off the paranoia and frustration of his life. His despair is such that he shouts "Objection! this can't be / Me!" and throughout the poem speaks of himself in the following tones:

[1] the Fear ordering peas in the French
    restaurant, with whole garlic

[2] I am afraid where I am

[3] Nothing but a false Buddha afraid of
    my own annihilation

[4] Leroi I been done you wrong
    I'm just an old Uncle Tom in disguise all along
    afraid of physical tanks.

[5] Saranam Gochamee Catchme quick

[6] dwelling in my mind "frightened ageing nagging flesh"

[7] Just a lot of words and propaganda
    I been spreading getting scared
    of my own bullshit

[8] "Make me ready—but not yet"
    No I am not "ready" to die when that Choke
    comes I'm afraid I'll scream and
    embarrass everybody—go out
    like a coward yellow fear I done left no
    Louis babies behind me Rebuke in
    Those 70 years eyes

And what Ginsberg suffers from, he also believes the world suffers from. Whether the paranoia and pain he sees in the world is a projection of his own or an accurate reading, the reader sees that the banyan Buddha is the symbol of Ginsberg caught in his own fears, the world caught in its loveless values, and the divinity in man and culture caught in the spiritless erosions of time.

Everywhere it's the fear I got in my own
    intestines—Kenyatta Prime Minister
    peacefully with his fly-wisk

and maybe the Mo Mo's underground
Mao-Mao—everywhere is my own Rhodesia
for Mysterious Choose Up Sides and Die
    like a "Man"

A prime cause of Ginsberg's fear and depression is his exposure to Saigon where he has met and talked with newsmen and military personnel and picked up the vibrations of moral death. Bits of Saigon conversation are caught in the stream of Ginsberg's consciousness: "I'm just doing my Professional duty," "I'm scheming murders," "I'm chasing a story." The ugliness he experiences moves him to a superficial vow, "I'm not going to eat meat anymore / I'm taking refuge in the Buddha Dharma Sangha." But the Buddha, Dharma, and Sangha are refuge for men more whole than Ginsberg, who can only flee in fear:

All the wire services eating sweet and
    sour pork and fresh cold leechee white-meat
        in sugarwater—
Discussing the manly truth Gee Fellers—
Even the fat whitehaired belly boy from
        Time and his Kewpiedoll wife
Could've been seen in the movies dancing
    the rainy night at the border
    Chinese cha-cha, Hysteria
That UP kid flown down from Vientianne
    Laos fugitive Hepatitis
    Scared of the Yellow Men, or the slow
        Alcohol red face of the Logistics
        Analyst—"I got the Eichman syndrome"
said he newsweekley—reporters who
never committed suicide like
    Hemingway had to, faced
    with the fat newsman with
        Seven children from
        Buddenbrooks
They were living in Greece while Pound
was taking a vow of silence
        "I knew too much"
    but it was all a mistake,

> I fled the Mekong delta, fled the 12,000
>   Military speaking hot dog guts on the
>   downtown aircooled streets

It is understated but clear in *Ankor Wat* that Ginsberg associates his and the world's ills with the evils of "Mind." The image of the Buddha of Mercy, engulfed as he is in tentacles that seem to grow out of his own head, suggests such a meaning. Ginsberg associates the image with his own "mind-snake":

> As I rode thru the forest Hari Hindoo and Lord of Mercy
>   struggled like Asur-Devas
>   with my mind-snake drifting
>   motorized under the trees—

Another snake image seems to pose this negative mind-presence against the power of D. H. Lawrence's living "Snake."

> So many grounds to cover the terrors of the day
> All got to do with snakes—and only one shy
>   tail, I saw disappearing behind a
>   rock, slow banded worm—

This may, of course, be pure narrative and a precise account of Ginsberg's day, but the fact that there are many symbolic mind-snakes and terrors and almost no living natural ones seems to speak perfectly to Ginsberg's poetic purpose. The image is closely followed by Ginsberg's regret that although the accusing voice of his mother, Naomi, is ever in his ear—"a sad case of refusing to grow up give birth to die"—he has not even the faintest desire for the "black silk girls in the alley of this clean new tourist city."

Guilt and anxiety so imbue these experiences that even as he catches a ride through Saigon with one of the "american husbands in sportshirts" on a "velocopedomotor" he tells himself and the soldier:

> You have no right being a Hitler repeating that
>   Abhya mudra reassurrance
>   Palm out flat, patting the airhide
>   of earth—

It is an undeniably poetic imagination that interprets and clothes in significance every casual act and move. The act of holding one's hand to the air currents is indeed a gesture of peace and well-being, and one who carries responsibility for war and paranoia perhaps has no right to engage in it. The gesture also resembles the *abhya mudra* of the multiple-armed, dancing destroyer, Shiva, who always raises one hand as a gesture of assurance to men that all the terror and threat is only a passing show and a game of the Gods. But Ginsberg in these months cannot find peace in this. The fear overwhelms him. The imagination that experiences all of this is extraordinarily aware, and its sensitivity validates what would otherwise seem merely political opinion or private pathology.

Ankor Wat (unlike "Howl," which does in fact have symmetry and order) is an amorphous vehicle for the poet's experience, and indulges again Ginsberg's propensity for describing his own spiritual and psychological battles in martial terms. His fate and that of the soldiers in Saigon are not really different, both originating in common disease. The effect or "shape" of the sprawling poem's meaning is similar to that which Robert Frost squeezes into sixteen careful lines in the poem "Bereft." Each poem expresses the moment of dread when the future looks poisonous and one stands shorn of all human support.

> Forward March, guessing
> which bullet which airplane which nausea
> be the dreadful doomy last
> > begun while I'm still
> conscious—I'll go down and get a cold coffee at
> > Midnight.

V

The best and most complete of Ginsberg's poems specifically about Vietnam is "Wichita Vortex Sutra." It is another sprawling poem with many portions having little to recommend them except their variety and wealth of particular information, scraps of news, numbers of soldiers, glimpses of Americana seen from a car window.

The poem is the transcript of consciousness of a confused and agonizing man driving across the Midwest with a head full of remembered news and a heart full of terror, listening to the radio and watching rural and neon America pass by. What makes it poetry at all is the fineness of Ginsberg's senses, the natural poet in him that finds surprising meaning in the commonplaces we ignore.

> American Eagle beating its wings over Asia
>   million dollar helicopters
> a billion dollars worth of Marines
>   who loved *Aunt Betty*
>   Drawn from the shores and farms shaking
> from the high schools to the landing barge
> blowing the air thru their cheeks with fear
>   in *Life* on Television[22]

Obviously when Ginsberg viewed these Marines "in *Life* on Television" his glance and concern were not casual. Here with casual expression (so casual and commonplace that we are also apt to under-appreciate it) he catches the nervous excitement of the boy-come-soldier, the metamorphosis of random high-school boys into billion-dollar fighting machines. The contrast and incongruity of these men "who loved *Aunt Betty*" and their role in Asia communicate the tragedy and travesty of the war better than any amount of prose. The Marines here are individuals, real men, not abstractions, and in the common gesture of "blowing the air thru their cheeks" Ginsberg vicariously experiences their fear.

The poem finds its force perhaps not so much in sublimity as in amplification and multitude of image and detail, and yet the effect of the whole is extremely moving and convincing. The passion and the amplitude rushes the reader along with it, so much so that the ending argument seems inevitably just:

> to the center of the Vortex, calmly returned
>   to Hotel Eaton—
> Carry Nation began the war on Vietnam here
>   with an angry smashing axe
>   attacking Wine—
> Here fifty years ago, by her violence

> began a vortex of hatred that defoliated the Mekong Delta—
> Proud Wichita! vain Wichita
>   cast the first stone!—
>   That murdered my mother
>   who died of the communist anticommunist psychosis
>   in the madhouse one decade long ago
> complaining about wires of masscommunication in her head
>   and phantom political voices in the air
>   besmirching her girlish character.
> Many another has suffered death and madness
>   in the Vortex from Hydraulic
>   to the end of 17th—enough!
>
> (*Planet*, pp. 131–132)

This passage, like so many of Ginsberg's, is richer than its deceptive spontaneity would suggest. It is a microcosmic expression of Ginsberg's philosophy. That it was the grape, the sacred fruit of Dionysus and ecstasy, that Carry warred against links her war with Vietnam in Ginsberg's propensity for counterposing the ecstatic and erotic against the Apollonian order of war. Her hatred, as Ginsberg sees it, was hatred of anything that would lift man out of that order, free him from the dead conformity and propriety of "righteous" living. The "demon Rum" was no other Satan than the kind invented by Urizen, who fears any power that weakens his repressive control and dominance. For Ginsberg, Carry's ax struck not at rum but at celebration, spontaneity, freedom of desire; for him, her hatred brought the burden of guilt upon everything that does not prostitute itself to the letter of an imposed and rigid law. Her determination to punish and destroy "evil" is the seed tumor behind Joseph McCarthy and napalm in Vietnam. "Proud Wichita!" The hand of righteousness is the hand of pride—the hand that punishes is the hand that is blindly certain that it, and it alone, holds the truth. For Ginsberg the defoliation of the Mekong is the child of American pride in its culture as the only true culture. "Vain Wichita / cast the first stone!" Wichita, in this echo of Christ's forgiveness of the prostitute, is without the sensitivity and love Christ had, and lacks the humility and sudden self-insight of the would-be stone throwers who knew that they were not worthy to cast the first stone. In the Biblical episode, had one stone been thrown, the avalanche of stones would have been unstoppable. Once a vortex of insensitivity and "judgment" is set in motion, it feeds upon and justifies itself; it creates the Absolute Reality in which only its own actions are rational and possible. Carry Nation's historical actions become the compressed and localized symbol of the character of the Western world. Historians, philosophers, and other poets might place the vortex further back, say in Plato's orderly republic, or Descartes's *cogito ergo sum*.

Wichita's "first stone" started, symbolically, the barrage of fear and guilt that slowly murdered Ginsberg's mother. Her paranoic delusion had been that the Communists had planted radio wires in her head and three mysterious long rods in her back. She lived in continuing fear of "phantom political voices in the air." Her terror serves the main theme of "Wichita Vortex" well, for Ginsberg, too, is one now driven to madness by the phantom voices in the air, the television, radio, and airprint that deal in "black magic language." It is a language of body counts, rationalization, prevarication, obfuscation, advertisement, money, materialism, "responsibility," punishment, fear, and death. The deaths that swirl from this vortex of judgment and language are physical (the carnage of the Vietnamese countryside), psychological, and spiritual (the tormented souls of America's poets, and all the souls "held prisoner in Niggertown" dying from inhibition and lacklove).

Such is essentially the Ginsberg position, and his explanation of the American disease also casts light on the deterioration of language. As a poet Ginsberg associates language with the deepest spiritual impulses of man. Language that has been made to serve the judgmental rational faculty rather than the imagination and the deeper self will necessarily become as superficial and dangerous as the master it serves. The proliferation and prostitution of language through the mass media has transmogrified the natural magic power of language, words to express the ineffable and the transcendent, into evil black-magic language that denies the ineffable and transcendent and elevates the spiritless untruths of modern politics and culture.

A chief virtue of "Wichita Vortex Sutra" is that it makes the reader *experience* the proliferation and abuse of language. Its technique is to notice and reproduce the language that inundates the senses everyday, and in doing so it makes one painfully aware that in every case language is used not to communicate truth but to manipulate the hearer. Language bludgeons the reader from every direction, on the sides of boxcars, from church lawns, neon advertisements, newspapers, television, radio, grain elevators, the sides of barns. The word "language" itself becomes a refrain in the poem, inserted again and again between the language of the mass media. Ginsberg might readily substitute "language" for "money" in Whalen's lines: "Nobody wants the war only the money / fights on, alone."[23] "Wichita Vortex" not only states but makes one feel how language has taken over and begun to control its controllers:

> Communion of bum magicians
>   congress of failures from Kansas & Missouri
>   working with the wrong equations
> Sorcerer's Apprentices who lost control
>   of the simplest broomstick in the world:
>   Language
>
> (*Planet*, p. 120)

"The war is language" because language is no longer poetic or close to its source in experience or particularity, but has become a language of mental constructs and abstractions:

> Black Magic language,
>   formulas for reality—
>   Communism is a 9 letter word
>   used by inferior magicians with
> the wrong alchemical formula for transforming earth into gold
>
> (*Planet*, p. 119)

In the alchemy analogy, Ginsberg's imagination captures the foolish and self-important character of politicians. Always the language goes on, removed and abstract while—

> Flesh soft as a Kansas girl's
>   ripped open by metal explosion—
> three five zero zero   on the other side of the planet

caught in barbed wire, fire ball
bullet shock, bayonet electricity
bomb blast terrific in skull & belly, shrapnelled
throbbing meat
While this American nation argues war:
conflicting language, language

(p. 121)

In the dynamics of the poem, language takes its place alongside the repressive and judgmental consciousness, and replaces the
erotic ecstasies the war mentality denies. That denial and that repression of ecstasy remains for Ginsberg the greatest sin. Even the
images of carnage emphasize that the flesh destroyed by war (flesh
soft as a Kansas girl's) is flesh formed for caress and passionate
touch. The young men forced into the army "throb with desire"
they are

boys with sexual bellies aroused
chilled in the heart by the mailman
with a letter from an aging white haired General
Director of selection for service in
Deathwar   (*Planet,* p. 124)

The obsession is larger than physical eroticism, and is tied to Ginsberg's own repeatedly confessed hunger for affection and tenderness:

All we do is for this frightened thing
we call Love, want and lack—
fear that we aren't the one whose body could be
beloved of all the brides of Kansas City,
kissed all over by every boy of Wichita—
O but how many in their solitude weep aloud like me—
On the bridge over Republican River
almost in tears to know
how to speak the right language—

(*Planet,* p. 125)

The effort of the poem and of Ginsberg's whole life is to

claim my birthright!
reborn forever as long as Man
in Kansas or other universe—Joy
reborn after the vast sadness of War Gods!   (*Planet,* p. 126)

"Wichita Vortex Sutra," the "Keystone section" of the "prog-
ressively longer poem on 'These States,' " says essentially all that
Ginsberg has to say about the war and America's culture, and says
it with greater passion and effect than any other of his poems. Vietnam enters Ginsberg's work elsewhere, but without anything like
the same power. The "Pentagon Exorcism" reiterates the torment
Ginsberg experiences from the "Governor's language," the "President's language," and the language of those who are otherwise busy
manufacturing death: "Corporate voices jabber on electric networks
building / body-pain, chemical ataxia, physical slavery" (p. 143).
Ginsberg's own use of language is a simple crowding together of
negatively connotative polysyllables—"Intelligence influence matter-
scientists' Rockefeller / bank telephone war investment Usury
Agency / executives"—or a pounding staccato of word-pairs and
compounds—"smog-shrouded metal-noised treeless cities / patrolled
by radio fear with tear gas, businessman! / Go spend your bright
billions for this suffering!"

Perhaps the most satisfying poem of protest, and one that most
reveals Ginsberg's compassion, advises us "Who Be Kind To"—
the self, the place, the neighbor, the mother, the politicians, the
fearful one, the hero, the Self of the universe—

> ... because unkindness
>   comes when the body explodes
> napalm cancer and the deathbed in Vietnam
> is a strange place to dream of   trees
>   leaning over and angry American faces
> grinning with sleepwalk terror over your
>   last eye—   (*Planet*, p. 95)

"Who Be Kind To" is full of Ginsberg's own childlike tenderness
and need for tenderness, his hunger and gratitude for

>   the kindness
>   received thru strange eyeglasses on
>   a bus thru Kensington,
> the finger touch of the Londoner on your thumb,
>   that borrows light from your cigarette   (*Planet*, p. 96)

Ginsberg's entire campaign against the "statue destroyers & tank captains, unhappy / murderers in Mekong & Stanleyville," against the many faces of Moloch is and has been from the first a campaign against *lacklove*, so that a new kind of man can "come to his bliss" and "end the cold war he has borne / against his own kind flesh / since the days of the snake."

Ginsberg's war protest is clearly an honest outgrowth of his biography and his experience of America. It is in no way an opportunistic espousal of a popular cause nor a whistling up of like-minded friends. And rather than being inferior, the poems in which the war and Moloch are the primary emotional focus are markedly superior to his other confessional ramblings. Ginsberg is not a great poet, but he is a great figure in the history of poetry. We do not win from him many new insights or subtle understandings, but we do take from his poetry a simple intensity and a certain freedom. His poetry has made it easier for others to speak honestly. His unabashed admission of his own insufficiency and anguish have helped make others aware of their own deprivations and insensitivity. Certainly we might have wished for a more tidy apostle of compassion, one who would spare us the unhappy details of his sex life, one who might combine reticence and discrimination with his genuine openness and honesty. (If thousands of lines and numerous poems like "Today" or "This Form of Life Needs Sex" had been left to mildew in Ginsberg's private journals where they belong, the positive emotional force of his poetry would be less clouded and he would find an immensely enlarged receptive audience.) But prophets do not come made to order. Ginsberg is a flawed but necessary prophet, a man desperately crying in the wilderness for love, searching the world's religions for a sustaining vision, witnessing nakedly to man's timeless spiritual and physical desires:

> And I am the King of May, that I may be expelled from my
> Kingdom with Honor, as of old,
> To shew the difference between Caesar's Kingdom and the
> Kingdom of the May of Man

> *(Planet,* p. 90)

3 DENISE LEVERTOV: PIERCING IN

I know I am solid and sound;
To me the converging objects of the universe perpetually
*   flow;*
All are written to me, and I must get what the writing
*   means.*

("Song of Myself")

Only the kernel of every object nourishes;
Where is he who tears off the husks for you and me?

("Song of the Open Road")
Whitman

I

Balanced and *whole* are words that have perhaps best characterized the work and the person of Denise Levertov—at least until the late sixties. The second line of her first volume of poetry speaks of the "systole and diastole marking miraculous hours," and it is inside just such a pulse of balanced polarities that her poetry finds its stable center. She knows that "Strength of feeling, reverence for mystery, and clarity of intellect must be kept in balance with one another. Neither the passive nor the active must dominate, they must work in conjunction as in a marriage."[1] Her poems seek the middle way not because they are dull or timid, but because the eye that finds the poetry inside the flux is sane and confident. There are no excesses of ecstasy or despair, celebration or denigration, naïvete or cynicism; there is instead an acute ability to find simple beauties in the heart of squalor and something to relish even in negative experiences. While her poetry experiences the world with a finely honed and precise sensibility, it accepts necessary human suffering and the world's imperfection with a deep strength that marks it as "masculine" and Jewish (that spirit that moves in the Book of Job as well as in the novels of Bernard Malamud and Saul Bellow). But it is more than just that—it is incomparable and unique poetry that tastes in the hard and difficult world a satisfying savor and at times a deep, if limited, joy.

Levertov's sanity and balance are not of the kind that excludes mystery—indeed, in addition to her interest in dreams, all her poetry seeks to discover the mystery that lies beyond the surfaces of things. Allen Ginsberg shares a reverence for mystery, but one realizes immediately that it means for him something different: Levertov is concerned with an internal and natural mystery rather than a transcendent or metaphysical one (though at their deepest core or supreme circumference they are the same).

If any of the three elements—feeling, mystery, and intellect—has outweighed the others in Levertov's poetics, it has surely been intellect, but intellect in its highest manifestation as *claritas*.[2] *Claritas* is more than oiled reason (though Levertov only partly shares Ginsberg's Blakean anti-intellectualism); it is the clean, precise perception that arises from attending closely while the will is quieted and the intellect is warmed by the emotions. *Claritas* arises from the unforced union of all the senses and faculties—but if one has to single out a primary synecdoche, the *eye* immediately recommends itself. Levertov's poetry is a poetry of the eye in that it is concerned with *seeing into* experience and discovering the order and significance that her poet's faith tells her is really there behind the surface chaos. Her poetry is of the mental and spiritual eye, however, and not primarily a poetry of phanopoeia or visual image.[3] She dislikes Robert Bly's poetry, in fact, insofar as it relies too heavily on the sense of sight and not enough on melopoeia or sound.[4] Her own work reminds us of Joseph Conrad's dictum that art is "to make you see," except that Levertov's intention hints less of indirect didacticism: her poetry is not so much to make someone else see as it is a *process of seeing* for the poet. Perhaps, "art is to make the artist see" or "art is the way an artist sees." Through poetry she reaches to the heart of things, finds out what their centers are. If the reader can follow, he is welcomed along, but although the poetry is mindful of communication and expression, its primary concern is discovery. Her poetry seeks *instress* or the *apperception of inscape* not only of natural objects but of emotional and intellectual experience as well. It seeks analogies, resemblances, natural allegories: "such a poetry is," as she has noted, "exploratory."[5]

Levertov's attitude towards art and experience is of primary importance in understanding her first reactions to the Vietnam War. Whereas Ginsberg sees war as the ultimate reification of artificial control and imposed order, the natural activity of a judgmental Moloch, she sees it as ultimate unreason and disorder, as the clouding of *claritas* and the violation of the innate order at the heart of things. In Ginsberg's hierarchy of values, *touching and experiencing* is preeminent; in Levertov's, *seeing into and understanding* is most important. Ginsberg does not seek *in-sight* so much as sensation, motion, and flexibility. His war is against pattern, restriction, limitation; her struggle is to discover the true patterns, to find the limits and definitions of things. He is concerned about pressures that impinge upon his flesh and space; she is concerned about forces that block and limit her vision. Thus in Ginsberg's poetry combat and orgy are juxtaposed; in Levertov's poetry carnage is juxtaposed against "my clear caressive sight, my poet's sight,"[6] and mutilated bodies are contrasted with the beauty of man's eyes, "flowers that perceive the stars."[7]

It is the loss and contradiction of vision that makes the war horrible to Levertov, and this may be said without any denigration of her compassion or humanity. Her concern is not a coldly aesthetic one: she cares not so much about the loss of the possibilities of art as an end in itself, but about the loss of the clarity that strikes to depths where the highest art and fullest life are inseparable. When vision reaches to that level, love and compassion are natural concomitants. The sight at that point is "caressive" by its nature, since at their core all things are orderly and love-ly (love-worthy and love-eliciting). *Claritas* and *caritas* are inseparable.

Allen Ginsberg also speaks of war and the war proclivities of Moloch as eating the heart out of the imagination and denying the possibilities of vision. But his "vision" is somewhat closer to "apparition" than to "clear-sightedness," and he is more interested in mind expansion than in mind composure. For him, the war mentality closes man into the *avidya* "illusion" of material things, keeps him from looking above and beyond, and *shuts him in* from vision. For Levertov the war keeps man at the surface of reality, keeps him from looking into, and *shuts him out* from vision. The first poet strives for transcendence and expansion of the mind, while the second seeks contemplation and the focus of the mind. The war is, however, equally antagonistic to either approach, and the approaches are, of course, not contradictory but complementary—both seek the "center that is everywhere and the circumference that is nowhere,"[8] that paradoxical point where far-out is the same as deep-in, where many become one, nothing becomes everything, and the ego is dissolved in the light of pure "seeing."

> Reduced to an eye
> I forget what
>   I
> was.   ("The Cold Spring," *Relearning*, p. 9)

Though the aims of Levertov and Ginsberg may be ultimately similar, their methods and forms are widely different. In general, we are likely to be more receptive to the techniques and achieved effects of Levertov because they are more familiar and more at home in the Western epistemology and mind-manner. There is something attractive in the solidity, the clean onyx of Levertov's lines, the propriety of her manner and composure. Ginsberg's poetry is often apt to seem distressingly messy. We would do well, however, to recognize that ours is a conditioned response, and that ultimately, as in the Zen understanding, one manner is neither better nor worse than the other, and that they are not validly open to comparison anyway. But we live in a world of relative consciousness, and poetics and literary criticism are founded precisely in the nexus of that relativity. Poetry itself stands in that world of relativity as a springboard into the world of transcendence; it is anchored in the "It-World" as a catapult for the imagination to cross out of that world into the Thou-awareness and relation.[9] The texture, body, and form of Levertov's poetry does seem to furnish a more substantial impetus into that relationship than does Ginsberg's passionate records of his own trips across the threshold.

Levertov tries to give her poems the shape and pattern she discovers outside the poem; the poems embody and concretize experience at the level of its orderliness, at the point where it touches the natural mystery in the heart of things. Though she might agree to some extent with Ginsberg that poetry can and should be "a transcript of consciousness," it must be of a consciousness composed and quieted to a deeper seeing, and not a random and undiscriminating "free-mind." Poetry should not be *prima materia* or liquid protoplasm: poems should "become definite bodies, as protoplasm becomes a living and solid creature, and moves as such a creature will move in its living."[10] Levertov dislikes the ossifications of Moloch or of poetic conventions as much as Ginsberg does, and yet realizes some kind of skeleton or integument is essential to all living things. She dislikes poems that are "mere quivering pieces of autobiographical raw material."[11] Giving the poem a structure or skin and keeping it "together" is a way of keeping the mind or consciousness together, and vice versa. Though it should not shape itself to external demands, every life and every poem must discover a form and attain a precise and substantial shape: it may grow its own organic hide but it cannot do without one. Levertov does not share Ginsberg's desire to "go naked" physically, psychologically, or aesthetically. While the "stiff brocade" and whalebone stays of imposed poetic and social conventions are also rejected by Levertov, she recognizes the aesthetic and practical value of properly fitting clothes, whether for poetry or flesh:

The best work is made
from hard, strong materials,
      obstinately precise—
the line of the poem, onyx, steel.

It's not a question of
false constraints—but
    to move well and get somewhere
wear shoes that fit.

To hell with easy rhythms—
sloppy mules that anyone can
    kick off or
step into.[12]

Going barefoot and nude through the litter of experience may be a noisy and sensational venture, but the distances one can explore are thereby sorely limited. The poet's integrity (in the literal sense of keeping in one piece) may be destroyed in such traveling: he may end hanging in shreds on the rough edges and briars of his experience. (Indeed, in reading Ginsberg one constantly fears the poet is in imminent danger of bleeding to death.)

II

The hard, clear form of Levertov's poetry since coming to America and until her most recent work was possible because she possessed a sense of self denied to many poets born and raised in the younger culture. In the fifties, Kenneth Rexroth found her poetry superior to that of Duncan, Olson, Creeley, Ginsberg, Cid Corman, and other "avant-garde" poets because "she is more civilized. One thing she has that they lack conspicuously is what Ezra Pound calls culture—and which he is himself utterly without. She is securely humane in a way very few people are any more."[13] Intending it, I suppose, as Matthew Arnold intended it in his criticism of the Romantic poets, Rexroth asserts that Levertov is a superior poet because she "*knows* more than her colleagues" (my italics). His seems a just appraisal: "securely humane" is an excellent description of Levertov's work in the volumes published between 1955 and 1965. She brought with her to the American experience a self-assurance and stability that kept her humanity strong and natural. The poetry offers no doubt that she is in control, moving attentively and perceptively through experience with a confidence more common to poets before the First World War. Not a naïve or romantic poetry, but a poetry of a healthy psyche, it is unlike much poetry written in the fifties and sixties.* Either because severe self-doubt did not exist or was kept outside of the poetry, the work before 1965 is able to devote its attention to the balanced seeing and savoring of life. Intensely personal and a "poetry of the immediate"[14] drawn directly from experience, it is yet a poetry in which the ever-present "I" is remarkably unobtrusive. The four volumes from *Here and Now* (1957) to *O Taste and See* (1964) are, in fact, admirable examples of Levertov's "negative capability." Because of the Vietnam War the same cannot be said of *The Sorrow Dance* (1967), *Relearning the Alphabet* (1970), and *To Stay Alive* (1971).

Alongside her obvious relish for life, Levertov's poetry has always carried a measured note of austerity and sadness. She finds beauty everywhere, yet it is seldom an effervescent or exaggerated outflowing; it is a beauty harbored deep within the heart of a paradoxical sadness and limitation. Such limitation is accepted as inevitable and good, not to be destroyed or rebelled against, but to be looked into to discover how beauty keeps its mysterious habitation there. Her eye has been able to find beauty in

the quick of the sun that gilds
broken pebbles in sidewalk cement
and the iridescent
spit, that defiles and adorns!
. . . .
. . . the fluted
cylinder of a new ashcan a dazzling silver,
the smooth flesh of screaming children a quietness, it is all

---

*Levertov acknowledged that though most American poets were busy trying to discover their "identity" (their poetry becoming the record of their struggle) British poets, having the benefits of an older and more insular culture, "know who they are"; and though she claims not to have felt the English identity (she was educated at home and has a unique European, Jewish, Anglican, and Welsh background), few poets have been so sure of their identities as Levertov has been of her own. See her remarks in an interview by Walter Sutton, *The Minnesota Review* 5 (1965):322–323.

> a jubilance, the light catches up
> the disordered street in its apron,
> broken fruitrinds shine in the gutter.[15]

Many such poems show us what "City Psalm" tells us: *"I saw Paradise in the dust of the street"* (*Sorrow Dance*, p. 72).

One notices in these and other poems the careful balance of the positive and the negative, of the off-setting "goods" that the "light" of the sun or of the imagination can always discover. In this equilibrium and balance Levertov finds her ordered reality, and extends her sanity and stability of soul. Whether balance produces the vision and form, or vision produces the form and balance, or the form produces the balance & vision—the cause-effect sequence cannot be determined, but the interrelationship is undeniable. The honest vision, precise form, and balanced view keep the poetry generally free of either pessimism or sentimentality. When a note of the sentimental creeps in, it is quickly annihilated by a swift stroke of the real:

> The cat on my bosom
> sleeping and purring
> —fur petalled chrysanthemum,
> squirrel-killer—
>
> ("The Cat as Cat," *Sorrow Dance*, p. 40)

This balance of the soft and the brutal, the beautiful and the ugly, the comic and the tragic is carefully maintained and developed, and in this poem it is further amplified in the cat's "dilating, contracting eyes" and the "flex and reflex of claws." The poet knows the cat is metaphor only if she makes her one, but that is just what the poet does with all things. Levertov does it not by using it and relating to it superficially as an object, but by coming into an "I-Thou" relationship with it, understanding it perfectly in both its faults and perfections, and seeing its flex and tension in herself and in all the world of being and knowing. Reality and experience is always an interaction, a dialogue, a balanced giving and taking. Joy does not come from eliminating the negative forces in the world, but from seeing them truly in their tension with the positive. Thus, the joy that comes from the poet's vision is for Levertov never orgiastic, but sparse, precise, fragile, tempered. The poet is like the hummingbird at the flower:

the fierce, brilliant faith
that pierces the heart all summer

and sips bitter insects steeped in nectar,
prima materia
of gleam-and-speed-away.

A passion so intense
It driveth sorrow hence...

("Revivals," *Sorrow Dance*, p. 41)

The bitter insects steeped in nectar are a telling metaphor of her understanding of life; and the poet's vision that finds joy and sustenance in this bittersweet food is indeed so intense that it keeps sorrow at a distance, even as it refuses to deny it. Levertov can even imagine, in another hummingbird poem, that in response to such a passionate intensity, nature sensuously desires to reveal itself, so that vision is again really an intercourse or dialogue:

The remaining
tigerblossoms have rolled their petals
all the way back,

the stamens protrude entire,
there are no more buds.

("A Turn of the Head," *Taste and See*, p. 32)

(Surely, here is a brand of subtle eroticism and refined ecstasy that Ginsberg is unable to achieve.)

While Levertov was never oblivious to pain and sorrow, she was always able through poetry to find in all experience an order and significance that explained and elevated it. At the least, poetry by speaking of sorrow was able to clarify and distance it so that it could be handled:

To speak of sorrow
works upon it
      moves it from its

crouched place barring
the way to and from the soul's hall—
("To Speak," *Sorrow Dance*, p. 63)

The shadow of the Vietnam War comes to alter all this: vision is clouded, form is broken, balance is impossible, and the psyche is unable to throw off its illness and sorrow.

III

The war poems in the 1967 *Sorrow Dance* are gathered at the end of the volume as broken and unredeemed notes coming suddenly after a carefully orchestrated progress through tragedy to restored wholeness.

The order of poems in Levertov's books is always careful and significant, and she herself has spoken of the "Olga Poems" (which work through the meaning of her sister's life and death) as the center of this volume.[16] In the Olga or "Sorrow Dance" chapter, the selections are of a darker tonal coloration and move from a fine crystalline hardness to poems of less composure and control, before the equilibrium is again reestablished in the "Perspectives" section. The first of the "Sorrow Dance" poems achieves a beautiful and horrible balance in the "headless squirrel . . . in rainsweet grass," and in "the first irises" with "dark veins / bruise-blue." Succeeding poems focus on beggars, furless dogs, mute and loveless men, memories of Olga, tortured faces. But the power of poetry is salvific and the poems do move the sorrow from "its / crouched place barring / the way to and from the soul's hall." Though the poems of the following "Perspectives" chapter are sometimes troubled, the last two, "City Psalm" and "A Vision," are poems that testify to a healthy soul, an integrity strong and unthreatened by the "dull grief, blown grit, hideous / concrete façades," and a power to find in all things an "abode of mercy," "an otherness that was blesséd, that was bliss."

So should end all symphonies perhaps, but *Sorrow Dance* disconcertingly adds to this otherwise rounded performance, eight, broken, jarring chords—eight poems on the war.

The first of the "Life at War" section poems is a beautifully enigmatic poem of multiple registrations. "The Pulse" encompasses one "life beat," one expansion and contraction. It begins in systole ("I knock my head / on steel petals / curving inward around me"), moves through diastole ("all is opened to me") and ends in systole ("I wait in the dark"). This archetypal cycle, common to nearly all things throughout time and space, whether seasons, civilizations, galaxies, or sea anemones, carries a multitude of meanings. The poet imaginatively imprisoned in the sea anemone finds it opened to a green half-light world of the imagination, a land where it is always morning, and where the currents of glitter and phosphorescence move the poet to song. But the song inspired by the fair world has a "ground bass," and it is not ecstatic and unrestrained—the singer's "feet are weighted" and "ache up from heel to knee." Even this tempered song, however, is soon denied by the reclosing of the steel petals, which condemns her to wait in a darkness she has no power to end. That "edict" must be given somewhere else.

Even before isolating any of the many possible readings of this poem, one feels convinced of the poem's rightness. It may apply to such highs and lows, expansions and contractions of being as each of us experiences, and over which we exercise so little control. It reflects also the progression of moods through "The Sorrow Dance," "Perspectives," and "Life at War" chapters; and it further suggests the experience of one who begins in inarticulateness, struggles out of confinement into the voice and vision of the poet, and finds that voice again restricted and destroyed even before the song's first refrain is reached. Subsequent poems point to the validity of a biographical reading. In coming to America and discovering its new rhythms and idioms, she had developed a poetic voice, but now forces from within that same culture threaten to destroy what had been brought to flower. Levertov's powers of sight and song are shriveled by the shadow of the war. This first of the "war poems," then, sets out the primary theme of her poetry on the war—the loss of vision and poetic power.

Those critics who have over the years complained that Levertov's poetry is too limited in subject matter have usually not been clear about what that limited matter was; but one can easily argue that too much of her poetry centers on the role and method of the poet, the experience of being a poet, and the act of creating poems. The propensity for *ars poetica* carries over into the war poems, as is already evident in "The Pulse." Both the inclination towards *ars poetica* and the concern for the effect of war on poetry reach back to *The Double Image*, her first volume of poems published at the end of World War II.[17] In a book review that praises H. D.'s insights into World War II, Levertov admits that she herself did not really experience that war as a poet: "I was too young— younger than my years—to experience, as a poet, the bombing of London: I lived in the midst of it but in a sense it did not *happen* to me, and though my own first book, in 1946, was written during the time, the war appeared in it only offstage or as the dark background of adolescent anxiety."[18] The neo-romantic *Double Image* is full of shadows and adolescent anxiety, but one poem speaks directly of a greater darkness. Its title, "The Shadow," looks forward to the title of *Out of the War Shadow: The 1968 Peace Calendar*, edited by Levertov, and to the spirit of her early poems on Vietnam. The poem (p. 32) begins: "I need a green and undulating line / the hill's long contours in my words." Most of the volume's poems achieve this British neo-romantic line, but, she argues, such lines are difficult or denied to her because the war atmosphere offers a contrasting landscape: "the ancient lines of mountains break in craters, / destructive skies crack like decaying plaster." Though she desires a positive language of springtime and love, poetry cannot carry on oblivious to the presence of the antipoetic: "music refuses to ignore the black confusion of war."

"Advent 1966" (published in *The Nation* as the *Sorrow Dance* poems were going to press) is a much more concentrated and powerful statement of the ravages of war on Levertov's poetic powers. A series of contrasts are built around Robert Southwell's mystical vision of the Burning Babe and Levertov's haunting imagination of the physically burning infants of Vietnam. Whereas the one vision prefigures redemption and purification, and increases the poet's spiritual powers and insight, the latter damns and destroys the imaginative powers. The one is "unreal" and speaks of the highest reality; the other is physically real and born of chaotic irreality. Southwell's burning babe is singular, unique; the babes of Vietnam are multiple "as off a beltline" and appear to the poet as the blurred and overlapping images of faulty vision:

> because of this my strong sight,
> my clear caressive sight, my poet's sight I was given
> that it might stir me to song,
> is blurred.
>   There is a cataract filming over
> my inner eyes. Or else a monstrous insect
> has entered my head, and looks out
> from my sockets with multiple vision,[19]

At what point and from what cause does the blurring of vision occur? Is it in the seeing, or in that which is seen? Is the insect in the head or is it an emanation and reflection of the chaotic facts of the war? The poem's realization seems to be, in fact, that the disordering of the sight and the disordering of reality are the same. Such is in keeping with Levertov's poetics. *Claritas* is possible only in the synapse of orderly mind and orderly object: the imagination does not add or change but discovers clarity, penetrates the order of its objects. The war, however, is without spirit or order, and the imagination cannot find the precisely focused image of the Burning Babe that is not there. The vision that is there

> will not permit me to look elsewhere,
>
> or if I look, to see except dulled and unfocused
> the delicate, firm, whole flesh of the still unburned.

Thus the poet's imagination, which before could see clearly through the surface chaos, now finds even the orderly surfaces (the "whole flesh of the still unburned") blurred by the impenetrable experience of the war. If the imagination is repeatedly defeated in its attempt to pierce through disorder, it becomes dulled and blunted, and loses its powers to do so.

The war casts a disabling shadow for Levertov because hers is a poetics of order and of the presumption of order: "my notion of organic form is really based on the idea that there is form in all

things—that the artist doesn't impose form upon chaos, but discovers hidden form by means of the poet's attentive listening, not
only his listening but also his feeling, his meditating upon his experience, and by means of his accurate transcription of that experience into words."[20]

Levertov would not normally speak in terms of what is poetic
and anti-poetic, or make the passé distinctions these terms call to
mind. But war is truly "non-poetic" within a poetry that discovers
order, inner truth, by piercing through the "shell" to the "kernel"
of reality.[21] Her tendency to see war as "black confusion" and
ultimate disorder suggests war is all shell and without the kernel
that poetry seeks.

The chaos of war is not the same as the surface confusion of
other things—these latter conceal but do contain an order that
poetry can extricate for life. Faith in the presence of this kernel
vitalizes all of Levertov's volumes before 1964. The poem "Pleasures"
is a beautiful example:

> I like to find
> what's not found
> at once, but lies
>
> within something of another nature,
> in repose, distinct.
> Gull feathers of glass, hidden
>
> in white pulp: the bones of squid
> which I pull out and lay
> blade by blade on the draining board—   (*Eyes*, p. 17)

"Pleasures" speaks further of the extricated seed of the fleshy
mamey, like polished walnut wood, "large enough to fill / the
hungry palm of a hand" (*Eyes*, p. 17). Levertov thinks also in
terms of the "palm of mind's hand" (*Relearning*, p. 101): poetry's
business is, for her, to disclose such seeds for its handling. She would
uncover the palpable nuclei of significance in all things.

Not only is the poem's form to be found "out there" or "in
there," but the content of truth, the metaphor of spirit, is also really
there somewhere under or inside the external phenomena. Numer-

ous poems attest to this belief: a good example is "The Palm Tree" where she studies the tree's frenzied tossing in the wind:

> At once the mind, agape,
> > scavenging:
> What's human here? What hope is there?
> thumbing the dry leaves
> eager, eager, for the fabulous
> poem there may be
> in this delight or battle[22]

It becomes clear that for Levertov nothing is more important than poetry: it is always and everywhere of the first consideration; and yet there is nothing of the *aesthete* in her, and no temptation to art for art's sake. For her, poetry is the way into life, *is* the life under the surfaces, and both life and poetry are diminished when either one or the other is diminished. Her concern for the demise of poetic powers during war in no way detracts from her compassionate concern for the people who suffer in war. They are inseparable. Poetry is close at hand and is what she knows; carnage and suffering are far away and are what she can know only secondhand. The horror of the latter manifests itself in its effect upon the former.

IV

Levertov's pre-Vietnam poetry shows us a capable and confident woman and poet avidly "reading" the world as she moves through experience. That world could be coped with and understood, and beauty lay along the path. She found it all, you may say, satisfactory. But war will not lie down to the imagination. It casts a shadow on all the other goings:

> . . . The feeling
> resembles lumps of raw dough
> weighing down a child's stomach on baking day.
> > ("Life at War," *Sorrow Dance*, p. 79)

One carries the war about as a burden, as if his heart were "balled into formless lumps." "War" here seems to have a slightly wider

extension than Vietnam (and applies, as in Ginsberg, to all that
is warlike):

> We have breathed the grits of it in, all our lives,
> our lungs are pocked with it,
> the mucous membrane of our dreams
> coated with it, the imagination
> filmed over with the gray filth of it: (p. 79)

But Vietnam is obviously the real sore: our "nerve filaments twitch
with its presence" and "nothing we say has not the husky phlegm
of it in the saying." It is perhaps not without significance that the
choice of images directly or indirectly relates to the making of
poetry: lungs, dreams, imagination, breath, saying.

A similar sense of blight finds expression in the work of other
poets. Robert Bly, for example, compresses it beautifully in a single
image: "we all feel like tires being run down the road under
heavy cars."[23] But the theme is unusually pervasive in Levertov's
own work and in work she selected for *Out of the War Shadow:
The 1968 Peace Calendar*. Of the poems of *The Peace Calendar*,
Dwight MacDonald writes: "Each one is original, a different voice,
and yet I think they share certain qualities which make the anthology a whole, and which perhaps reflect the taste of its compiler.
They tend towards the laconic and hard."[24] MacDonald's is sensitive
and accurate analysis, for in addition to their economy and their
onyx hardness, these poems share certain themes, not the least of
which is the spiritual blight of the war.

In 1961, Levertov had objected strenuously in *The Floating
Bear* (number 11) to Robert Kelly's comment on the need to restore a "poetry of desperation." If poets are desperate, she argued,
poems will be; if not, not, so why "restore" it. Such poetry has
existed before and will perhaps exist again, "but spontaneously and
of necessity." Surely, desperate poetry was at that time foreign to
the imagination of the poet of *Overland to the Islands*. But the
Vietnam War restored the poetry of desperation by making Levertov
and other poets desperate.

Yet desperation does not really describe the feeling flowing
out of Levertov's poems on the war. A few notes of *The Sorrow*

Dance sound something like hysteria, and later poems move beyond desperation, through mild catatonia toward intransigent rebellion. One fact is apparent in the changing moods: evil has been encountered by Levertov in a way it had not been encountered before, and the effect has been profound. "Life at War" shows it in the images of raw dough and husky phlegm, but even more dramatically in the descriptions of carnage:

> . . . the scheduled breaking open of breasts whose milk
> runs out over the entrails of still-alive babies,
> transformation of witnessing eyes to pulp-fragments,
> implosion of skinned penises into carcass-gulleys.   (p. 79)

One thinks immediately of Siegfried Sassoon's "Counter-Attack":

> The place was rotten with dead. Green clumsy legs,
> High-booted, sprawled and groveled along the saps,
> And trunks, face downward in the sucking mud,
> Wallowed like trodden sandbags loosely filled,
> And naked, sodden buttocks, mats of hair,
> Bulged clotted heads slept in the plastering slime.
> And then the rain began, the jolly old rain.[25]

But though Sassoon's experienced vision is more horrible than Levertov's imagined one, its expression nevertheless possesses a detachment and a distance that her lines do not. The last line of Sassoon's, of course, helps this impression, but it would be apparent without it. His images are reported, observed, seen in all their grotesqueness, but the poet's psychic integrity is not threatened. That characterizes all of Sassoon's poetry and the bulk of the poetry of the First World War. It is a poetry of the eye, the outer eye. Levertov's images are here seen with a visceral eye different from the inner eye of her earlier poems. These images are not seen into or through, but experienced with the "mucous membranes" mentioned earlier in the same poem. Duncan says of these images that, though the poet believes she is writing anti-war sentiments, the war is really only an irritant that knocks the scabs from already present psychological sores. He feels her choice of images here and elsewhere suggests a repressed obsession with sexual violence. Whether this is more than can be safely seen in the lines, they do certainly reveal that the poet's agitation is more than superficial.*

The two *Sorrow Dance* poems after "The Pulse" and "Life at War" are titled simply "Didactic Poem" and "Second Didactic Poem." They *are* didactic, and differ from her non-war poems in that they are not primarily poems of discovery or exploration. They are not a means of seeing into, but of expressing points the poet already understands and holds. The first is prose-like, and argues the need to create our own lives and invent our own deeds, rather than carry out the will of the dead spirits who preceded us and still permeate us. The legacy of debt and undone deeds passed from generation to generation perpetuates the unreal and the inhumane. Those debts must be disowned and new actions taken up.

The "Second Didactic Poem" is the better poem, more imaginatively conceived, and an important reiteration of an article of Levertov's faith. It teaches "The honey of man is / the task we're set to." Though difficulty and evil are everywhere, they can be transmuted just as bees make honey in the presence of corruption: "Beespittle, droppings, hairs / of beefur: all become honey" (*Sorrow Dance*,

---

* Duncan's appraisal is actually even more stringent than this. He says, "There's another field of feeling that frequently comes up when she means to write a protest feeling, and that is her own sadism, and masochism, and so the war becomes like, becomes a not gloating but almost as fierce an expression as the fantasies of Dickey. She'll be writing about the war and suddenly—in one of the earlier poems that's most shocking—you get a flayed penis, and . . . when she reads it you get an effect and tone of disgusted sensuality. And when you look at her poetry it tells more to look at that flayed penis and realize that her earlier poems are talking about stripped stalks of grass! She's got one that loves peeling [perhaps the "Pleasures" poem quoted above]. Suddenly you see a charged, bloody, sexual image that's haunting the whole thing, and the war then acts as a magnet, and the poem is not a protest though she thinks she's protesting" (personal interview, 9 May 1969). Duncan's analysis will appeal to Freudians. There is indeed even in the few poems quoted in this study a great deal of peeling and digging and probing into, but I believe these are best seen as aesthetic and epistemological concerns (a desire to get at the "center," the "kernel") rather than sexual ones. (But if Freud is right, our aesthetics and epistemology may be sublimated sexuality anyway.)

p. 82). It is as though in face of the threat expressed in the first poems of the "Life at War" section, Levertov is reasserting her position, witnessing to her faith in the possibilities of men, and in pattern and purpose in the world. Just as the desire and intensity of the hummingbird can find life in the bitter insects steeped in nectar, so man can cultivate a spirit in which the ugly and negative will have a part but no power: "Virulent micro-organisms cannot / survive in honey." The "Second Didactic Poem" is momentarily the old voice of equilibrium and secure humanity speaking again. That security does not survive long.

Though Levertov's initial reaction to the war was that it clouded her poetic eyes, in another sense it perhaps opened them forever. In her more recent poetry she has much of the temper of the Vietnamese woman whose eyelids were burned off by napalm:

She saw
her five young children
writhe and die;
in that hour
she began to watch you,
she whose eyes are open forever.

("Two Variations," *Sorrow Dance*, p. 85)

V

After the violent images of "Life at War," "Two Variations," and "Advent 1966," Denise Levertov comes to avoid specific description of the war's horrors, "the crimes of war, / the unspeakable—of which, then, / I won't speak" ("Interim," in *Relearning*, p. 26). But knowledge of them is ever present and forms, as Bly warned, "Particles / The grass cannot dissolve."[26] Her poems find enough other outrages—the imprisonment and fast of Courcy Squire, the immolations of Norman Morrison and Alice Hertz, the indictment of her husband, Mitchell Goodman, and the multitude of grotesqueries that have haunted the news during the years of the war. The result of these is a profound change in the attitudes and techniques of Levertov's poetry. New eyes and a new voice are in evidence. And a new imbalance.

Because poetic vision and poetic form are so closely allied for Levertov, it is natural that her verse about and during the Vietnam conflict should be troubled with a loss of form as well as a loss of vision. Thus, just as "The Pulse" and "Life at War," dealing with loss of vision, introduce the war poems in *The Sorrow Dance*, so "The Broken Sandal," concerned with the loss of form, introduces the long section of war-related poems in *Relearning the Alphabet*.

> Dreamed the thong of my sandal broke.
> Nothing to hold it to my foot.
> How shall I walk?
> > Barefoot?
> The sharp stones, the dirt. I would
> hobble   (*Relearning*, p. 3)

Considered in the light of the much earlier "Art" (*Eyes*, 1960) quoted on p. 90, this poem, too, asks to be read as *ars poetica*. It is of course also more than that, except that for Levertov the art of poetry includes the whole art of living. Howsoever that may be, the poem witnesses to a disabling predicament, an impediment to desired activity and growth, and a time for retrospection, introspection, and circumspection.

> Where was I going?
> Where was I going I can't
> go to now, unless hurting?
> Where am I standing, if I'm
> to stand still now?   (*Relearning*, p. 3)

This moment has been created by the last five or six years of her life, years in which the war has been the largest presence; and the entire volume of poems suggests a reconsideration and change of perspectives and assumptions. Moreover, the poems offer evidence formally and rhythmically that the poet's old composure and equilibrium have been lost, that a new period has been entered. Equilibrium and balance, the earmarks of Levertov's poetry and person, have finally given way to new doubts and new involvements and poems that have lost much of their quality of "onyx, steel."

"The Cold Spring," the volume's third poem (after "The Broken Sandal" and "Advent 1966"), displays a loss of faith in the assurances of the "Second Didactic Poem" and questions the sufficiency of a poetry of the immediate. The rhythms display a new barrenness that is neither desperation nor despair, but lassitude. It is a poetry of disillusionment, and very nearly of complete defeat:

> Twenty years, forty years, it's nothing.
> Not a mirage; the blink
> of an eyelid.
> Life is nibbling us with little
> lips, circling our knees, our
> shoulders.
> What's the difference,
> a kiss or a fin-caress. Only sometimes
> the water reddens,
> we ebb.   (*Relearning*, p. 5)

Life is here not, as in earlier poetry, a vital movement, "intently haphazard" where "every step is an arrival." Rather life is something that happens to one; the one who lives is passive and acted upon, immobile, drifting. This is in sharp contrast to Levertov's self-instructions in "The Five-Day Rain":

> Wear scarlet! Tear the green lemons
> off the tree! I don't want
> to forget who I am, what has burned in me
> and hang limp and clean, an empty dress—   (*Eyes*, p. 13)

On the contrary, the voice of "The Cold Spring" is like the empty dress, acted upon by external forces that threaten to drown but hold the helpless non-swimmer upright, her toes barely touching the muddy bottom. And though a fin-caress need not be terrifying, it is so here, and sounds as threatening as the fins in "Sharks" (*Overland to the Islands*). The statement about the difference between a kiss and a fin-caress—"only sometimes / the water reddens"— suggests almost manic depression.

Section II of "Cold Spring" doubts the importance of a poetry of natural mystery and the particular. What the broken sandal image suggests about insufficiency of form, this and the following section suggest about content:

What do I know?
  Swing of the
  birch catkins,
  drift of
  watergrass,
  tufts of
  green on the
  trees,   (*Relearning*, p. 5)

"It's not enough," she fears, for the poet to go on playing his
meager five notes, relishing "some certainty / of mordant delight,"
while the firing resumes on the other side of the world, and science
begins to speak of human obsolescence in the promise of computers.
Somehow poetry and poets are failing and need a new voice and
vision. Poets "who grew up toward utopias" suffer from an amnesia
of the heart, and the American dream, now come to, is not the
place we sought. The spirit has left it and us. In this quandary
the poet finds herself drowning and wounded, and sounds much
like the Ginsberg of *Empty Mirror:*

Forty years redden the spreading circles.
Blink of an eyelid,
nothing,
obsolete future—   (*Relearning*, p. 8)

The poet fears she will "find [her] poem is deathsongs," and that
she is without the spiritual resources to give life significance.
Nature is still constant, still real, but somehow empty, too, and
without the meaning or purpose that the poet's own fire had before
found or placed in it.* She feels "reduced" to a cold eye that sees
but sees and sings death.

---

* Though Levertov's attitudes toward nature are generally quite different from those of the Romantics, there is here a new realization that nature
and experience can be as much a source of doubt as of faith, and that though
the reading of nature is not wholly subjective, nevertheless the same sights
and sounds can sometimes sustain, sometimes destroy. The awareness resembles Percy Bysshe Shelley's in "Mont Blanc": "The wilderness has a
mysterious tongue/Which teaches awful doubt, or faith so mild" or "Mont
Blanc yet gleams on high—the power is there,/The still and solemn power
of many sights/And many sounds, and much of life and death." The well-

Reduced to an eye
I forget what
     I

was.   (*Relearning*, p. 9)

The poet's extremity is underlined by the fact that this statement
ought to have an exactly opposite significance. It is very close to
the language of the *Hasidim* and Christian and Zen mystics. In a
more positive context "reduced" would be paradoxically synonymous
with "magnified," and the forgetting would be the desirable loss
of ego or relative consciousness. Even here there is perhaps a kind
of death of will that in later poems will make possible a movement
into purer consciousness and ecstatic seeing. Implicit here again is
the idea that these years of war cannot be pierced with the inner
eye, or if pierced are no different in the kernel than in the shell.
The inner eye, having no proper object, becomes like the outer eye.
In the passive, cold, sterile aura of this poem one feels that the
"eye" is locked, inactive, glazed, and staring. Defeat in "Cold
Spring" is both internal and external. The universe is empty and
the will is dead, and neither possess the spark to rekindle the other.
This emptiness and hopelessness echoes throughout *Relearning the
Alphabet*:

no hope: Don't know
what to do: Do nothing: ("Biafra," p. 18)

While the war drags on, always worse,
the soul dwindles sometimes to an ant
rapid upon a cracked surface;   ("An Interim," p. 21)

. . . this year
    only cloudless flushes of light, paleness
        slowly turning to rose,
        and fading subdued.
We have not spoken of these tired
risings of the sun.

("What Wild Dawns There Were," p. 29)

---

springs of meaning in the universe and in the individual are alike mysterious
and uncertain. This is a modification of her faith in the benevolent order
behind or in phenomena.

> A dark time we live in. One would think
>> there would be no summer.   ("July 1968," p. 64)
>> Is there anything
>> I write any more that is not
>> elegy?
>>
>>> Goldengrove
> is unleaving all around me; I live
> in goldengrove;   ("From a Notebook," p. 96)

Poets and idealists who grew up equating utopia with "living in the present" and who now find the present intolerable are indeed facing a gulf like that faced by the black boy in the Detroit riots who stole "armfuls of gladioli" from the florist's only to find them without perfume, white man's flowers:

> Breathless he halts to examine
>
> the flesh of dream: he squeezes
> the strong cold juicy stems, long as his legs,
>> ("The Gulf," *Relearning*, p. 15)

Levertov can see his flight and his actions in her mind's eye, but she cannot see further than the gulf he faces, cannot see whether he throws the flowers away and goes in search of another dream, or keeps them nevertheless. He is frozen in his dilemma in her imagination, and she is similarly paralyzed in the face of her own crisis of life and poetry.

The remaining poems of the first chapter of *Relearning the Alphabet* are less important statements of the poet's psychology, philosophy, and aesthetics in crisis, and deal with topical or occasional matters. The fine poem "Tenebrae" counterposes the mindless and artificial quotidian activities and artifacts of our culture against the reality of the war:

> And picnic parties return from the beaches
> burning with stored sun in the dusk;
> children promised a TV show when they get home
> fall asleep in the back of a million station wagons   (p. 13)

There is an innocence in what we do, but a "grim innocence"; our actions are not of desire but of etiquette, and grow only out of a

need to be proper and accepted. Further lines suggest why Robert
Bly especially likes this poem's illumination of American life.

> Their parents at night
> dream and forget their dreams.
> They wake in the dark
> and make plans. Their sequin plans
> glitter into tomorrow.   (p.13)

A similar voice begins to surface in other poems. Political faces
on the TV remind the poet of Bosch's paintings, and certain lines
begin to take on the qualities of the surreal:

> . . . no room
> for love in us: what's left over
> changes to bile, brims over: stain on the cushion: (p. 17)

Different poems begin to look like an attempt to go barefoot
or put on a different sandal in quest of greater sufficiency of content and form. Two long political poems in *Relearning the Alphabet*, "An Interim" and "From a Notebook: October '68–May '69,"
mix stanzas of various lines and rhythms, handbills, news stories,
prose letters, much in the manner of Williams's *Paterson* or Pound's
The Cantos. They are marked too with a new spirit, a new
polemical subjectivity. Though she is not completely comfortable
within the "revolution," she knows that it is "revolution or death"
and that

> It's in the air: no air
>   to breathe without
> scent of it,
>   pervasive:
> odor of snow,   ("From a Notebook," p. 102)

The revolution is at least an activity in a time when activity
seems impossible, a way out of darkness and lassitude. If a poetry
of the swing of the birch catkins seems trivial in the shadow of
Vietnam and People's Park, then poetry must find a revolutionary
voice. The poetry of "discovery" no longer satisfies the hunger for
meaning when what it discovers are objects without meaning. The
earth does not satisfy the needs of man, and life must become more

than the intently haphazard tourism of the senses. Though the polished seed of the mamey, the extracted bones of the squid, or "Black beans, white sunlight. / These have sufficed," she knows now "a hunger there is / refuses. Refuses the earth" ("A Hunger," *Relearning*, p. 51). That Denise Levertov has been politicized and radicalized by the war seems clear.

Marge Piercy praises *Relearning the Alphabet* for its richness of revolutionary imagery, and sees it as evidence that Levertov now fully belongs to "the movement."[27] Levertov is not, however, fully at ease within the movement, and her hunger is somewhat different or larger than that of most of those within it. She is not comfortable in verse that is not "exploratory" and is uneasy with the "few flippant rhymes" she is able to "bring forth out of . . . [her] anger" ("An Interim," *Relearning*, p. 26). Subsequent poems reveal her awareness that the idiom and traditionless iconoclasm of the revolution are not hers. The new shift in poetic manner further complicates an already alien predicament: she has changed continents and cultures and is "without a terrain in which, to which, I belong" (p. 97); and because her roots are in the nineteenth century she is not only without a country but without an era.

> Language itself is my one home, my Jerusalem,
> yet time and the straddled ocean
> undo me, maroon me,
> (roadblocks, the lines down)—
>   I choose
>   revolution but my words
> often already don't reach forward
>   into it—
>   (*Relearning*, p. 97)

Even her language is not at home or in tune and makes her untrue to her time; but if she were to change it sufficiently, she would be untrue to herself (p. 98). That this predicament (the pressing needs of the revolution weighted against the strong need for poetic integrity) is the cause of great anguish can be seen, despite the carefully modulated rhythms, in her echo of St. Paul's tortured cry, "For the good that I would, I do not: but the evil which I would

not, that I do. . . . O wretched man that I am! who shall deliver
me from the body of this death?" (Romans 7:19 and 24):

> Whom I would touch
> I may not,
> whom I may
> I would
> but often do not.   (p. 97–98)

"Snail" is almost a retraction of her movement toward a new
manner of poetry:

> Burden, grace,
> artifice coiled
> brittle on my back, integral,
> I thought to crawl
> out of you   (p. 77)

But she knows still that "in my shell / my life was" and remembers
the values of objectivity and balance: "my eyes adept to witness /
air and harsh light / and look all ways." There is, then, in *Relearning the Alphabet*, a "politicized poet" and a "pure poet,"
which are at times distinct, at times indistinguishable. The one has
not replaced the other, but they exist side by side. There are poems
here that would be interchangeable with any of the poems of *The
Jacob's Ladder* or *O Taste and See*: "The Singer," "The Open
Secret," "Bullfrogs to Fireflies to Moths" are positive and crystalline,
clear caressive sight preserved in amber. Onyx.

But though the old poetry is still for a while a possible poetry
for Levertov, the war and the revolution have opened new fields
and new spiritual understandings. Certain poems of *Relearning the
Alphabet* at last show the spiritual depth that one might always
have looked for from a poet of such extraordinary fortitude and
strong *Hasidic* background. One cannot be sure whether the understandings here evident are new to the poet or are only now allowed
to manifest themselves because of a changing aesthetic. But the
title of the 1970 volume, the tentative manner in which some ideas
are set forth, and the long tradition of exploratory poetry lead one
to believe that the shape of the book is not a matter of art alone,

but of spiritual autobiography, a true relearning. The book is not an aggregation of separate poems but an admirably unified work: its shape is that of a *Bildungsroman* or, better, a mystical hagiography. The voice moves through defeat and death of the will to a new peace and hope, a new sense of human possibility. Though every life changes under a multitude of influences (the mere passage of time alone having profound effects), it seems clear that the war and the social malaise have occasioned the darkness, and that "the movement" and Levertov's spiritual heritage have brought on the new light. Such at least is the configuration of the poetry in *Relearning the Alphabet.*

It should not be surprising that a volume of poems written in years when death seems ubiquitous should be heavily colored by its influence. Death invades these poems in a variety of meaningful ways. It is there from the beginning in the burning babes, the broken sandal, the spreading circles of red, the graveside poems, the starvation in Biafra, and indeed in the chapter heading "Elegies." But there are also the remarkable deaths of Norman Morrison and Alice Hertz, the near death fast of Courcy Squire—where each death testifies to a deeper life. And there is the death-in-life of the consumer with his station wagon full of kids, Mayor Daley, and "the coprophiliac spasm / that smears the White House walls with its desensitized thumbs" (p. 93). But more importantly, there is everywhere in the volume the death that Keats evoked in "Ode to a Nightingale." Levertov has elsewhere said that "Ode to a Nightingale" was the first and only poem she ever learned by heart. Phrases from it recur throughout *Relearning the Alphabet,* and the reader frequently picks up from her own words a life-fatigue, a longing for the soft, funeral darkness of the forest glade, a drowsy numbness that would sing to death a sweet song, a voice that evokes pictures of sad last grey hairs shaken with palsy. Perhaps the poet's extremity *is* this exaggerated; otherwise one could hardly excuse the inclusion of such a poem of sentimentality as "Souvenir d'amitié." Would Keats at his weakest moments, too, have been gratified by a dog sharing a flea with him? The death longing that surfaces through the book seems to be larger than the poet's conscious artistic intentions.

Indeed, if one can trust the long poem "From a Notebook: October '68–May '69," Levertov seems actually to have come near death by running obliviously through traffic to reach a taxi. Handled in the poem as it is, it appears she intends it to be seen as an action prompted by a subconscious death desire. She emphasizes ironically that instead of fear, she was more "strenuous to convince" the driver that she was not "a habitual public danger": "So close to death and thinking only / of being forgiven by strangers" (p. 94). Flirtation with death seems part of a desire to escape the burden of guilt and inadequacy imposed by the war and the culture—"(Unlived life / of which one can die)" (p. 92). The incident is made to work poetically as a longing to escape the fever and the fret of the examined life, as a desire to be free at last from the disappointment and disillusionment that evil and decay constanly impose on us. And, lastly, it is part of the dark night of the soul forcing it toward the necessary cessation of struggle, the passivity needed for the rekindling of the fire. The change has not been an instantaneous or cataclysmic affair, but the years of the war have forced Levertov to find a new relationship with the world, and have made it impossible for her to go on spiritually or poetically wearing scarlet and tearing the lemons from the tree. The ineffective struggle against the war has brought a new desolation, and

'. . . desolation is gestation. Absence
          an absolute
          presence
          calling forth
          the person   (the poet)
     into desperate continuance, toward
     fragments of light.'

                    ("Dialogue," *Relearning*, p. 91)

It would be easy to read too much spiritual biography into the poem; but spiritual allegory is there, and even the title should lead us to look for it. "From a Notebook: October '68–May '69" begins in the growing darkness of fall, moves through the darkness or colorless whiteness of winter, to the reawakenings of spring. The progression is never simple or imposed, but is, nevertheless, there.

The first five cantos of Part I explore the choices between revolution and death—death of not one but several kinds. The tone is predominantly elegiac and the poet's own death-longing will not stay below the surface despite her assertions of life desire. Canto vi explores the poet's alienation from the culture and the time, employing the image of one marooned in a snowstorm. The "Entr'acte" between Parts I and II tells of the thinning light of October, the November that is suddenly there without one's knowing it, and

> . . . into the first snowstorm (marooned)
> the lines down
> no phone
> no lights
> no heat
> gastank for cooking about to give out
> car stuck in the driveway.
>   We find candles   (p. 99)

There is here also a coldly frightening description of black and white emptiness and silence:

> hemlock and cedar a toneless black,
> snowtufted trunks and boughs
> black, sky white, birches
> whiter, snow
> infinitely whiter: all things
> muted: deprived
> of color, as if
> color were utterance.
> A terror
> as of eclipse.
> The whites graying.   (p. 100)

These together, along with the way the phrases of the first excerpt are broken for emphasis, bring to mind the Buddhist mantra "no mind, no hands, no eyes, no touch" and suggest that the spiritual state shadowed forth is a parallel emptiness and dying away of the self. There is also in the "Entr'acte" a curious, grayed, shriveled fly that the speaker had "thought dead" but which still "slowly waves" on his back on the windowsill.

> Yes, what would be its right arm
> dreamily moves—out—in—out again
> twice, three times.
>   It seems
> flies dream in dying.   (p. 99)

The elegiac tone and the fervorless images of fatigue and death give way in Part II. It begins:

> Can't go further.
> If there's to be a
> part, it's not
> a going beyond, I'm
> still here.
> To dig down,
> to reexamine.

The poem then proceeds to rethink the implications and possibilities of the revolution, and of the persons that give it life. An awakening of sorts occurs in Levertov's account of her work with students on the clearing of People's Park:

> O happiness
> in the sun! Is it
> that simple, then,
> to live?   (p. 106)

From this point to the end of the volume the descant of death and the drowsy numbness of death-longing are gone, and are replaced by a note of joy and positive strength. The rest of "Notebook" is vigorous and truly revolutionary, and "Relearning the Alphabet," the final long poem that follows, puts this new vigor and optimism into its larger spiritual and philosophical context. "Notebook" ends with three powerful images of revolution; and these no doubt account for Marge Piercy's excitement about the book. The first is of a tree floating up in floodwaters, raising a branch to the sky, and stirring mud from the bottom with the other side of its crown; the uplifted branch, in what the imagination sees as a kind of cinematic technique, is suddenly refocused as an arm raised in a crawl stroke, and the waters are suddenly alive with swimmers;

and at last, by a similar cinematic transmutation, the mind watches "Islands / step out of the waves on rock feet." Thus the vigorous last twenty-two lines of this poem are such as every revolution has longed for. They are poetry deserving the definition of "language with which nothing more can be done."

The title poem and last long poem of *Relearning the Alphabet* is an application and amplification of its prose epigraph by Heinrich Zimmer:

> "The treasure . . . lies buried. There is no need to seek it in a distant country . . . It is behind the stove, the center of the life and warmth that rule our existence, if only we knew how to unearth it. And yet—there is this strange and persistent fact, that it is only after . . . a journey in a distant region, in a new land, that . . . the inner voice . . . can make itself understood by us. And to this strange and persistent fact is added another: that he who reveals to us the meaning of our . . . inward pilgrimage must be himself a stranger . . ."
>
> (p. 110)

"Relearning the Alphabet" is rightly neither protest poem, war poem, nor political poem, and yet there can be no doubt that its experience is shaped in the matrices of war, politics, and protest. It is in many ways an "Ash Wednesday" poem in which the poet "relearns" the joy of simplicity; accepts the cycle of

> Endless
> returning, endless
> revolution of dream to ember, ember to anguish,
> anguish to flame, flame to delight,
> delight to dark and dream, dream to ember   (p. 111)

and realizes that transcendence is not a matter that may be forced by the will or "sharp desire." The holy place that one comes to, the inseeing into things that one finally achieves, is not what the poet, the revolutionary, or the "vain will" "thinks to construct for its testimonies" (p. 119).

> Vision sets out
> journeying somewhere,

walking the dreamwaters:
arrives
not on the far shore but upriver,
a place not evoked, discovered.   (p. 119)

The "far shore" is the language of Zen and mysticism, as is the
realization that

Only the vain will
strives to use and be used,
comes not to fire's core
but cinder.   (p. 120)

The seeing or the peace that one strenuously seeks comes only in
defeat and passivity:

The door I flung my weight against
was constructed to open out
                    towards me   (p. 117)

The poem moves beyond the aesthetics of *claritas* to a more
emotional and spiritual seeing:

the heart an eye looking,
the heart a root
planted in earth.
Transmutation is not
under the will's rule.   (p. 119)

Claritas is still important, but now comes after and through *caritas*
rather than vice versa:

Caritas is what I must travel to.
Through to the fire's core,
an alchemy:
                    caritas, claritas.   (p. 113)

VI

Denise Levertov's poems on war and written during that time
are for the most part not poems of the same viability or aesthetic
autonomy as the earlier precise poems of immediate experience.

Those were "made objects" with a life of their own, true to experience, true to a moment and to a context, and once made were able to walk off on their own power, no longer dependent. In place of the earlier sonnet-sized *closed* and ordered poems, her later work moves to long *open* and unbuttoned poems, which are very much, in Robert Duncan's sense, "Passages" of a continuing larger Poem in which the order is the constant shifting of orders. In some sense the early poems are undoubtedly more perfect and enduring works of art, more timeless and less datable, but they are, for all their fineness, only teacups, and of sorely limited capacities. The war-shadowed poems are less clean and symmetrical but are moral and philosophical schooners of some size. Though Levertov felt a need to apologize, in effect, by labeling them didactic poems, some of the earliest of the Vietnam-provoked poems assume a new moral weight. And for our moralist, whom better could we desire than a poet of Levertov's culture and humanity, integrity and equilibrium. Perhaps Richard Howard was right in 1963 when he complained that "her imagist mode" and her concern for the primacy of objects and experience kept her from doing what she does best, writing poetry of profound moral and spiritual statement. "She is a moralist whose manner forbids her to develop what she knows."[28] Whether or not "moralist" is a satisfactory appellation, it is true that her full moral power could not enter the poetry under the more restrictive aesthetic. *O Taste and See* is incomparable poetry, but one would be dissatisfied if it were the only kind of poetry: and one would ultimately be dissatisfied with Levertov if it were the only kind of poetry she could write. The war, by offering much that was distasteful and unsightly, prompted a poetry that asks the poet to add the light and weight of her moral and spiritual powers to the fine sensibility of her palate and eye.

VII

Though we should like to end on that up-note, Levertov's more recent volume, *To Stay Alive* (New York: New Directions, 1971), does raise further questions about the direction of Levertov's poetry and personal protest. At times a note of something too hard, too intransigent rises in these poems: "There comes a time when only anger / is love" (p. 58, and again on p. 81). Levertov's growing bitterness about the war and the state of the American soul has prompted Robert Duncan to see her as Kali, the black goddess of terror and destruction, and has moved William Stafford to comment:

> Denise Levertov, to move to another, different kind of protester, I like to talk with, but I find myself differing with her not just in terms of style (as happens with Bly) but in terms of apparent aim: I feel that her protest is part of a way of life, rather than a chosen issue as in Bly's case. My impulse, even in protest, is toward some kind of redemptive move toward the opposition, and I do not detect that readiness to find common group in some protestors, and I guess Denise would represent the intransigent position, or the unforgiving position.
>
> (In a letter to this writer, 31 Jan. 1972)

There has been indeed a growing note of alienation, an increasing sense of unbridgeable distance between Levertov and her opposition, the amorphous *they* who in one way or another are to blame for Vietnam. She and the war-makers have become more and more estranged, and her humanity no longer reaches out in the poems to enfold them as "beespittle, droppings, hairs of beefur" into the honey of the human. But her own humanity is still very much warm and alive. Both revolution and anger are still essentially foreign to her nature, and she would almost prefer death rather than immersion in the intransigent and aggressive acts of revolution:

I lug home
the ham for Christmas Eve, life
whirls its diamond sparklers before me.
Yes, I want
   revolution, not death: but I don't
care about survival, I refuse
to be provident, to learn automechanics,
    karate,
    soybean cookery
    or how to shoot.   (p. 80)

So, although the war has driven her into an alien stance, tone, and poetic form, I believe she is speaking the truth when she claims "I am not Kali, I can't sustain for a day / that anger" (p. 81); and that the desire for "humankindness" and the honey of the human is still strong and struggling to push through the detritus and fatigue of life at war.

4 ROBERT BLY: WATERING THE ROCKS

I am the poet of the woman the same as the man;
And I say it is as great to be a woman as to be a man;
And I say there is nothing greater than the mother of men.
. . . .
I am he that walks with the tender and growing night;
I call to the earth and sea, half-held by the night.

Whitman, "Song of Myself"

The energy with which the Minnesota poet Robert Bly unreservedly gives himself to his ideas, or in some cases, his prejudices, makes him both one of the most annoying and most exciting poets of his time. Objectivity and judiciousness are not nice words in Bly's vocabulary: "Men like Whittemore or Nemerov can never write anything new because they are on-the-other-hand-men. If you say, the Christian Church is corrupt, they would say, 'On the other hand . . . .' If you say, 'John Foster Dulles was as close to being crazy as most statesmen get,' they would say, 'On the other hand . . . .'"[1] There is little danger that Robert Bly will ever be ridiculed as an "on-the-other-hand-man." Compared with the intense flex and balance of Denise Levertov, Bly sometimes seems like a frenetic farm-boy shying rocks impulsively at anything that moves; but he can often be stingingly on target, and has probably brought home more game politically than any other poet besides Allen Ginsberg.

113

Bly is a natural *antagoniste*. From the first issue of *The Fifties* in 1958, it was evident that Bly was a noisome gadfly to be reckoned with. Readers could sense that no one and no thing was to be immune from criticism, which instead of observing the polite rules of "on the other hand" attacked with what sometimes seemed a sophomoric energy. Though "Crunk," who is usually the pseudonymous shadow of Bly as Thersites, is here particularly mild, this first *Fifties* nevertheless draws blood from Yvor Winters, Allen Ginsberg, Henry Wadsworth Longfellow, *The Western Review*, John Ciardi, Chicago newspapers, and *The New York Times Book Review*, and gets in shots at rhyming, imageless poetry, universities, advertising, Christianity, the Atomic Energy Commission, and, indeed, everyone, because "everybody" thinks "America is in strong moral condition." Bly and Crunk warm to their task in subsequent issues, taking on poets, institutions, and ideas of every kind with a wit that, though sometimes shallow, is always vigorous and exciting. Bly is, like the Supersabres he campaigns against, a "knot of neurotic energy"; and his voice, like "the whine of jets, pierces like a long needle" whether in prose, in person, or as "voice" in his poems. Bly is skilled both with needle and with ax, for to describe what happens in the shambles of "Madame Tussaud's Wax Museum," "Wisdom of the Old," and "The Order of the Blue Toad" (regular features of *The Sixties*) one has to reach for the metaphor of the ax. Whether or not it is true that Bly "started out completely surrounded by enemies," he has over the years offered nearly everyone an excuse to claim that status. "It's a wonder he's alive," exclaims Kenneth Rexroth.[2] But Bly has not only survived, he has thrived.

I

Most artists are, of necessity, "outsiders" to the larger society and its values, but Bly has been something of an outsider to his fellow poets as well. He has come by this chiefly for two reasons. The first can be called by different names: integrity, independence, stubbornness, egoism. One suspects that many of the critical remarks offered against Bly by his colleagues during the sixties (his theatricality, carelessness of form, lack of music, dilettantism) are only "acceptable" expressions of "unacceptable" irritations and antagonisms they felt toward him. Bly is "no respecter of persons," and often does not play according to the polite rules, whether the game in question belongs to the establishment or the anti-establishment. He is like the pesky student who keeps asking the professor troublesome questions and will not be intimidated. Such traits alone are sufficient to alienate many, but even beyond this, there is something about Bly in person or print that often makes people uneasy. He is a man with disturbing energy and self-confidence, and an unreserved commitment to the things he does. Earmarks of integrity? or egoism?

Secondly, Bly stands as an "outsider" in that he has been without the support of anything like a Black Mountain, San Francisco, or New York coterie of fellows and followers. (Though a few poets have had affinities with Bly's poetic manner and ideas—Robert Kelly, James Wright, Louis Simpson, Jerome Rothenberg—he stood mostly alone before the *Kayak* poets began to make themselves heard.) Bly's allegiance has been to poets of other languages and of another imagination—the German poets Georg Trakl and Gottfried Benn, the French René Char and Michaux, the Swedish Ekelof, and especially the Spanish Cesar Vallejo and Garcia Lorca, and the Chilean Pablo Neruda. This inspiration, and the "new imagination" of the poetry that Bly promotes and practices, demands more than casual reading. Bly's poetry is perhaps not so much misread or unread as shallowly read and put easily aside as poetry of the *deep* or *subjective image*. It has been an uncrowded and easy category, a convenient pigeonhole for disposing of poetry that challenges poetry-reading habits. Because the form is strange, it can be focused upon for comment and used as an excuse to avoid a difficult and profoundly unsettling content. Bly has been, then, generally regarded as that poet whom one wishes would take more care "with how things go together,"[3] whom one hopes will take more notice of *melopoiea* and *logopoeia* and give up his obsession with *phanopoeia*,[4] whom one wishes would put a little more trust in the power of "art," and give less energy to polemics.[5]

Bly's interest has always been with content rather than form, and life rather than "art." (Though these pairs are properly not polarities but are related as *ends* and *means*, poets and schools of poetry persist in arranging themselves on one side or another of the dichotomy.) His quarrel with traditional forms and their recent American substitutes is that they cannot carry the content of modern life. That content, he feels, is "the sudden new change in the life of humanity, of which the Nazi Camps, the terror of modern wars, the sanctification of the viciousness of advertising, the turning of everyone into workers, the profundity of associations, is all a part."[6] The "men of 1914" and Eliot in *The Waste Land* made one large raid into this life, but did not persist or widen their foraging; and, in fact, they finally retreated. Bly's view of the modern world is one, then, that focuses on an ugliness that is wider and deeper than that exposed by *The Waste Land*, and which in 1958 had "still not been described."[7] That reality, he suspected, could never be described in the restraints or prettinesses of rhyme, the decorous regularity of iambic meter, the four-letter words of Beat-poetry, the vague suggestiveness of the *symboliste* mode, the impeccable order of poems for *Kenyon Review*, the narrowness of personal or confessional poetry, or the abstract tendencies of contemporary British poetry. What was needed was something at once more vigorous, more powerfully physical, more capable of reaching down into the darknesses and nightmares of the modern sickness. All these are implied in the metaphors with which he describes Spanish poetry, where he finds a power that "grasps modern life as a lion grabs a dog, and wraps it in heavy countless images, and holds it firm in a terrifically dense texture."[8] American poetry was incapable of this because it had sidestepped and never really gone through the experience of surrealism:

> Beginning with Baudelaire, French poetry went through a dark valley, a valley filled with black pools, lions, jungles, turbid rivers, dead men hanging from trees, wolves eating the feathers of birds, thunder hanging over doors, images of seas, sailors, drunken boats, maggots eating a corpse with the sound of a sower sowing grain, endless voyages, vast black skies, huge birds, continual rain. This immersion has given French poetry its strength, its

rich soil, whereas our soil is thin and rocky, and the poetry of the 30's and 40's increasingly resembles a flower cut off above the ground and slowly withering.[9]

The last line hints at Bly's bias against the conscious mind, against the cerebral and the abstract. A poetry that grows from the intellect is like the plant deprived of its soil: true poetry springs from a deeper self, unknowable by the machinery that sorts and labels the produce at the top of the head and makes rational cases for whatever it wishes. The deep imagination swells up from the edges of hallucination and fantasy to produce Picasso's "Guernica," while the superficial imagination finds satisfaction with the usable representational art of Marines planting the flag on Iwo Jima. The images that Bly calls for are not, then, the pictures of Ezra Pound and the Imagists, "petals on a wet black bough," but the images that writhe in the fogs halfway between deep and inarticulate passions and conscious thought. For Bly, the Chilean poet Pablo Neruda is the greatest poet of the deep consciousness and imagination, the possessor of a gift "for living in the unconscious present. Aragon and Breton are poets of reason, who occasionally throw themselves backward into the unconscious, but Neruda, like a deep sea crab, all claws and shell, is able to breathe in the heavy substances that lie beneath the daylight consciousness. He stays on the bottom for hours, and moves around calmly without hysteria."[10] Bly, one feels, is not by nature such a deep-sea crab, nor entirely or always securely beyond the tentacles of hysteria; but if he remains a poet of reason—as his heritage and Harvard experience perhaps force him to be—he does nevertheless sometimes swim deeply into the dark waters of the individual and the national psyche.

Bly chooses the poetry of the subjective image because it can carry the content he wants. But is there, perhaps, a closer relationship between the form and the nature of the content it carries? Does the deep image by its very nature, as revealed in the metaphors with which we describe it, lend itself necessarily to a dark, pessimistic, "anti-" or protest poetry? One does not swim downward into light, but into darkness; and one expects the ocean floor to be inhabited not by delicate and docile creatures, but by horrifying and grotesque forms. Thus a mode chosen to reach into these depths may end by compelling one to stay there, and a way of expressing what one sees may end in becoming a way of seeing whatever one would express. In other words, if we draw images and metaphors from an irrational and chaotic field, will the world they attempt to express be found to be more grotesque and horrible than it perhaps really is? (One thing is at least beyond question— the deep image is by its nature not well suited to saccharine, romantic, or patriotic poetry.) The importance of the question is that, ultimately, one wonders whether Bly's form is a result of his vision, or his vision the result of his form; whether he achieves a more powerful protest because his agonies are deeper, or whether they only seem so because expressed in a more profound form. One is at least confident in claiming that the two influences have reinforced and deepened one another, and that content and form join with a potency that justifies Bly's emergence as one of the most important poets of the sixties.

II

Bly's first book of poems, *Silence in the Snowy Fields*, is full of rural quietnesses, farmyards, fields, solitudes, and silences.[11] Peaceful and strangely satisfying, the poems attest to a wholeness in the poet who speaks them. The few troubled poems are easily carried by the calm of the rest. But there are touches of discontent here already, and, though far from the spirit of protest animating later work, they do raise themes that become important in *The Light Around the Body*.[12]

In "Unrest" (*Snowy Fields*, p. 25), Bly offers us a "state of the nation": youth blighted in a landscape of cold darkness, barren trees, baboons, and insects. Stereotyped bankers and businessmen appear first as culprits, and ultimately as fellow sufferers. The poem speaks of a "lassitude" that "enters into the diamonds of the body," and thus looks forward to "the light in children's faces fading at six or seven" ("Those Being Eaten by America," *Light*, p. 14), and to Bly's magnificent images of defeat in "Come with Me" (*Light*, p. 13).

In "Awakening" (p. 26), the poet communicates a fear and foreboding that evokes Yeats's "Second Coming" and the beast moving its slow thighs. A storm is coming, a darkness, apocalyptic, threatening, creeping through the grass, making the water in wells tremble, piling up in the shadows of church doors, seeping into the corners of barns, coming, coming. Indeed it is a darkness that makes us "want to go back, to return to the sea" ("Return to Solitude," p. 12), or to dive into that other darkness and "sea of death, like the stars of the wheeling Bear."

Unlike Levertov, in whose poetry death becomes alluring only after the war has undercut a previous vitality, Bly seems always to have sung soft songs to death. "Return to Solitude," "Depression," and "Night" are a few of the poems in *Snowy Fields* where death enters more as friend than intruder. It is as if death were at last the full granting of the solitude and silence that man grabs fleetingly from the night and the fields when he is able momentarily to forget his daylight awareness of man's inhumanities to man. To die is also to be absolved from returning to the agony of moral confrontation and impotence. Death is, moreover, an escape from the self ("My body hung about me like an old grain elevator, / Useless, clogged, full of blackened wheat" p. 37), and from the future into which

> . . . we are falling,
> Falling into the open mouths of darkness,
> Into the Congo as if into a river,
> Or as wheat into open mills.   (p. 31)

But despite these signs of a Marlovian consciousness, the dominant vision of *Silence in the Snowy Fields* is convincingly positive. Much more prevalent than shadow is luminescence; much more prominent than negation is affirmation:

It is good also to be poor, and listen to the wind.	(p. 28)
I am full of love, and love this torpid land.	(p. 33)
There is a privacy I love in this snowy night.	(p. 38)
It is a joy to walk in the bare woods.	(p. 45)
I have awakened at Missoula, Montana, utterly happy.	(p. 47)

> How beautiful to walk out at midnight in the moonlight
> Dreaming of animals. (p. 54)

Nor is it nature alone that Bly finds satisfying. There are also friends, "men and women I love," the human face that "shines as it speaks of things" (p. 58). The poet's peace is extremely attractive and yet perhaps a peace "in spite of," a "separate peace" concluded between the poet and a world that is necessarily restricted. This personal and local poetry is at times very much like Levertov's "poetry of the immediate." Just as one eventually learns from Levertov's poetry what can be seen from her kitchen window, one learns in reading *Snowy Fields* that nearly all the trees in Bly's farmyard must be box-elders.

The apparent contradiction between the personal poetry of *Silence in the Snowy Fields* and Bly's *Fifties* campaign for a poetry that grasps the whole of modern life like a lion can perhaps be explained as his attempt to set his own house in order before setting out to correct the world's. Or it may be that, prior to the political assassinations of the sixties and the onset of the Vietnam war, Bly still secretly hoped that a private poetry and an escape from ugly political realities were possible. He doubted from the first, however, that "The small farmhouse in Minnesota" would be "strong enough for the storm" (*Snowy Fields*, p. 26). The tornadic emotions of Vietnam destroyed the "farmhouse," and convinced Bly that the inward man could not survive unless the outward man spoke out. Poets could not, like trees, be nonpolitical and flourish as well under one Administration as another.[13]

Whatever explanation accounts for the private and personal nature of the early poetry, that poetry no doubt increased Bly's understanding and furnished the reservoir of spiritual strength to sustain his political and public energies in *Light Around the Body*. The epigraph to *Snowy Fields*—"We are all asleep in the outward man" (Jacob Boehme)—suggests Bly was digging inward, exploring the solitary "insular Tahiti" of the soul, in order to *awaken* the self. He later argues that "paradoxically what is needed to write true poems about the outward world is inwardness."[14]

III

In *Light Around the Body* the specific detail of *Snowy Fields* becomes the generalized subjective image, the inwardness becomes a window on the world, and the "I" becomes "we" or appears only as a point of vision ("I hear," "I see") or means of introducing the image. The "I" of the private vision and of the self apart from the mass of men becomes the "we" of public vision and of the self as part of the community of mankind. Just as there is an inner and an outer man, there is a private and a public man, and similar laws of union and alienation apply to both: "For according to the outward man, we are in this world, and according to the inward man, we are in the inward world. . . . Since then we are generated out of both worlds, we speak in two languages, and we must be understood also by two languages" (Jacob Boehme, epigraph to Part I, *Light*, p. 7). In *Light Around the Body* Bly is speaking in the other of his two necessary languages, about the other of his two necessary selves. The private vision of *Silence in the Snowy Fields*, if persisted in, would have atrophied into a wrinkled Wordsworthian natural mysticism evasive of modern realities; the focus of *Light Around the Body*, pursued exclusively, threatens to deteriorate into noisy rhetoric.

Maintaining a healthy balance and interchange between inner and outer worlds is not easy: most men eventually fall toward an "other-worldly" pseudomysticism or a "this-worldly" utilitarian cynicism. True mystics—St. Paul, Meister Eckhart, St. John of the Cross, Jacob Boehme—are distinguished by their ability to use the resources of the inner world for the practical concerns of everyday existence. The inner world is not a rejection or escape but a source of strength and illumination that transforms the outer world. The genuinely spiritual man accepts both worlds; "he knows that his mortal life swings by nature between Thou and It [the divine and the mundane], and he is aware of the significance of this. It suffices him to be able to cross again and again the threshold of the holy place wherein he was not able to remain."[15]

Bly may not be a mystic, but he seems to be a genuinely spiritual man who has learned to use the resources of the inner life to energize his work in the outward world. Furthermore, there are convincing signs that Bly at least *understands* mysticism. That is itself a rare gift. He also seems to have learned, in Eliot's words, "to care and not to care," that difficult passivity that leads to revelation. His poem "Watering the Horse" records one such instant of clarity:

> How strange to think of giving up all ambition!
> Suddenly I see with such clear eyes
> The white flake of snow
> That has just fallen in the horse's mane!
>
> (*Snowy Fields*, p. 46)

That kind of "letting go," generally foreign to rational Western man, is usually learned through pain and defeat. Bly, who nowhere shares with his reader the details of his particular personal suffering, has somehow come to the mystical wisdom of passivity:

> There is a joyful night in which we lose
> Everything, and drift
> Like a radish
> Rising and falling, and the ocean
> At last throws us into the ocean,   (*Light*, p. 62)

This understanding, necessarily experiential and not the mere acceptance of the idea by the conscious mind, is for Westerners, if not "mystical," at least a great epiphany. (Denise Levertov's denial of the vain will is a parallel illumination. Allen Ginsberg may not yet have learned to float like a radish, and continues to fling himself against the door that, as Levertov has learned, opens outward.) If the reader bothers to become aware of this spiritual depth in Bly, he is less apt to assume he has read Bly when he has read him only superficially.

IV

Bly's great energy has often earned for him the image of reckless dilettante. In the few public poems of *Snowy Fields* and in nearly all poetry during the war, Bly set for himself the task of jumping up out of the self "like a grasshopper" into the larger soul of the nation to "entangle" in words and bring back some of the strange plants and animals that inhabit it.[16] By seeking to explore the origins and effects of the impulses that make America and Americans physically and psychically what they are, Bly has found himself in the role of "psychologist." Armed necessarily with only a layman's knowledge of Freud and Jung, an imperfect secondhand knowledge of his patient's history, and an inability to hide the simplicity of his thought in arcane official jargon, his analyses have inevitably struck many as foolish and simplistic:

> I think the Vietnam war has something to do with the fact that we murdered the Indians. We're the only modern nation that ever stole its lands from another people. And killing the Indians seemed like a wonderful idea at the time: everybody used to shoot them out of trains and have a grand time. But it doesn't seem so funny anymore.
>
> But as Freud says, when you commit a crime . . . . Supposing you're a five-year-old boy; you beat up some kid next door—he's two years old—and you put out his eye and what happens? Your parents smooth it over and everything, and it's all o.k. and you forget about it, and everything goes fine—until you get about thirty-five years old and you get married and it turns out that everytime you get in a quarrel with your wife, you beat her up. So finally you both go to the psychiatrist and the psychiatrist talks for about six years and finally the story about the little boy comes out, and then he says, "Could I see a photograph of the little boy?" and you go back to your mother and get a photograph of the little boy, and then the doctor says, "Did you ever notice the resemblance between that little boy and your wife." As Freud said, when we commit a crime we don't atone for it as the Catholic Church thought we would. What you do first when you commit a crime is you forget it and then you repeat it. So therefore in my opinion what we're doing is repeating the crime with the Indians. The Vietnamese are our Indians. We don't want to end this war! We didn't want to quit killing the Indians but we ran out of Indians, and they were all on reservations.[17]

Similar readings of American history are behind many of Bly's poems, and have frequently been offered between poems at his readings. Moreover, in exploring the American psyche Bly sometimes comes to conclusions that, contrary to all accepted rules of poetry, he baldly offers in the poems themselves free of charge. These must be acknowledged as disturbing weaknesses: in *Light*, "Men like Rusk are not men" (p. 30), "We distrust every person on earth with black hair" (p. 36), "No one in business can be a Christian" (p. 43); and in *Teeth-Mother*, "The ministers lie, the professors lie, the television lies, the priests lie" (p. 10). Even though perhaps true, these are prose opinions and not poetic insights. Political poetry is always in danger of being taken literally as prose, and the presence of prose passages such as these has helped insure misreadings of Bly's poems. Read as prose, the poems seem more strident and fantastic than they really are.

It is not difficult to understand why many have been offended by Bly and why his efforts have sometimes been dismissed as "theater." But are the faults just mentioned really the source of the dissatisfaction? Or is it that we suspect it is "highly improper" for "a poet" to talk and act as Bly does, "forgetting his art" and speaking out in areas where he is "not qualified"? Would we readily embrace the same analyses, garbed in an esoteric lingo we only half understand, coming from an "experienced psychologist" with "credentials"? Is it perhaps that our culture has always assumed and tacitly demanded that its poets should "stick to 'poetry'" and remain political eunuchs? Is it perhaps that Bly's openly subjective readings offend against New Criticism, value-neutrality, and "the myth of the objective consciousness"?

But Bly and his work are deeper than they at first seem. Bly may simply be wrong in asserting that we kill the Vietnamese because we have run out of Indians and because "Underneath all the cement of the Pentagon / There is a drop of Indian blood preserved in snow" ("Hatred of Men with Black Hair," *Light*, p. 36); but there can be less doubt that the two are connected, and that killing of Indians and Vietnamese are both related to the same complex disposition and world-view. In fact, even the objections to Bly's political energies grow out of the very same set of values, and it is at these values as much as at the war that Bly directs his protest.

Like Allen Ginsberg, Bly began his protest against the war long before this country's fighting in Vietnam began. He sensed early that although oppression in all countries was increasingly invisible, it was nevertheless increasingly experienced—"even in America, [oppression] is as common as beauty, for those who have senses which can grasp it."[18] The protest against the war has been for Bly as for Ginsberg (as it was not for a long while for Levertov) part of a larger revolt against the disposition that occasions war and oppresses the human spirit. Bly senses that somewhere hidden in present values and in the American psyche is a dark and terrible cancer, a core of rottenness and disorder. Louis Simpson feels the same truth and suggests that just when America seems to have realized its dream—

Priests, examining the entrails of birds,
Found the heart misplaced, and seeds
As black as death, emitting a strange odor.[19]

It is this darkness and disorder that Bly seeks to explore, understand, and expose—toward the end that it may heal.

Does this darkness grow out of the black seeds of a national and international malaise, or is it something so pervasive as to hint of a darkness in human or cosmic nature? Is this darkness and this terror, which eventually drives man to "tear off his own arms and throw them into the air," innate in man and the cosmos or in man's political and social structures? The question of Bly's philosophy of man and nature is not immediately easy to answer. He is neither a Hobbesian who believes that man is, except for law, a wolf to man, nor a Rousseauist who sees man as a noble savage diseased with civilization. Nor can he be easily categorized as a Jeffers or a Conrad or a Hardy—he is neither a skeptic nor a pessimist, but senses a darkness in both man and the cosmos that he does not understand. The third stanza of "Johnson's Cabinet Watched by Ants" gives the reader a feeling that evil may be timeless and very much at home in the universe, that it is an old story, ineluctable, cotemporal with the primeval ooze:

Ants are gathered around an old tree.
In a choir they sing, in harsh and gravelly voices,
Old Etruscan songs on tyranny.
Toads nearby clap their small hands, and join
The fiery songs, their five long toes trembling in the soaked earth.

(*Light*, p. 5)

Perhaps man has always alternated between demonic nights in the forest and days of faith; perhaps he always will. Bly knows that evil is real, and should not be underestimated. Thus in Bly's protest, visions of a New Day (Ginsberg's *TV Baby Poems*, and Lawrence Ferlinghetti's "After the Cry of the Birds") give way to more modest visions:

The world will soon break up into small colonies of the saved
("Those Being Eaten by America," *Light*, p. 14)

They will abandon their homes
to live on rafts tied together on the ocean;
those on shore will go inside tree trunks,
("Written in Dejection near Rome," *Light*, p. 15)

Generally, of course, Bly's poetry does not seek to uncover the ultimate nature of the universe, but to find the more immediate sources of darkness in man's present society. Some evil may be inevitable, but the poet of *Silence in the Snowy Fields* knows also that man is capable of peace, wholeness, and joy, and that most of the darkness and joylessness of modern man is unnatural. The American psyche Bly finds especially afflicted.

V

Before we approach Bly's poetic diagnosis of the cause of America's illness, we will do well to examine the symptoms he notices. The most egregious symptom is, of course, the Vietnam involvement itself; but closely related are manic fatigue, hysteria, and desire for self-mutilation and death.

The war and the unavailing protest against it has deepened the "lassitude," and that dulls "the diamonds of the body" (one recalls

Ginsberg's "Moloch that enters the mind early"). This oppression-spawned acedia has been especially pervasive in the anti-war movement and poetry itself. It coexists in a schizophrenic tension with outrage: the uncontrollable necessity of "raging out" (as Robert Duncan puts it) and the sense that it will do no good, that the evil is too large and inexorable. Or perhaps the soul corrodes into the catatonic depression of Levertov's "Cold Spring" because it is overcome with the surfeit of ugliness and horror. In the protest poets themselves, and in their vision of America, there is a prevalent taint of "the Bartleby syndrome," the despair that comes from impotently facing up to the massive wall.

Apathy and paralysis can result from conflicting impulses, from frustration of intense desire, and also from alienation of one part of the self from another. In our culture we are paralyzed and defeated because the outer man has lost touch with the inner man. The only images that now express us are "those things that have felt this despair for so long," things that man has used, worn out, given to the refuse heap, or simply ignored like "curly steel shavings, scattered about on garage benches" (*Light*, p. 13).

Despite his own personal energy and strength, Bly is the supreme poet of defeat—defeat expressed in deep images of maniacal fury and total inertia. Poems such as "Come with Me" make their impact immediately without need of explication. Something in us readily identifies with

> Those removed Chevrolet wheels that howl with a terrible
> loneliness,
> Lying on their backs in the cindery dirt, like men drunk, and
> naked,
> Staggering off down a hill at night to drown at last in the pond.
> Those shredded inner tubes abandoned on the shoulders of
> thru-ways,   (*Light*, p. 13)

These images are so right and familiar that we are apt to pay too little attention to their richness. Not only in his choice of image, but in his choice of particular words, Bly exactly captures the loneliness, degradation, defenselessness, disorientation, suffocation, defeat, and isolation of modern man. Moreover, we see in these images that man is impelled headlong by forces he does not understand or control, that instead of being in the driver's seat he is driven by a larger impersonal machine and is a commodity that has no value except that it can be used up. The appropriateness of Bly's images are perhaps proven by the fact that we can hardly speak about them without falling into puns. Men are the wheels of a society that oppresses, and they carry its burdensome machinery on their backs. Like the inner tubes, they are worn down or defeated in time because the pressure is too great. Like any expendable material, valuable only as it serves the great work of commerce, progress, or the Gross National Product, the defeated and destroyed individual is left by the roadside to rot while the great business of the world roars on. If even this much explication seems too much, it may at least suggest that the "rightness" we feel in Bly's images is not accidental. One can no more rationally explain how it feels to be a tire than one can explain the oppression the Vietnam War has brought to the human spirit, yet both are immediately known when the poet writes, "We all feel like tires being run down roads under heavy cars" (*Teeth-Mother*, p. 16). And even the use of the passive voice here could not be otherwise. Man no longer acts but is acted upon by external forces.

Bly's deep images, so well suited for carrying the sense of the grotesque, light up other dark corners of American life, and make the reader feel he is watching strange old movies out of the American past:

We have a history of horse-beaters with red mustaches
knocked down by a horse and bitten.[20]

... these are the men who skinned Little Crow!
We are all their sons, skulking
In back rooms, selling nails with trembling hands!

(*Light*, p. 36)

The janitor sits troubled by the boiler,
And the hotel keeper shuffles the cards of insanity.

(*Light*, p. 17)

Though these images are still close to the surface imagination, one

can already feel in them an ominous and terrifying note that elsewhere explodes from the deep unconscious with hysterical force:

> One leg walks down the road and leaves
> The other behind, the eyes part
> And fly off in opposite directions
>
> Filaments of death grow out.
> The sheriff cuts off his black legs
> And nails them to a tree   (*Light*, p. 31)
>
> Wild dogs tear off noses and eyes
> And run off with them down the street—
> The body tears off its own arms and throws them into the air.
>
> (*Light*, p. 6)

Such images haunt *The Light Around the Body* and carry a fantastic
horror and degradation. The impossible spectacle of the body tearing off its own arms and throwing them into the air (it has all
the mind-crushing–paradox qualities of a Zen *koan*) is the ultimate
expression of extreme self-revulsion and longing for mutilation
and annihilation.

Because we have been captured by "death," the death-in-life
of the outward man cut off from his vital center, Bly believes we
long for real death, an annihilation of the alienated self. Undoubtedly influenced by Freud,[21] Bly finds in our hatred and desire to
kill others a double proof of our own self-hatred and death wish.
According to Freud's theory of projection, we attribute to our
enemy the hatred for us that we feel towards ourselves. We thus
need to destroy the enemy because we are paranoically sure he is
trying to kill us. And by a second law of sublimation and trans-
ference, we satisfy our desire for self-destruction by violence against
our enemy. Out of such understandings come those sections of
The Teeth-Mother Naked at Last in which Robert Duncan thinks
Bly has captured the truth behind the Vietnam War.[22]

> It is a desire to eat death,
> to gobble it down,
> to rush on it like a cobra with mouth open,

It's a desire to take death inside,
to feel it burning inside, pushing out velvety hairs,
like a clothes brush in the intestines

(*Teeth-Mother*, p. 10)

An even more powerfully haunting version about death occurs in
a portion of the poem published in *The Nation* but strangely does
not appear in the City Lights edition of the larger poem:

As soon as Rusk finishes his press conference,
    Black wings carry off the words,
bits of flesh still clinging to them; somewhere
in Montana near Hemingway's grave,
they are chewed by timid hyenas[23]

Bly's poems suggest multiple reasons for his and America's
obsession with death. Death is variously looked on as the complete
solitude and silence, as escape from self and weary realities, as
schizophrenic catatonia, as avoidance of the imminent apocalyptic
darkness and cataclysm, as annihilation of the alienated outward
self, as projected and sublimated self-hatred. Bly further suggests
that we desire death as punishment for the guilt of past evils, and
as the culmination of our strong anti-life impulses.

We seek death as expiation of the burden of guilt accumulated
from the rape of the frontier and the ecology, from Puritanic morality and discipline, from killing Indians, from a history of violence
and socioeconomic inequities—Bly's hysterical images of mutilation
seem to spiral out of guilt-frenzy. There are anti-life forces at
work throughout the modern world, but Bly senses that they have
developed most strongly in America because our "progress" has
been more rapid.

VI

The temptation is to throw sticks at someone, to blame someone for all this guilt and evil, and Bly does not resist. The nearest
targets are "merchants," "executives," "bankers," "dentists," and
"sportsmen." Michael Goldman and Louis Simpson are right when
they complain that Bly's executives and bankers are all stereotypes,

and that his depiction of them is full of clichés.[24] But Bly, of course, is not interested in the psyche and personality of the individual banker; he is interested in the national psyche, of which "banker" is one aspect. It is nonsense to imply that Bly's poetry fails because all bankers are not really the bad men Bly paints them to be. Bankers as stereotypes ("stereotypes" are after all formed by induction) do after all have common values that *are* indeed the clichés that keep the machine of state running. Moreover, Bly's poetry everywhere *intends* to imply that life in America *is* a cliché: "Dentists continue to water their own lawns even in the rain" ("The Great Society," *Light*, p. 17).

It is true that poetry, ever since Pound and Eliot, has been overrun with images of philistine bankers and joyless typists; but because the evils of commercial society are still upon us, poets are probably impelled to rage on against them even if there are no longer fresh ways to do so. Still, we are rightly tired of hearing "No one in business can be a Christian," even if, in the way Bly means it, it is undeniably true.

There is in Bly also a Poundian tendency toward easy economic readings of political and social evils. In *The Teeth-Mother Naked at Last*, after a description of the massive armaments that crush Vietnam, we are told: "This is Hamilton's Triumph. / This is the advantage of a centralized bank." We have a right to feel less pleased with this element of Bly's poetry because it may seem to us, as Pound's economic theories seem to Louis Untermeyer, "not only ineffectual but absurd."[25] But, although it is easy to overlook, Bly's analysis goes further than Pound's and in an exactly opposite direction. Pound was, after all, a reactionary and eventually a fascist of sorts; Bly has none of his tastes for "kulchur," power, order, or violence (see "Sestina Altaforte"). Moreover, unlike Pound, Bly sees the centralized bank and commercialism as a symptom rather than a cause of the modern disease:

> It's because a hospital room in the average American city
>   now costs $60 a day that we bombed hospitals in
>   the north

It's because the aluminum window-shade business is doing
so well in the United States that we roll fire over
entire villages

. . . .

It's because we have new packaging for smoked oysters
that bomb holes appear in the rice paddies
(*Teeth-Mother*, p. 14)

Though these and other such lines seem to be a condemnation of material wealth, they are something more than that. Added together they show an artificiality, a passion for order and precision, a remoteness from experience, a coldness, a hardness, and an antiseptic quality in our lives. What seems at first an inane economic prose argument—"It's because taxpayers move to the suburbs that we transfer populations"—becomes, with the added thought we grant to poetry, a statement about attitudes that grow out of our own rootlessness and externality, our loss of sense of place, our distaste for the darker, more sensual (less external) "uncivilized" populations of the inner cities, and the loss of uniqueness and identity that makes us forget "populations" are composed after all of individuals.

It is the externality, the living in the outward man, that Bly quarrels against: "O dear children, look in what a dungeon we are lying, in what lodging we are, for we have been captured by the spirit of the outward world; it is our life, for it nourishes and brings us up, it rules in our marrow and bones, in our flesh and blood, it has made our flesh earthly, and now death has us" (Jacob Boehme, epigraph to Part IV, *Light*, p. 39).

VII

The inward/outward, spiritual/material dichotomy in Jacob Boehme's writings eventually merges for Bly with the parallel *anima/animus* dichotomy important in the psychology of Carl Jung. Marx made us aware of the laborer's alienation from his labor; Ivan Illich now shows us, in his "deschooling" campaign, the learner's alienation from what he learns; Robert Bly, taking his inspiration from Boehme, and ultimately from Jung, helps us understand the present alienation of the inward and the outward man.

In perhaps the most finely realized poem of *Silence in the Snowy Fields*, "A Man Writes to a Part of Himself," Bly serendipitously "figures" the inner and outer selves as wife and husband— the wife starved, hiding in a cave, "Water dripping from . . . [her] head, bent / Over ground corn . . ."; and her husband

> On the streets of a distant city, laughing,
> With many appointments,
> Though at night going also
> To a bare room, a room of poverty,
> To sleep among a bare pitcher and basin
> In a room with no heat—   (*Snowy Fields*, p. 6)

The contrasting images are of primitive and modern man, of primitive and native spirituality neglected and atrophied in favor of commerce and a joyless sensuality that, in the end, is barren and unsatisfying even to the outward man.

We cannot know how much Bly consciously intended in this poem, but like any good poem it continues to throw off multiple radiations. Bly claims not to have read Jung until later, but the poem is nevertheless rich with the symbology of Jungian psychology and offers something of a key to the rest of Bly's work.* Rather than being consciously influenced by Jung, the poem is probably another piece of spontaneous evidence for the validity of certain Jungian archetypes. It is, first of all, significant that Bly should choose to represent the inner self as a woman and the outer self as a man. If we look closer, we notice that the wife is hiding in a "cave," and though she may be starving, is nevertheless bent over

---

* This poem and also "The Busy Man Speaks" were written, Bly claims, before he started reading Jung. But the Jungian influence on the rest of *Light Around the Body* is at least partly conscious, and Bly seemed pleased (personal interview, 28 Oct. 1971) to confirm the patterns that I had discovered in his imagery (as developed here in the last half of this chapter). In his new book, *Sleepers Joining Hands*, Bly himself briefly explores in prose his fascination with Jung and the earth and stone mothers.

a bowl of grain (the bowl, though not named, is necessarily imaged in the adjective of "ground corn"). Water drips from her head and she looks out over another concavity or bowl, "into rain that drives over the valley." Despite her loneliness and poverty in her husband's absence, these are images of fertility and life, of soil to be planted, of seeds waiting in the dark earth, of sensuousness and female sexuality. Though it is evoked with amazing economy, one even senses deep emotion in the wife: "you raise your face into the rain."

In contrast to the fertile valley are the "streets" of the city; in contrast to the visceral emotions of the wife are the superficial emotions of the husband "laughing, with many appointments." The husband's room, furthermore, is one "with no heat" and no running water. The pitcher and basin, important parallel symbols for male and female, are barren—"bare" being twice repeated in the stanza. Instead of returning at night to the wife's warm, dark, wet, fecund cave, he goes to the "bare room," light, dry, antiseptic, without heat or water.

Though the outward man may necessarily seem to bear the brunt of the blame for the loneliness and estrangement, Bly's poetry seeks a balance that refrains from disparaging the outward man. In this indirect "dialogue of body and soul" there are no recriminations: the spiritual/emotional/sexual is not put on a pedestal, the material/active/external is not damned—both are deprived of the natural ecstasy that can come only when they are united as one. Even the central metaphor of marriage indicates Bly's understanding of the necessary balance of masculine and feminine forces in all considerations of life. This awareness saves his protest from the antinomian heresies of fun, flesh, and frolic marking Ginsberg's work. Bly, too, knows that the flesh is holy, yet he shows no signs of Ginsberg's excessive, almost tantric faith in sanctity through sexuality, nor any utopian visions of mankind made ecstatic by schooling in the "college of the body." The Beat Generation's treatment of the order-orgy dichotomy sometimes forgets that the two are simply out of balance and that order is not all bad or orgy all good. Bly shares a similar revolt against the "intellect" and a campaign for restoration of emotional and sensuous life, but with the implicit understanding that order, objectivity, law, restraint, authority, material goods, and social conventions are not to be destroyed and abandoned, but brought back into proper proportions with freedom, subjectivity, impulse, spontaneity, and spirituality.* Perhaps this makes Bly a traditionalist, yet the "balance" he seeks is not a lukewarm half-way point; he seems to understand that such polarities are not really antagonistic but can paradoxically come together in a union that increases and enhances both.

When Bly in later poems condemns the outward world, it is never the physical and social "man" that he condemns, but rather the implicit assertions of modern life that this is the only man there is. Though the modern world gives itself to the "husband," the outward man, he too is nevertheless starved, and like so many things "howls outside the hedges of life" ("Smothered by the World," *Light*, p. 7), because he cannot really *live* except in union with his "wife."

Importantly related are the series of contrasts in "The Busy Man Speaks," the second poem of *Light Around the Body*. Here the modern busyness-man, like the accountant of stars in Antoine de Saint Exupéry's *Little Prince*, is devoted to *matters of consequence* and refuses to give himself to the "mother" (significantly) of solitude, tears, ocean, sorrow, humility, suffering, open fields, night, crickets, Christ. He will give himself instead to the upright "father" (significantly) of all things hard, angular, and artificial:

> But I will give myself to the father of righteousness, the father
> Of cheerfulness, who is also the father of rocks,
> Who is also the father of perfect gestures;
> From the Chase National Bank
> An arm of flame has come, and I am drawn

---

* Bly complains in an early issue of *The Sixties* about the abstract language of modern poetry, and includes a portion of *Howl* as an example. He has consistently claimed that Beat poetry, in spite of its predilection for four-letter words, uses an abstract diction. Perhaps proof that Bly has found a more concrete language—we are very much aware that Ginsberg's poetry is about the two long strings of abstractions listed in the above paragraphs, but we have first to carefully analyze the images and motifs of Bly's poetry before we see that it is equally concerned about these same abstractions.

To the desert, to the parched places, to the landscape of zeros;
And I shall give myself away to the father of righteousness,
The stones of cheerfulness, the steel of money, the father of rocks.

(*Light*, p. 4)

Bly parodies the modern religion of commerce and money by suggesting a mystical relation between the busy man and his modern God: the flash of holy fire comes not from the heavens but the Chase National Bank. Though devotion to this God surrounds modern man with a "desert," his days in the desert, unlike Christ's, bring him not spiritual food, but spiritual starvation.

Such divisions of the masculine and feminine occur under subtle and sometimes covert forms throughout Bly's protest poetry, and become the most important unifying theme. What for Ginsberg becomes an Apollonian-Dionysiac or order-orgy conflict, becomes for Bly a conflict between masculine and feminine, hard and soft, rigid and flexible, rock and water. The related polarities or subforms are many, and include reason-emotion, active-passive, barren-fertile, cold-warm, angular-curved, stars-moon, frozen-fluid, domination-submission, discipline-love, power-weakness, and light-dark.

Never an "on the other hand" poet in his commitment, Bly characteristically uses an "on the other hand" conjunction and contrast of images that involves some aspect of the masculine/feminine tension. Sometimes they are subtle and concealed, and yet they are usually strange enough to make us think they can hardly be accidental: "The Marines think that unless they die the rivers will not move" (*Teeth-Mother*, p. 18).

While a good deal of the symbolism one finds as a result of the *anima/animus* key may be fortuitous rather than consciously managed by Bly, it is nevertheless part of a particular disposition and consistent manner of seeing. The opening image of *Light Around the Body*, for example, may have been chosen for no other reason than its signification of great numbers: "Merchants have multiplied more than the stars of heaven" ("The Executive's Death," p. 3). Perhaps Bly was not at all thinking of the connotations stars have in Blake's "Tyger," Yeats's "Who Goes with Fergus" (and Yeats's system), or Stephen Crane's "Open Boat," yet these meanings work perfectly with the poem's juxtaposition of high and low, cold and hot, sterile and prolific; with the contrast of merchants and executives against crane-handlers, taxi-drivers, and commuters. The executives walk "High in the air" on "cool floors" and dream of a death that calls up thoughts of Hemingway's leopard in "The Snows of Kilimanjaro"; the commuters are compared to "moles" and "hares" living close to the earth, with the "sound of thousands of small wings."

VIII

What does Bly see as the historical roots and parallels of the lopsided masculine emphasis of modern life? Among others, the poetry seems to implicate such figures and forces as Plato, the Old Testament, the Roman Empire, Hegel, the Catholic Church, Puritanism, Locke, Andrew Jackson, and Teddy Roosevelt. It seems most convenient here to start with the more recent and move backwards in time.

Theodore Roosevelt is one of the "Three Presidents" (*Light*, p. 19) along with John Kennedy and Andrew Jackson. The advocate of carrying a big stick is here imagined as wanting to be a stone laid down thousands of years ago, one so dry that it is filled with invisible cracks. It is apparently an anti-orgiastic stone, too, for it "gets up and runs around at night, / And lets the marriage bed fall"; and though it leaps into water, it does so only for the purpose of "carrying the robber down." To the Rough Rider who "crushed snails with . . . [his] bare teeth," Bly contrasts Kennedy. (Bly wanted to idolize Jack Kennedy—see the sorrow of "Listening to President Kennedy Lie about the Cuban Invasion," *Light*, p. 16.) When he reads the "Three Presidents," Bly's voice shifts from a harsh, aggressive, mocking energy in the Roosevelt section to a liquid, smoothly flowing serenity in the Kennedy portrait. Unlike Roosevelt, Kennedy does not want to be a stone, but a "stream of water falling," "able to flow past rocks," to "carry boulders with me to the valley."

Andrew Jackson appears in "Three Presidents" only briefly,

and although his desire to be a white horse is perhaps muscular and masculine enough, it is not really a negative image. But there can be little doubt of Bly's intentions in "Andrew Jackson's Speech" (*Light*, p. 24). Jackson has been reading Virgil, who, we recall, wrote the *Aeneid* in behalf of "duty," "law and order," the divine right of Augustus Caesar, and the glory of the Roman Empire; and who was chosen by Dante to serve as "Reason" in the Divine Comedy. The passage of Virgil at hand—"I have broke faith with the ashes of Sichaeus!"—argues a loyalty to the dead past at the cost of sensuous love and domestic happiness. Andy Jackson, known for his quarrels and duels in defense of the "sacred name" of his wife, Rachel, here claims he would kill to save the honor of his people as readily as he did for his wife. The poor of Detroit are pictured, interestingly enough, as people who had been warned by Washington "Never to take another husband." The Detroit riots, it is implied, must be put down at whatever cost to save the honor of the dead and moldering American dream, the attitudes toward enterprise and order that no longer serve the people's present needs any more than the dead Sichaeus serves Dido's daily needs of spiritual and sensual love.

Bly's obsession with Jackson erupts again in his National Book Award acceptance speech. Bly remarked that, of late, books concerning the killing of Indians seemed to jump into his hands when he entered bookstores, and from them he discovered that Andrew Jackson was the "Westmoreland of yesterday," one who was guilty of a scorched-earth policy and "recommending murder of a race as a prudent policy, requiring stamina."[26] Both "prudence" and "stamina" are, in such a context, obviously distasteful "masculine" qualities that remain as forces behind the mentality of the Vietnam War.

In "The Current Administration" (*Light*, p. 22), Bly employs his favorite technique of contrast, posing the hard and abrasive against the soft and the yielding, the spiritual and the humane against the material and the mechanical. Among other signs revealing blindness and lack of understanding during the Current Administration, "A rose receives the name of 'The General Jackson.'" Here in nine words Bly catches the insane unreality of official thinking, the corruption of language, the refusal to see any meanings beyond one's own purposes and prejudices. The rose, the symbol for poets of Eternal Beauty, of Love, of Absolute Good, of Dante's mystical vision; the rose, in nature the most fragile, soft, delicate of flowers—here, with the complacent mindlessness of pseudo-Southern charm becomes "The General Jackson," both "Old Hickory" and "Stonewall" himself. ("O rose, thou art sick, / the invisible worm / That flies in the night . . .")

No doubt Jackson was "not all bad," but the point is that Jackson is, for Bly, an effective shorthand symbol of certain qualities that decimate American life. That, too, is the case with most of the other figures and institutions Bly implicates. The Roman Catholic Church in Bly's poetry is not the church of Thomas Merton, Teilhard de Chardin, or Good Pope John, but the hierarchical, authoritarian, excommunicating, fear- and guilt-instilling church of the Inquisition. Bly knows that this Church is not the whole reality, but that it still is a *part* of the reality and feeds the attitudes that create Vietnams. It is also a ready symbol of the establishment and of the past, against which may be posed the revolutionary anti-war "Protestant tied in the fire" (*Teeth-Mother,* p. 22). The Inquisition affords a convenient parallel to the questioning of Viet Cong prisoners (*Teeth-Mother,* p. 9, and *Light,* p. 37), and the Church's guilt, historically, of simony can be used as excellent indirect criticism of modern governments that are likewise guilty. Thus, President Johnson might expectedly be a defender of the Church, and include in his "lies," "that only the Protestants sold indulgences" (*Teeth-Mother,* p. 12).

With this general attitude in mind, one sees the significances Bly intends in the following lines: "and with a lily the Pope meets / a delegation of waves, and blesses the associations / of the ocean." More strange occurrences of "The Current Administration"! The first contradiction is between the symbolic Pope and the lily-waves-ocean. Here is the "rock" that so often finds juxtaposition with water in Bly's protest poetry. The rock of Peter, the foundation of the Church, itself a rock against which floods shall not prevail, here officiously blesses the waters and inevitably thinks of them as "delegations" and "associations." Not only is there a provocative contrast between the static and fluid, the motionless and the motionfull, but also, seemingly, an insidious encroachment of the institutional order and hierarchy into the realm of the wet and the free.*

Sharing the guilt with Roman Catholicism is Puritanism: whereas the first is the primary symbol of institutional evil, the second is the primary symbol of a harsh and repressive morality. Puritanism imposed both a terrible guilt and a terrible need to punish; promoted a judgmental disposition; caused men to look on one another with jaundiced eyes; encouraged a hiding of the inward self by external masks; outlawed ecstasy and denied the flesh; reduced the world to blacks and whites; and sent men on hunts for witches and Communists. It is partly responsible for the darkness haunting Bly's poems:

> It is that darkness among pine boughs
> That the Puritans brushed
> As they went out to kill turkeys
> ("At a March Against the Vietnam War," *Light*, p. 34)

That same darkness, fear, and guilt make Bly, during the march on Washington (27 November 1965), imagine

> . . . . something moving in the dark somewhere
> Just beyond
> The edge of our eyes: a boat
> Covered with machine guns
> Moving along under trees   (*Light*, p. 34)

Because the Puritan's devil is after us always, we must always seek to kill the "devils." Bly, were he to comment on this poem, might as easily say (as he did about "running out of Indians") that we kill the Viet Cong because we have run out of witches and devils.

Behind both Catholicism and Puritanism, as Bly conceives them, is an essentially Old Testament mentality. Old Testament

---

* William Everson, in David Kherdian's *Six Poets of the San Francisco Renaissance* (Fresno: Giligia Press, 1965), pp. 131–151, has some brief but interesting remarks on the Church's masculine spirit, and her neglect of the feminine Sophia, the Divine Wisdom.

Yahweh was a jealous God, a God of the Hebrews who demanded complete obeisance, and in return helped the righteous Jews slay their enemies. He was the God who asked Abraham to slay Isaac (see Marge Piercy's "Fathers and Sons" in her *Hard Loving*), who sent plagues upon evil-doers, and who might, to embarrass the devil, send plagues upon just men. These are the images, tending toward caricature, that Bly intends in "The last haven of Jehovah, down from the old heavens, / Hugged a sooty corner of the murdered pine" (*Light*, p. 22); and "They are dying because the President has opened a Bible again" (*Teeth-Mother*, p. 18).

The Old Testament Yahweh was a God of patriarchy and hierarchy, was a God above and remote, having the relation to his people that a Victorian father had to his children. This hierarchical pattern or pyramidal structure mirrors that of a strong President to his constituency (and, in fact: of a professor to his pupils all in rows; of the Pope to his laymen; of reason to the other faculties in the renaissance–neo-classical scheme of "order and degree"; of God to the Great Chain of Being; and of the powerful U.S. to the lesser nations). Though he never poses *hierarchy* against *community* as Robert Duncan does, Bly similarly revolts against such "fathers" and such hierarchy. Bly apparently intends to pose the President and Yahweh as interchangeable entities in his Jack-and-the-Beanstalk description of "the giant's house."

> . . . Chairs
> In the great room, hacked from redwood.
> Tiny loaves of bread with ears lie on the President's table.
> Steps coming! The Father will soon return!
> ("The Current Administration," *Light*, p. 23)

The Bible that the President "has opened" again and which causes the dying is obviously an Old Testament. But there is more to the Bible than the Old Testament—Christ brought a new covenant of *grace* that was to replace the covenant of *law*:

> I know that books are tired of us.
> I *know* they are chaining the Bible to chairs.
> Books don't want to remain in the same room with us anymore.

> New Testaments are escaping! . . . Dressed as women . . .
> they go off after dark.
>
> (*Teeth-Mother*, p. 17)

Presumably the Old Testament would not have to be chained, but would be comfortable in the same room with modern man. Is it accidental that Bly has this book—of forgiveness, freedom, and the love that counsels "resist not evil," "if a man takes your coat, give him also your shirt," and "move as the Wind of the Spirit moves you," that teaches strength in weakness, victory in defeat, and life in death—can it be accidental that Bly has this book go off "after dark" dressed as a "woman"?

There are forces in the secular realm as well that oppose the spirits of the wind and the water:

> I walk with a coarse body through winds
> That carry the birds on their long roads to the poles,
> And see the ghost of Locke above the railroad tracks.
>
> (*Light*, p. 22)

The poet obviously regrets his coarse body and his inability to share the fluid wind-paths of the birds, and almost implies that this ability is not foreign but has been lost. The road of the birds, the river of wind, contrasts with the iron rails, heavy cross-ties, and inflexible direction of the modern railroad. The ghost of Locke that hovers over this hard fact is not the Locke who sometimes defended religious and political liberty or battled against Cartesian abstraction, but the Locke associated with the "association of ideas," the "tabula rasa," materialism, and positivism. The Holy Spirit quietly implicit in the images of birds and wind has been replaced for modern man by the spirit of Locke—anti-mystical, anti-miraculous, anti-Enthusiasm (*en-*, in + *theos*, God; in God or possessed by God; poetic ecstasy). The "coarse body" here deserves comparison with the "heavy body" in "Smothered by the World" (*Light*, p. 7) and the "body burdened down with leaves, / The opaque flesh, heavy as November grass, / Growing stubbornly, triumphant even at midnight" in the poem "In Danger from the Outer World" (*Light*, p. 47). Locke and his ideas have helped as much as Puritan morality to reduce the body to joyless mass and rob it of the light that both *lights* and *lightens* it (Bly obviously understands the idea of grace in Dante, and in Simone Weil's *Gravity and Grace*):

I have risen to a body
Not yet born,
Existing like a light around the body,
Through which the body moves like a sliding moon.

("Looking into a Face," *Light*, p. 53)

Significantly, the body moves through and with a light not like the sun, but "like a sliding moon" (Diana, not Apollo). It is the light of the imagination and the interior mysterious soul that gives all things an awesome significance, and not the hierarchical sun of reason that denudes all things with cold analytical light.

Rather than unifying or synthesizing, science analyzes, dissects, reduces things to components and numerical quantities, and is concerned with bodies as mass. The "heavy body" figuring so prominently in Bly's poetry, and the persons reduced to numerical quantity ("Arabic numerals / walked the earth, dressed as bankers and sportsmen" [*Light*, p. 22]) are perhaps related to Locke's teachings that matter can be expressed in terms of mathematical quantity, and that even the secondary qualities of bodies ultimately depend upon "the bulk, figures, number, situation, and motions of the solid parts of which the bodies consist."[27]

What Locke effected in the world of physics, Hegel effected in metaphysics. Hegel's teachings, when overly simplified, reduced man to a small cog in a vast scheme and pattern. The universe had purpose and direction, and man was part of the process, but not the end and *raison d'être* of creation. Hegel, now generally out of favor, has been replaced by Sören Kierkegaard, the father of modern existentialism, who argued against the Hegelian Grand Design and for the freedom and responsibility of the individual. But Bly evidently still finds Hegel culpable for the modern inclination to make external abstract considerations—honor, progress, power, "national purpose"—more important than persons:

Accountants hover over the earth like helicopters,
Dropping bits of paper engraved with Hegel's name.

> Badgers carry the papers on their fur
> To their den, where the entire family dies in the night.
>
> (*Light*, p. 8)

Here again in characteristic association are the numerical, commercial, mechanical, military, external, and abstract hovering over and bringing death to the underlings, here "badgers" (elsewhere moles and hares) living underground but nevertheless fatally tainted and infected. Hegel's killing power is indeed frightening, for even his name on a scrap of paper can kill the whole family of badgers.

In the Roman Empire, known for its persecution of early Christians, its lust for power, order, duty, propriety, and in its later stages, its corruption and disintegration, Bly finds an apt commentary on the present United States. The Romans were the first people to get along without gods; having lost any real interest in their pagan deities, they were nevertheless determined to suppress the God of the Hebrews and Christians. They are ready images for modern pragmatism and coercion and for contemporary persecutions of any lingering or fresh spirituality. The time-setting within poems where Bly uses the Romans cannot be determined, and, one may infer, is unimportant: the American enterprise and the Roman enterprise are the same. Thus in lines obviously dealing with the torture of Viet Cong prisoners, "excellent Roman knives slip along the ribs" (*Teeth-Mother*, p. 9), and in "Romans Angry about the Inner World" (*Light*, p. 9), executives, executioners, and Romans blend as one. The young girl the "Angry Romans" torture could as well be an early martyr, a modern occultist, or a trans-temporal symbol. In the last-mentioned poem it is once again noteworthy that the poet, who might have chosen a St. Stephen, picks a female as his advocate of the inner life, as the victim of the stern hardness of the Romans for whom

> The other world is like a thorn
> In the ear of a tiny beast!
> The fingers of the executives are too thick
> To pull it out!
>
> (*Light*, pp. 9, 10)

These executioners, who know nothing of children, of ecstasy, of "a leaping of the body, / the body rolling,"

Move toward Drusia, They tie her legs
On the iron horse. "Here is a woman
Who has seen our mother
In the other world!"   (p. 9)

The horse has often been used as a symbol of masculine sexuality, certainly in D. H. Lawrence and Robinson Jeffers. The horse here, however, is not an image of living and sensual potency, but an iron horse, an instrument of torture, an appropriate symbol of a cold and barren force, a masculinity gone awry. On this iron horse the devotee of the inner world is broken because she continues to testify that these men have a "mother" in the inner world.

Because modern Western society has wrongly associated masculinity with toughness and power, Bly connects it with images of irons, teeth, rocks, mountains, ice, and passionlessness. The defective modern attitude thinks of Christ as "effeminate," in sharp contrast to the insights of Hopkins or Donne. For Hopkins, Christ is both the falcon riding the river of wind and "a stalwart stallion, very-violet sweet." Biblically, Christ is the sensual lover prefigured in the *Song of Solomon* and the bridegroom for whom the maidens light their lamps. In Donne's holy sonnet number 14, God is a phallic force or battering ram seeking to enter the walled city that "labors to admit" him. This masculine vitality, however, by ravishing and enthralling the city (the self), makes "her" chaste and free. In place of this potent and fertile masculinity, compatible and in fact paradoxically identical with femininity, the modern world poses a harsh and sterile travesty. Ironically, the very railroad over which the spirit of Locke hovers carries, too, its "iron horse," as much an incarnation of the God of Science and Industry as the "stalwart stallion" of the God it replaces.

If proper masculinity is somehow an incarnation of spiritual power mysteriously *creating* through warlike "destruction" and *making whole* by "annihilation," then we might readily expect a pseudomasculinity to destroy what it would pretend to create, and annihilate what it would make whole. Such reflections throw an interesting light on war, including the first war in literature, Homer's Greeks on the beaches of Troy. Though Achilles may have been the offspring of the sea-goddess Thetis, he is inflexible, intractable, armored man. As barren, barbaric, alienated power, who treats women as concubines, Achilles chases Hector, the devoted husband and Troy's physical and spiritual bulwark, around the walled city and, embarrassingly, through the "laundry" (the hot and cold springs where the women do their washing when the city is not under attack). One kind of masculine power defeats another, and associates it disgracefully with the feminine. Furthermore, Odysseus, the man of reason, in the artificial wooden horse —pretended as a spiritual offering to the gods—gains entrance to the walled city, not surely to make it chaste and free, but to rape and destroy. In place of the seeds of life, the false and hollow horse carries the forces of death.

Because Bly has been a busy student of America's history since deciding to "leap up into the psyche of the nation," he is probably well acquainted with *The Education of Henry Adams.* Adams's chapter on "The Virgin and the Dynamo," if not a source of influence, at least offers parallel perceptions about the American Temper. Adams himself feels the strong and almost mystical attraction Americans have for the dynamo and the wonders of science, and realizes that these represent for us the kind of force that the Virgin held for the builders of the Gothic cathedrals: "The force of the Virgin was still felt at Lourdes, and seemed to be as potent as X-rays; but in America neither Venus nor Virgin ever had value as force—at most as sentiment. No American had ever been truly afraid of either."[28]

Though "the Virgin had acted as the greatest force the Western world ever felt, and had drawn man's activities to herself more strongly than any other power, natural or supernatural, had ever done" (p. 388), "yet this energy was unknown to the American mind. An American Virgin would never dare command; an American Venus would never dare exist" (p. 385). St. Gaudens, a famous American sculptor in Paris at the time Adams wrote these words, could not appreciate the cathedral sculpture nor the power of the virgin. "St. Gaudens' art was starved from birth, and Adams' instinct was blighted from babyhood. Each had but half of a nature, and when they came before the Virgin of Amiens they ought both to have felt in her the force that made them one; but it was not so" (p. 387). Instead Adams felt "the forty-foot dynamos as a moral force, much as the early Christians felt the Cross" (p. 380). As for the sculptor, "for a symbol of power, St. Gaudens instinctively preferred the horse, as was plain in his horse and Victory of the Sherman monument" (p. 388). The horse St. Gaudens "preferred" as a symbol of force was not just any horse, but a war-horse thrusting forward under the legs of the General in pursuit of the airy-winged female Victory. In St. Gaudens's most representative work, "The Puritan," the male figure grasps a Bible to his chest with one hand and carries a heavy oak cudgel in the other, ready to conquer any evil, any frontier, and any feminine witchery.

Alongside the ghost of Locke and "The Puritan" one can, with some violence to the full truth, place the effigy of Plato. This it seems is Bly's intention, when after cataloguing the horrors of modern war in Vietnam, he tells us

And Plato! . . . . Plato wants to go backwards . . .
He wants to hurry back up the river of time, so he can
  end as some blob of seaflesh rotting on an
  Australian beach.   (*Teeth-Mother*, p. 17)

Plato might want to go backwards because he sees how men have fallen short of his vision, or he may be filled with revulsion at what his own teachings have brought. At first look, one cannot be sure whether Bly's attitude toward Plato here is positive or negative; but other lines of a parallel pattern afford the necessary clues: "The dams reverse themselves and want to go stand alone in the desert" (*Light*, p. 14). Plato, too, seems here to be experiencing a change of heart and would undo what he has done. Apparently, for Bly, Plato has been like the dam, holding back the stream of life and passion. There is, to be sure, a poetic Plato, a mystic Plato, a sensuous Plato, but these elements have been largely neglected and misunderstood by his less great-souled followers. The Plato that helped to shape the Western world is the Plato who saw material reality as a pale imitation of the pure ideas, art as a copy of a copy, and poetry as detrimental because it "feeds and waters the passions instead of drying them up" (*Republic*, Bk. X). From this "copy" of the real Plato comes the definition of man as rational animal, the antipathy between mind and body, the emphasis on control and discipline of the lower nature, the hierarchical structures of governments, social classes, education, epistemology, and psychology. Plato was guilty, too, no doubt unforgivably so for Bly, of equating emotion with effeminancy. After witnessing the horrors of the Vietnam War—the evolutionary success of mind over emotion, of reason over instinct—Plato would supposedly flee backwards in time away from mind, back to mindless primitive organism, senseless and rotting on a primeval beach.

For Plato the state was the individual writ large. There could be then no conflict between what was good for the state and what was good for the individual. (This can easily degenerate into the logic of fascism, communism, and capitalism—"what is good for General Motors . . . .") Plato thought the individual soul consisted of three qualities, each with a proper role and activity: Reason, Spirit, and Appetite, or wisdom, courage, and moderation (meaning obedience to reason), respectively. These were mirrored in the state by the three classes: Legislators, Warriors, and Tradesmen, who handled matters of government, defense, and production. Physiologically, whether in the individual or the imagined Leviathan of the state, the three qualities of the soul were located in the head, upper chest, and lower body; or more simply: head, heart, and genitals.

Alongside this threefold division there came to be a simpler twofold one—the spiritual and the material. Actually, Plato thought of courage (heart) as growing from the union of the spiritual and material souls, so that a familiar trinitarian pattern emerged—as in the Spirit generated between the Father and the Incarnation, or the love (or child) generated between male and female. So long as the heart belonged to neither reason nor appetite, and the warriors belonged to neither the legislators nor the people, but to both, all were joined in fruitful union instead of destructive conflict. But the middle term—spirit/courage/heart—became associated with reason and the "spiritual soul," while emotion and appetite remained alone in the "material soul." (Plato promoted that imbalance because his own will, volition, or "heart" was with reason and against appetite. Similarly, in his ideal state both of the "upper" classes were to enjoy communism so that they might avoid distraction with material concerns and could devote themselves to the spiritual, the abstract, the One; the "lower" class was not admitted to the communal scheme and was expected to engross itself with the material, the particular, the Many.)*

Thus the ideal three-part harmony where mind and matter were reconciled in heart became bifurcated lopsidedly into warring forces—"higher" and "lower" natures. Women, who have never been logical, and, until modern Israel, seldom good warriors, were quite naturally associated with the appetite and the material body. "Emotion," too, belongs in that lowly company, for not only is it of the body, but, as Plato reminds us, it is by nature "effeminate." Physiologically, then, the twofold division cuts man along the dotted line at the waist. For women, who are neither intellectual nor courageous, the waist is located just a few inches above the top of the head. Reason and judgment take for themselves the task of repressing the "appetites," and within the state the rulers and their soldiery keep law and order among the workers, women, and "bleeding hearts."

The associations inherent in Plato's system from the first carried certain liabilities now made apparent in the modern experience and illuminated by the symbols of Bly's poetry. The diagram of a simplified and corrupted Plato given here adds new registrations to Robert Duncan's "swollen head of the nation" and Ginsberg's "college of the body." It especially clarifies the structure of Bly's work. The twofold division works naturally with Bly's use of juxtaposition and contrast, and the lopsided imbalance of forces accounts for the

---

* Where does the heart belong? Plato of course was right originally: it belongs equally with both mind and body. But the modern split is typified in the slogan "Make Love, Not War." Each side makes us a dangerous syllogism of an either/or nature: "War goes with reason and the mind, 'love' with the body and the emotions. But reason and the mind are (good/bad); and body and emotions are (bad/good). Therefore it is good to make (war/love), but evil to make (love/war)."

violence and sterility of modern life. Balanced, voluntary union is creative; coerced imbalance and submission is destructive. Bly's poetry gives the higher-lower, dominance-subjection pattern a spatial expression, and sets it reverberating on sexual, political, economic, physical, psychological, and philosophic levels: flexible tires under heavy machines, lake water pressed down by ice, vegetable walls destroyed by steel from the sky, burrowing animals killed by symbols dropped from helicopters by accountants, executives in cold skyscrapers or on icy mountainsides while the poor keep under or close to the ground. What is high is cold, hard, abstract, powerful, violent, oppressive, masculine; what is low is fluid, warm, damp, earthy, oppressed, feminine. In other poetry in other times rain may fall from the sky to impregnate the valley, the sun's rays may penetrate the soil to bring forth life, Sky may stir life in the Earth-Mother, and the masculine Logos may impregnate feminine Chaos; but in this poetry the interchange is coercive, unsatisfying, barren. Love has been replaced by rape, the stallion by the locomotive, and the Lover at the city gates by the Trojan Horse.

Bly's attitudes about the masculine/feminine forces are interestingly related to those of Robert Graves, who in *The White Goddess* argues the sanctity of the female, the moral force of matriarchy, and the goddess of love as the muse of true poetry originating in sacred matriarchal rites. In an interview in *Playboy* (Dec. 1970, pp. 103–116), Graves further draws the lines along the "male/female" split involved in "Make Love, Not War." He implies that the poetry of love and of war are associated with the male and female: "Piracy and acts of violence—wars—are a male affair." True poetry should emphasize "the extreme dependence of man upon woman for her moral guidance and of woman upon man for his practical doing": "Patriarchal or Apollonian poetry started with ballads about war. Beowulf and the Icelandic sagas are examples. Such poems were enough for the men of the time when they sat together in a mead hall, throwing plates and bones at each other. But they lack lasting emotional value, because they are centered on war, not love. All poetry of value is matriarchal in its origin" (p. 114).

D. H. Lawrence, on the other hand, though he agreed with
Bly and Graves about the nature of modern evils, tended to make
somewhat different associations. His own life experience and conse-
quent pathological suspicion and fear of women caused him to see
the female and the Magna Mater not as a benevolent life-force, but
as an anti-life force that seeks to destroy true masculinity and Holy
Spirit in the male. "Knowing" and mentalizing were not for him,
as for Bly and Graves, masculine traits, but were feminine, and
were embodied in such women as Edgar Allen Poe's Ligeia (see
Lawrence's *Studies in Classical American Literature*). But many
aspects of Lawrence's thinking are just what Bly would attack
and see as evil. Lawrence would never "lose his leaves," never let
himself float like a radish, never give himself to Whitman's democratic love (which he saw as a self-sacrifice, a death of self). Law-
rencian thought is in some ways too masculine (certainly hierarchial,
superior), too Apollonian (in spite of his campaigns for "blood-
knowledge"), and tends to encourage the rise of Hitlers, violence,
and war. See John R. Harrison's *The Reactionaries: A Study of
the Anti-Democratic Intelligentsia* [on Yeats, Lewis, Pound, Eliot,
Lawrence] (New York: Schocken Books, 1967).

Also interesting in connection with masculine/feminine images
and associations are Frederick Karl's and Marvin Magalaner's remarks on James Joyce's novels:

> If a woman—or, at least, the Female principle—might be repre-
> sented in Jungian psychology as a body of water (in *Finnegan's
> Wake*, Anna Livia Plurabelle, the sparkling wife of Earwicker,
> is actually the river Liffey, as it flows through Dublin), then a
> smooth-flowing verbal stream, poured out with spontaneity and
> almost without check, might most effectively simulate the essence
> of Molly's being. Moreover, Molly's special type of femininity
> fits easily into the scheme. Lacking mind, missing the hardness
> and angularity which logic, reason, and judgment add to the
> total personality, Molly substitutes physical softness. Her amply-
> flowing curves are matched by the flimsiness and lack of definite
> structure of her thought processes. To approximate this liquid
> flow of emotional sensuousity, Joyce surrenders almost all punc-
> tuation. The monologue is an overwhelming continual outpour-

ing. For the eye to attempt to separate the word groups into sentences is like trying to pick up a handful of water.

(Great Twentieth Century English Novels
[New York: Noonday, 1959], p. 229)

Mutatis mutandis, these same ideas say much about anti-war poetry's rejection of structure, its impetuous and free-flowing energies, its fascination with images of water and sea, its rebellion against logic and hardness.

Bly's understanding of the history of ideas may not be minutely sophisticated, and his knowledge in many areas may by some criteria be dilettantish. But his pretentions are no greater than those of every other poet: he may venture into fields others avoid, but he makes no claim to professional expertise in any matter except poetry. As Robert Duncan has said, the goal of the poet and the poem "is to feel how things compose."[29] Bly does this. He stands with senses awake and takes the shape and measure of the forces impending on his body and spirit now, in this place. Whenever possible he has tried to let the language generate itself, adding what understanding his conscious mind could supply. *Light Around the Body* is a book of many perceptions, and the larger unifying patterns are perhaps largely subconscious rather than calculated. But there is everywhere below the immediate surface of these poems a consistency, integrity, and *coherence* that makes them worthy of the National Book Award. In the award citation the judges, Theodore Weiss, Harvey Shapiro, and Donald Hall, wrote: "If we poets had to choose something that would be for us our Address on the State of the Nation, it would be this book."[30] Not only has he succeeded in giving us the psyche of the nation, but he has articulated what our individual psyches feel—our oppression, hysteria, and deep sadness have found a tongue.

IX

If all failures are failures of the imagination, certainly the greatest impediment to change is the failure to see the larger picture, or to envision how not just a part but the entire picture might be altered. New wine cannot be contained in old skins, and any desired new element in society will seem impossible and irrational in the old context. War indeed is the only "reasonable" possibility of action within the system of forces now at work. Those forces are of the outward man and are hollow travesties and brittle shells of the vital inner potencies they usurp. Bly not only helps us see the nature of this outward "giant," but also imagines a new human possibility. Wendell Berry, reviewing Lowenfels's *Where Is Vietnam?* claims it is a desperate book in spite of its new involvement; its poetry looks at the horror but is incapable of any alternative vision.[31] But what will satisfy us as an alternative vision? One senses that the only possible alternative is neither immediately acceptable nor even comprehensible to the Western mind. Though Bly's poetry is essentially wasteland poetry—his purposes are to give that landscape fuller expression—he does offer such an alternative. It seems at first a private and personal alternative, but it is open to every private person and thus ultimately to the society at large. Indeed, the great revolutionaries have understood that changes in individual consciousness are what is needed, and that changes in the outward political structures are otherwise irrelevant. Those structures are merely the body for which our attitudes are the spirit. Changes in consciousness are difficult, and, as Aeschylus and Sophocles and Shakespeare understood, are most often brought about by suffering sent from the Gods. But changes of heart and consciousness can also to some degree be cultivated.

Bly believes the outward and the inward man can be brought again into communion, and envisions this in mystical/sexual images of rocks falling into water. In a poem significantly titled "A Journey with Women," he imagines us going

... at night slowly into the tunnels of the tortoise's claws,
Carrying chunks of the moon
To light the tunnels,
Listening for the sounds of rocks falling into the sea ...

(Light, p. 56)

There seem to be two *ways* to promote this reunion: one is to "give up desire," the formula of all spirituality; and the other is to accept the person as sacred. (These have some relation to the thunder-over-the-wasteland's *datta* (give) and *dayadhvam* (sympathize), though *damyata* (control) never sounds here; "control" is already momentarily in over-supply.)

The first "way" involves a "death" and a "defeat," for it is "in the deep fall, the body awakes." "The wind rises, the water is born" when "white tomb-clothes" are spread "on a rocky shore." If man is to become again the amphibian he properly is, the too-powerful shore must undergo some death so that the sea may rise again to fullness. "We did not come to remain whole. / We came to lose our leaves like the trees." Man must learn to lose, to spend less energy on being invulnerable and invincible, "And swim in the sea, / Not always walking on dry land" ("A Home in Dark Grass," *Light*, p. 44). The "leaves" we refuse to lose are strangely like scales that weigh down the heavy body, "the body burdened down with leaves" (*Light*, p. 47). Leaves and scales were once perhaps needed when primitive man had to endure hardships of nature:

Man cried out—like the mad hog, pierced, again,
Again, by teeth-spears, who
Grew his horny scales
From sheer despair
("The Fire of Despair Has Been Our Savior," *Light*, p. 48)

But the same "Fire of Despair" that formed the scales must now cause their shedding: "O holy trees, rejoicing ruin of leaves." It is no longer the Middle Ages ("iron ringing iron," "chill," "clatter," "stone") or the Ice Age (ice, "bone stacks," "snow," "snow-bound valley"), but "autumn" in man's history, a time for shedding of leaves, when the "spring coming in your black branches" is much easier to see. Yet man cannot find the road; and the monolithic Pentagon blocks our moving on beyond the drop of Indian blood and the military posture that at one time in man's history may have been a part of the way:

Underneath all the cement of the Pentagon
There is a drop of Indian blood preserved in snow:
Preserved from a trail of blood that once led away
From the stockade, over the snow, the trail now lost.
(*Light*, p. 36)

The shell, the ossified outer protection must fall away, for we are all, like the State Department, becoming "exhausted crustaceans." Such symbols are Bly's own, though he occasionally expresses the same ideas with what seem borrowings from Zen Buddhism:

> The dying bull is bleeding on the mountain!
> But inside the mountain, untouched
> By the blood,
> There are antlers, bits of oak bark,
> Fire, herbs are thrown down. (p. 57)

Even as the bull, the outward man, the relative consciousness, dies, new life flames inside the mountain cave:

> The green leaves burst into flame,
> The air of night changes to dark water,
> The mountains alter and become the sea. (p. 57)

The second way to a new life is through the rediscovery of the awe-full, wonder-full person. The importance of the person was visible already in *Silence in the Snowy Fields*; in *Light Around the Body* the value of humans "standing over against one another" (Buber's phrase) is emphasized in a number of poems. In "Evolution from the Fish" (*Light*, p. 59), we are reminded that man is, after all, the "grandson of fishes" and only the "nephew of snails"; and sometimes man still "lies naked on a bed / With a smiling woman." We still feel "What a joy to smell the flesh of a new child! / Like new grass!"

"Suddenly Turning Away" studies the sad truth that man's sensitivity, clarity, and gypsy joy are destroyed by fear and "not-love" (recall Ginsberg's "lack-love"). When someone "comes near," we close in, "the jaw / Tightens, bullheads bite / The snow," and the half-developed faculties of intimacy and communication are scarred again and again, "Half-evolved antennas of the sea snail / Sink to the ground."

"Looking into a Face" praises the spiritual warmth and strength that may be gained from intimate human contact

> ... Opening
> The surfs of the body,

Bringing fish up near the sun,
And stiffening the backbones of the sea!   (*Light*, p. 53)

To be noted are Bly's choice of "surfs," and the difference between backbones or endoskeletons and exoskeletons. Bly does not advocate fleeing from all stiffness, all order, backward in time to the jellyfish, but forward to a sense of the inner infinite, to an order of personal volition. To be contrasted with these images are those of the State Department crustaceans who are also like confused squids in the heavy jellies near the bottom (*Light*, p. 36), and the people living under the shadow of the detective "Who sleep restlessly as in an air raid in London; / Their backs become curved in the sloping dark" (*Light*, p. 6).

X

Hundreds of fascinating related images surface in Bly's work. What is most amazing is that they *cohere*. Here, in a poet frequently accused of superficiality, dilettantism, and "theater," is in fact a poetry that "grasps modern life as a lion grabs a dog, and wraps it in heavy countless images, and holds it firm in a terrifically dense texture." There is no way of telling whether the unity of the images results from meticulous conscious effort, or springs spontaneously from a deeper well where things are, despite their seeming chaos, mysteriously orderly. But as the reader draws closer to the poetry, he often discovers that what seem arbitrary and random figures are either intentionally or serendipitously full of significance. For example, in Part II of *The Teeth-Mother* Bly intends us to understand that the President lies about everything and anything; but it seems strangely significant that he should happen to have him lie about the date the mountains rose, the number of fish taken in the Arctic, the acreage of the Everglades, and the composition of the amniotic fluid!

Bly's is a strange new poetry, more deeply involved, more superficially raucous and polemical. It will not be readily embraced —the rocks on the shore do not easily submit to the sea. It campaigns for a deeper, more spontaneous life, and follows its own advice in its volatile and "uncivilized" subjective images. And yet in the midst of its energy, it understands a tranquil center, a letting go, so that at last, naked as a radish, "the ocean . . . throws us into the ocean." The mountain has not yet altered and become the sea, but partly perhaps because of Bly and other poets against the war, some rocks are falling.

5 ROBERT DUNCAN: IRREGULAR FIRE —EROS AGAINST AHRIMAN

The war is a mineral perfection, clear,
unambiguous evil within which
our delite, our life, is the flaw,
the contradiction?   Duncan, "An Essay at War"

Taking myself the exact dimensions of Jehovah,
Lithographing Kronos, Zeus his son, and Hercules his
*   grandson;*
Buying drafts of Osiris, Isis, Belus, Brahma, Buddha,
In my portfolio placing Manito loose, Allah on a leaf,
*   the crucifix engraved,*
With Odin, and the hideous-faced Mexitli, and every
*   idol and image;*
Taking them all for what they are worth ....
                                Whitman, "Song of Myself"

                    I

Robert Duncan is sometimes spoken of as not only the most talented
but also the most intelligent of modern poets. Though both claims
may be close to the truth, part of the credit for intelligence surely
grows out of the unintelligibility of much of his poetry. Duncan's
esoteric erudition frightens most critics and reviewers into submission, or sets them railing against his "tediousness,"[1] "incantatory
monologues," "debilitating preciosities of mannerism," and "overt

159

pedantic scholarship."* Most readers will agree that Duncan "must certainly be our most difficult active poet," a poet "for the strenuous, the hyperactive reader of poetry; to read Duncan with any immediate grace would require Norman O. Brown's knowledge of the arcane mixed with Ezra Pound's grasp of poetics."[2] In reading Duncan "it simply helps to be familiar with Dante, Blake, mythography, medieval history, H. D., William Carlos Williams, Pound, Stein, Zukofsky, Olson, Creeley, and Levertov."[3] To this list we might add Cabalistic literature, Hermetic writings, Indian lore, *The Golden Bough*, the pre-Socratic philosophers, Christian mysticism, and the *Oxford English Dictionary*. Lacking these familiarities the reader can penetrate some distance into the complex syncretism of Duncan only by a dogged persistence.

Fortunately, for most purposes an exact understanding of every allusion and action in the poems is unnecessary (fortunate, because impossible). It is not only that Duncan's mythic foragings are incredibly wide-ranging: gods and goddesses, songs and rituals may with patience be traced down. But more difficult is the aura of the mythic that invades the language at all levels. There is in Duncan's work "an endless ribbon of eloquence flowing out of his 'jungle' [the forces, creatures, and faces projected out of his own inner life and his reading] and finally diluting it. Rarely is Duncan's imagination anchored in a true bodily intensity. . . . the skin of his vision floats out; it becomes a vast eloquent surface, but the body has been left behind; the body rots out of sight somewhere, beneath the airy

---

*Lawrence Lieberman, "Critic of the Month: VII, a Confluence of Poets," rev. of *Bending the Bow*, *Poetry* 114 (1969):40–58. Among others who have attacked Duncan's work are R. D. Slavitt and James Dickey, respectively (excerpts here from *Book Review Digest*): "a toned down imitation of Ezra Pound, full of private allusions to his chums and their books, undigested clots of autobiography, puerile incantations, improbable allusions, and insufferable arrogance in its privacy. What is not obscure is slovenly, and does not give much incentive to go back and puzzle out the rest" (*Book Week*, 14 Mar. 1965); "one brings away from it only a sense of complicated inconsequence, of dilettantism and serene self-deception, of pretentiousness, of a writer perhaps natively gifted who has sold himself the wrong bill of goods" (*American Scholar*, Autumn 1965).

spaces of the poem which seems to be talking about it."⁴ Trouble-some abstractions such as "reality," "essence," and "truth" may be expected in any poetry; but the mythic tones of Duncan's voice infuse an abstract quality into a multitude of words that would normally be fairly concrete in character: night, day, light, darkness, flower, heart, bird, sea, eye, tree, song, poem, etc. Moreover, since Duncan's thoughts and perspectives are rarely simplistic, the sym-bolic weights of such words may not be handily determined. Night and darkness may in one poem be negative qualities; in another, positive counters of a totally different resonance. The poetry of Duncan consistently defies habitual orders and delimitations.

Duncan's *mythos* and spiritual orientations are ambitiously syn-cretic and omnivorous. Syncretism *à la* Duncan is a different thing from eclecticism. An eclectic mythology or religion picks the best bits from the myriad of available systems, reordering them into a spartanly viable whole; Duncan's syncretism seems to see all aspects of all systems as vehicles of the one Truth, and embraces them all. The result is a swirling cauldron of systems and images. Bits and pieces, subtly flavored by the poet's private sense of their meanings (the reader doesn't have the recipe), are combined at will to fit the purposes and brew of the moment. The result all too often is ob-scurity and, for the reader, the kind of frustration that provokes James Dickey's unsympathetic explanation of Duncan's complexity: "As he keeps telling us, he is a mystic, which of course allows him to say anything in any order."⁵ (Of course, Dickey's difficulty is further exacerbated because he is unsympathetic with mysticism itself.)

Is this poet a mystic? One must admit he talks a good case. But in the midst of the abundant "God-talk" we somehow feel that the *body* of the God-experience is missing. The reader gains no sensation of any unique union or rapture, no sense that Duncan writes from experience instead of erudition. I am not inclined to agree with Rudolph Nelson that "we may grant that Robert Dun-can's complex vision is essentially ineffable."⁶ There is in Duncan certainly an intense intellectual and spiritual concern for the Be-loved, but the Beloved is usually a complex and abstract formula-tion rather than an experienced entity. What and who the Beloved is, we will have more to say of later; but for now it suffices to remark that the Beloved remains an *idea*, remote to Duncan's experience, no more sensuously present to him than the physical lover of his poems becomes for the reader.

From Duncan's redundant mythologies, then, we are not apt to distill any private mystic vision, but perhaps we may discover a private *mythos*, shaped by the circumstances of the poet's life and time. If it is to be distilled, it will be, one expects, in the alembic of Duncan's poetic—for in the study of Ginsberg, Levertov, and Bly it has become evident that the poet's world-view is intimately bound up with his poetic, and that that poetic is inextricably tied to the poet's reaction to the Vietnam War. And it is, after all, an understanding of Duncan's reaction to Vietnam that we ultimately hope to come to.

II

From the retrospective of nearly twenty years, Duncan can look back on his early poems and assert of them what only his later poems could reveal to the assiduous reader. Writing in the Preface to his *The Years as Catches: First Poems 1939–1946* he tells us: "These are poems of an irregularity. From the beginning I had sought not the poem as a discipline or paradigm of my thought and feeling but as a source of feeling and thought, following the movement of an inner impulse and tension rising in the flow of returning vowel sounds and in measuring stresses that formed phrases of a music for me."[7]

"Irregularity" proves to be a word of many registrations, and a key that unlocks many locks. Duncan's youthful decision for poetry was a stepping aside from the regular conduct and mind of his society, a relinquishing of the goals it offered him, goals which brought him so much pain in the pursuit. The nature of that pain is revealed in "Letter," Duncan's dream that looks back to his boyhood struggle (age 13) in a high-school shop class to plane a breadboard "level" and hide or obscure the ugly flaw in the imperfect

splice he had made in the dark and light wood.* Already his irregular vision—eyes crossed from a childhood accident—hopelessly
defeated his frantic efforts to make the board level; and that failure,
as well as the symbolic flaw deep in the grain, made him despair
of the expectations of manhood the world asked of him. No matter
how intense the desire to impose an external form, no matter how
deep the planing, the grain in the wood remains true to its own law.

Nor could Duncan's own irregularity be effaced. In poetry he
found an oasis of freedom amid a desert of prohibitions and demands, and was drawn by "the promise of a feeling I had found
in certain poems and the permission given for feeling in poetry"
(*Years*, p. i). The word "permission" is especially significant and
occurs again in a similar context on the jacket of *The First Decade*,
where he suggests that the true critic will find in all his poems "a
crisis of truth and permission."[8] And in the "Venice Poem" of the
same volume he writes

> Never in living
> but here, here,
> all felt things are
> permitted to speak. (p. 105)

Looking back on these early poems Duncan is able to understand that "Perhaps the sexual irregularity underlay and led to the
poetic; neither as homosexual nor as poet could one take over
readily the accepted paradigms and conventions of the Protestant
ethic" (*Years*, p. i). His parting of the way with the Protestant
ethic was more than an abandonment of its paradigms and conventions, a turning away from its contents; it was also a turning away
from its forms to a new form, a new process. In poetry the process,
the shaping, was to be true to its own self, whatever warp that might
display—it was a permission to feel whatever one really felt, and an
area where one's inner nature could unfold, one's own law be dis-

---

* "Letter" in *Roots and Branches* (New York: Scribner's, 1964), pp.
16–21. "What I remember is some utter misery in me that showed up in
whatever I did there, so that all could see I was not somehow a man, showed
up my crying and being afraid of what a man must do" (p. 17).

covered. Ginsberg's homosexuality brought him into open revolt with society, and to poetry as a voice of that revolt. Duncan's homosexuality brought him to poetry as an area of freedom, a private order that demanded no revolt—society and its systems could be disregarded. Moloch need not be bearded, he could be ignored. But not easily ignored—for the early poems are haunted with images of disease, self-doubt, loneliness, and isolation. But they are a beginning toward the mature poetic of Duncan, exploring the possibilities of love and growth, and finding in eros and the beloved a step on the ladder toward the Primal Eros and the Beloved.

III

Love is the first interest of Duncan: he sees his own life as a struggle to learn to love, and the life of the universe as an unfolding toward the Perfect Form of Love. Love is the one Law (Gospel, "God-Spell") written in all things, but a law that is brought to flower only with great travail. Much of what passes for love is not "good news" at all. In the early Berkeley poems the poet admits, "Among my friends love is a painful question." They "do not burn hotly," they " question the fire." It is more like a lovelessness that they seek somehow to exhaust.

> We do not fall forward with our alive
> eager faces looking thru into the fire.
> We stare back into our own faces.[9]

Their own faces look back at them because all men seek love, seek to take from the fire, but are neither contributors of fire nor enraptured with the fire itself. In his mature essay in "essential autobiography," Duncan writes that he would now

> understand sin as Man's refusal of Love Itself, his refusal to love in his desire to have love—my own human refusal of the love that strives to speak in the poem. Not only the loss of love, which confronts us, where we admit the suffering, with the reality of love, but the recognition of love moves us to tears. Our daily affections are a gentle practiced removal from a reality that threatens to overcome us. Our sexual pleasure is a protective

appetite that distracts us or blinds the psyche to the primal Eros, as all the preoccupations of our poetic craft preserve a skin of consciousness in which we are not overtaken in fear of the Form that works there.[10]

Man's half-life, then, is an escape from the intensity of Love—a protective shield against an ecstasy so profound that man fears it. It would demand that he lose himself in it, fall forward "into the fire." He refuses the fire, refuses to dissolve his ego into the Ego, his selfish self-love into Otherness. He would instead deny the numinous, the divine presence in stones and trees and men. *Scientia* (which Duncan intends not as wisdom, *sapientia*, but as knowledge that destroys) would look upon love and all spiritual things with the cold eye of scrutiny, causing them to vanish as Cupid vanished when Psyche, driven with curiosity, looked upon the Love that nightly visited her:

> Scientia
> holding the lamp, driven by doubt;
> Eros naked in foreknowledge
> smiling in his sleep; and the light
> spilld, burning his shoulder—the outrage
>   that conquers legend—[11]

Apollo's mouthpiece, the Pythian oracle (the voice of sunlight, of rationality), told Psyche that her visitor was the Serpent-Desire who spread pain, and cautioned her not to seek after him. Having lost her original innocence, Psyche must now seek Eros through the world, suffering and struggling with the many tasks Venus sets for her.

Duncan's own psyche similarly struggles to win the right to Eros, to say "I love."

> I could not speak
>   the releasing
> word. For into a dark
> matter he came
> and askt me to say what
>   I could not say. "I. ."

> All the flame in me stopt
>> against my tongue.
> My heart was a stone, a dumb
>> unmanageable thing in me[12]

Love is not a matter that can be coerced, not even by one's own rational will, but is a Form that must be discovered, uncovered, unfolded in the self during time, much as the poem must unfold in its own imperatives. It demands a submission of the "I" just as the poem demands a certain submission of the poet—a falling off, a giving in.

> When I say *Love* the word comes out of me
> like a moan—life-sap. From broken wood.
> Yet I would not have it come easily.
> The word, the truth and the light of it
> are one I have not won in myself.[13]

In poems dedicated to Jack Spicer in *The First Decade* he can offer only a "swindle of the heart" in the words, for

> ...I do not think I can say
> *I love you* and not know
> the hurt of roses as they die,
> humiliation-bright uncertainty of the rose.   (pp. 47–48)

Duncan is painfully aware that the love he is able to give is not worthy of the word (or Word), not equal to his idea of what Love participating in Primal Love should be. Alluding to lines from Marianne Moore's "In Distrust of Merits," Duncan realizes that "There is no / not making the vow / and breaking it."[14] Even though "we are not competent to make our vows" of love, we must make them anyhow, for as Moore wrote, they are vows "without which no man is king." The anguish of making and breaking these vows is the Cross, or as Duncan likes to call it in various poems, "Christ-crossed" on the rood of Time.

Eros has two roles in the history of mythology. In a degenerate form he is the mischievous godling of erotic love (the Roman Cupid), son of Venus, as he is in Apuleius's narrative of "Cupid and Psyche." In the "Poem Beginning with a Line by Pindar," Duncan restores Cupid to his status as Cosmic Eros or Love, and sees Psyche as both the soul of every man and of all men. Those are the roles they enjoy in early Greek cosmogony[15] and in "Chords: Passages 14" (*Bow*, p. 46). An important realization of "Chords" is that if Psyche is to awake Primal Eros from the World-Egg, which Chronos has planted in the bosom of Chaos, Psyche will have to allow the winds to carry her where he is sleeping. The winds are the winds of poetry, and only they can bring the Soul to the place where it can awaken the Beloved that sleeps in the core of all things. Poetry lifts her "as the line lifts meaning and would / light the light, the crack of dawn in the Egg." This is the apocalypse Duncan promotes and desires, the birth, the hatching of Eros in the World-Egg. (The emblem or picture of the cracked egg must be borne in mind, for it is echoed or mirrored in a number of other emblems.) Duncan sees himself as a priest bringing the Lover to the Beloved, and his work as a half-way house, "a station on the way" toward the realization of Divine Eros. In a personal interview he reveals that even as a boy of ten or twelve he turned away from war and violence because he realized he really wanted to "convert" people, and saw that killing and coercion changed nothing, except perhaps living matter into compost.[16] He wants instead to lead people to a wisdom, a wonder:

> For them may there be a special green
> and flowering of life in these words—
> eager to be read, taken, yielded to.
> Yes, though I contrive the mind's measure
> and wrest doctrine from old lore,
> it's to win particular hearts,
> to stir an abiding affection for this music,
> as if a host of readers will join the Beloved
> ready to dance with me, it's for the
>   unthinking
> ready thing I'm writing these poems.　　　　　(*Field*, p. 61)

IV

The above poem adumbrates three important related motifs in the phrases "*green* and *flowering,*" "ready to *dance* with me," and "the *unthinking ready thing.*" The plant, the dance, and the irrational are recurrent figures and governing ideas in Duncan's poetry and poetics. All three are related to the Olson–Black Mountain idea of "composition by field," but they are also uniquely tied to Duncan's biography and values. Each image deserves consideration at some length.

The "green and flowering of life." Duncan's is, of course, an organic theory of poetry—few poets today do not claim that sobriquet for their poetic, though it often means only that they do not impose strict traditional forms upon their work. Poets like to think poems grow like plants; though in almost every case they grow more like gardens in the hands of careful gardeners. But Duncan's organicism goes beyond Emerson's "ask the fact for the form" or Creeley's "form is the extension of content." It not only claims that the poem unfolds according to its own law, but envisions a compatible cosmology in which it may do so. It is not the poem alone that must grow as freely as the plant: the life of the person, the state, the species, and indeed the cosmos itself follows a parallel law. All must follow their own imperatives and volition; all activity must be free of external coercion. But first the poem.

Like Keats, Duncan thinks that unless the poem comes as easily as the leaves to the tree, it had better not come at all. Behind his poetry he sees something like the divine afflatus of Plato's *Ion*. When the spirit is upon him, the "I" or voice of the poem is something larger than Robert Duncan. "When that 'I' is lost, when the voice of the poem is lost, the matter of the poem, the intense information of the content, no longer comes to me, then I know I have to wait until the voice returns" (*Truth*, p. 26). That this is not merely poet-talk is proven by poems in which he loses inspiration in the middle, runs down, grinds to a stop—then picks up the flow at a later time when the afflatus returns. A good example is "The Collage: Passages 6" where he gets only as far as this block with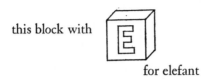

for elefant

when "the play runs down." (One fears it ran down some lines
earlier.) On another day, however, the spirit apparently

> runs away with me
> and I enter the wave of it.
> How long have I been waiting,
> the language, the sea, the body
> rising above
> sleep   (*Bow*, p. 20)

In "The Performance We Wait For" (*Field*, p. 55) he tells us
"there is no greater wrong / than to force the song." Every poet
and every king needs a garden even if it is only "a single plant
tended in the evening" because in it he will see the "signature that
is the ground of all delight." And in another poem we find

> The force that words obey in song
> the rose and artichoke obey
> in their unfolding towards their form.   (*Field*, p. 60)

There is here, then, something more than a simple organicism;
there is a statement about the nature of order in the cosmos. And
in the rose and artichoke there is symbolically a comment about
the order of all Beauty and Divinity. In his ideas of cosmic order,
Duncan appears to be a Platonist by natural inclination, an Aristotelian by choice, and an evolutionist (Darwin/Chardin) by desire
and necessity of circumstance. As already implied in my comments
about the *bodilessness* of his poetry, he tends to deal with the material world as though it were but a copy of the divine *eidos* and
interesting chiefly as the metaphor or signature of the spiritual.
He does so in spite of his intentions and assertions to the contrary.
With Aristotle he insists, however, that this world is the real world,
and that its Form is innate rather than remote. In his study of
Dante he emphasizes and endorses Dante's insistence upon the literal
as the primary meaning, ahead of the anagogic and metaphysical

significances of "polysemous" poetry. The real world, he adds, is the source of all our knowledge and devotion; we take our revelation from it, and it is not to be despised as it was by the Gnostics. The actual, the literal, is the primary ground out of which we create the linguistic, the universal. Creation "is the Divine Presentation, it is the language of experience whose words are immediate to our senses; from which our creative life takes fire, *within which* our own creative life takes fire."[17] Plato, too, he insists here and elsewhere, understood this—to him *ideas* meant "things seen." The etymology of "ideas" seems to bear this out (it comes, like "species," from a root meaning "to see"), but that does not change the fact that Plato thought the objects he saw around him were unreal shadows of real Ideas.

Like Levertov, Duncan believes that the "actual" world is very real and full of its own Form and mystery. Unlike Levertov, however, he fails in poetic practice to convincingly ground the transcendental within the proximate and actual. As Rudolph Nelson has clearly understood, Duncan is a poet of the threshold between the two worlds; but in practice he crosses the threshold horizontally, leaving one world for the other, instead of crossing it by going deeply into the real in the manner of Levertov.[18]

If Duncan does not *show* us the mysterious and transcendent in the quotidian commonplace, he repeatedly tells us that it is there. We have only to realize (come to know) it, and allow it to realize (come to be) itself. The divine presence, the *numen*, the Hebrew *Shekinah* is with us, in stones, in trees, in the broom-vendors of Denise Levertov's poems; but men shield themselves against it because it "is not only awe-ful; it moves us to tears" (*Truth*, p. 29). "The numinous is felt as the presence—it *is* the presence—of an overwhelming power of a stone, of a snake, of a man, of a fate, of a word, so that it becomes personal. The numen of the universe is its awful and overwhelming reality as an entity, its *genius*" (*Truth*, p. 45). Poetry can open men's senses to this *genius*, but men flee the poetic experience because "assent and thrill so enter into dramatic utterance, that the threat of the poetic reality to take over all other realms of human reality is fearful" (*Truth*, p. 15). They refuse the poetic awareness for the same reason they refuse love—they do not want to give themselves to that which is greater than themselves. But Duncan "After Reading Barely and Widely" has immersed himself sufficiently in this destructive element (the Other) to know that "there is that to which we would give ourselves wholly" (*Field*, p. 89).

Duncan wants to believe the cosmos is itself unfolding like a plant; that it is alive and a God in the process of becoming. Hermes Trismegistus, or "Thrice Greatest Hermes," so speaks of the world in his "Perfect Sermon of The Asclepius,"[19] and Duncan reads a parallel significance into the myth of the Primal Eros in the World-Egg. A similar idea has been put forward by Teilhard de Chardin and is echoed essentially in Duncan's idea of the world growing toward Christhood: "Christ's life is the immediate historical reality of the Form, or the proclamation of that Form, happening in this poetry of process; and the Second Coming is the Form of Forms from which all Judgment and redemption of events flows" (*Truth*, p. 62). The unfolding of the plant, the poem, the self, the earth is toward the ultimate end of Christform. Or the cosmos is thought of as a Book of Poetry in the process of writing itself, searching for its final form.[20] Whatever one chooses to call the One—God, Poet, Poetry, Eros, All-Father, Brahma—Duncan sees the One not as remote from, above, or behind the cosmos, but the cosmos itself. "That One is the Cosmos—as early as *The Unresting* I seem to have begun to see that; and Man, one of the many poems in which the Cosmos seeks to realize its Self" (*Years*, p. xi).

Duncan is not unaware that the Greek *kosmos* meant "order," and his own poetry takes its dramatic center in the tension between order and disorder, *kosmos* and *kaos*. The manner in which these seeming polarities are related is perhaps the knottiest critical problem his poetry poses. In ordering chaos one creates cosmos and participates in the original work of the Grand Designer. Yet Cosmos is for Duncan not an eradication of Chaos, but an awakening of and an awakening to the harmony with which Chaos is already suffused. His poetry intends not an ordering of experience, but an experiencing of its order. The divine harmonies with which Chaos is pregnant are of an order different from our human order, and it is precisely for this reason that the poet must, so to speak, keep his hands off his poem. Pythagoras did not invent the perfect order of musical consonances but discovered them already mixed in the apparently amorphous spectrum of sound. It is not hard to understand how the Pythagoreans, with their sacred *tetraktys* and their belief that "all is number," should experience something like a mystical revelation in the discovery that the perfect consonances can be expressed in terms of the ratios of 1, 2, 3, and 4, numbers which when combined form the perfect number 10 wherein the very nature of number resides. (The octave is produced by the ratio of 2:1, the fifth 3:2, and the fourth 4:3.)[21] Duncan likewise experiences the consonances he discovers in life and story as joyful revelations of cosmic vitality. Like those of music, they exist not apart from but in the very veins of chaos. Or rather they *are* the very *veins* of chaos.

I choose the word *veins* purposively, for although neither image is to be found in the poetry (there are too few sensuous images), the picture of veins irregularly swarming through a denser medium, or of lightning jaggedly honeycombing the night sky, accurately expresses the kind of order Duncan seems to intend in his abstract manipulations of "harmonies," "diversities," "mistakes," "concords," "irregularities," "disorderly excitements of a dream," "consonances beyond our knowledge of consonances." The order that men would impose upon chaos would resemble a gridwork of regular lines—a graph-paper sky (or a rectangular and "level" breadboard). But nature supplies the body's needs by an altogether erratic (seemingly) branching of arteries; and the tree spreads its branches through the chaos of monotonous air with an order that is excitingly disorderly. For Duncan, such is the difference between life and death. The dead matter of the universe science dissects into tidy stackables; the living significance of creation, the angel with which the poet wrestles, is a volatile whirlwind of sharp knees and elbows threshing with a grace beyond our knowledge of grace.

If there are in Duncan's poetry few images that convey this idea of the world, there are a number of what are perhaps more properly called "emblems" that do mirror it. The epigraph at the head of this chapter is one example—and here, significantly, it is "our delite, our life" that is the ragged cross-hatch, the flaw that threads through the mineral perfection of "war" just as the cracks of age give beauty to the crystal pitchers of the Hapsburg's that Duncan saw in the early fifties.* Another is the rivering fissures in the shell of the World-Egg visioned in the mind's eye as Eros is awakened, "the crack of dawn in the Egg / Night's nature shelters before Time." The title of the "Passages" themselves suggest such a mapping of ways, and the "pyramid" of "Passages 6" into which Duncan would "cut ways" is another. "The Collage" and the Grand Collage mentioned elsewhere likewise carry the idea of the universe as a disorderly, irregular order. In the link between the pyramid, the Greek Delta Δ, the river delta, and the "life-door, the cunt," we are led finally to the wound in Christ's side ("Passages 8")—all of which are images of an order, a life, that is a "break," a flaw, a disruption, a door. The flaw as a *door*. The irregular as a *way*. Duncan's poetics, biography, and cosmology come together.

Duncan's organic order is a disorder within a larger order. That statement might be read as an assertion about his personal life as well as about his poetry and philosophy. It also characterizes poets in relation to other men; poetry in relation to more mundane activity; and ties of Love in relation to an essentially loveless landscape. There is another sense that the Greeks understood, in which we may say that the disorder of order is *the* order. Music is a matter of differences, measure a matter of ratios, and life a matter of disequilibrium. Ordering the chaos that exists prior to cosmos

---

* Cf. Yeats's beautiful "Lapis Lazuli," where the flaws of the stone add to the beauty of the delicately carved art:
"Every discoloration of the stone,
Every accidental crack or dent,
Seems a watercourse or an avalanche,
Or lofty slope where it still snows."
And similar flaws no doubt account for the final beauty and wisdom of the two Chinamen and their awareness: "Their eyes mid many wrinkles, their eyes,/Their ancient glittering eyes, are gay."

is a matter of disturbing its sameness, destroying its equilibrium, drawing its elements into irregular agglomerations and differentiations.* Entropy is the natural tendency of things to fall back toward sameness and equilibrium. The organism, the plant, the poem, the cosmos creates a new order by throwing things out of order; the new order is by comparison spontaneous, irregular, erratic, disorderly—the branching of trees, veins, lightning against a shapeless sky.

"Ready to dance with me." The discussion of order and disorder has thus far been largely in terms of spatial images. The organism or plant is a creature of time, but is experienced in space. Unlike the plant, the poem, though also created in time, is experienced in both time and space. For this second dimension of poetry, the Dance becomes a more apt metaphor. The dance, too, is a kind of disorder of movement in time, a temporal field of ratios. One of the essentials of "modern dance," I believe, is that the dancer must relinquish something of his control and his will to the dance itself; he must lose himself in it, give himself to it until, as Yeats would have it, we "cannot tell the Dancer from the Dance." Duncan's poems are replete with references to the dance, and his description of how the form of poetry takes shape must surely be also an accurate law of the dance: "For the poet, It, the form he obeys in making form, the very revelation of Art, is not strictly so [that is, never exact, complete, accurate, orderly, finished]. Creativity, as I have suggested, means such a change in the meanings of every

---

* W. K. C. Guthrie, in *Orpheus and the Greek Religion* (London: Methuen & Co., 1935), p. 75, writes of the Orphean theogony/cosmogony: " 'Everything comes to be out of One and is resolved into one.' At one time Phanes, at another Zeus contained the seeds of all being within his own body, and from this state of mixture in the One has emerged the whole of our manifold world, and all nature animate and inanimate. This central thought, that everything existed at first together in a confused mass, and that the process of creation was one of separation and division, with the corollary that the end of our era will be a return to the primitive confusion, has been repeated with varying degrees of mythological coloring in many religions and religious philosophies."

See also Duncan's essay, "Towards an Open Universe," in Howard Nemerov, ed., *Poets on Poetry* (New York: Basic Books, 1966).

part in the creation of each part that every new strictness is also a charm undoing all previous strictnesses, at once an imperative and at the same time a change of imperative" (*Truth*, p. 66). In other words, the poem, the dance (and life itself as a poem and dance when fully lived) is like a snake in almost perpetual need of shedding its skin. Indeed, we find just such an image in *Roots and Branches*; always and everywhere the living moment sheds the last moment's order:

What is
hisses like a serpent
and writhes
to shed its skin.   (p. 30)

The poem, one's life, the life of the cosmos, the dance of things in time, have no plan or end or pattern or goal, other than the imperatives of the unfolding law of their own activity in space and time. The only law the dance has is love of the Dance itself, which in practice means love of all persons and objects that are a part of it. Evil is that which is antagonistic to the dance, the resistant medium through which the dance honeycombs its erratic patterns. Life, Poetry, Godhead is the light coming out of darkness, cosmos radiating through chaos, the God's eye opening in the murky ambience ("Eye of God: Passages 29," *Bow*, p. 124). Love is the First Caller and the First Partner of the Dance and man must be an "unthinking ready thing" "delighting in *His* numbers" (italics mine). For just as God's order is different from man's, so Love's measures are syncopated, the notes coming slightly off the regular beat:

. . . our feet
dance to be true to the count,
repeating the hesitation, the
slight bow to His will in each change,
the giving up, His syncopation,
the receiving   an other
measure again.   (*Bow*, p. 5)

"The unthinking ready thing." If the plant, the dance is to

be right, man must subdue both his will and his propensity toward cold analytical reason; he must recognize a mystery larger than his own powers. In Duncan's children's-fable allegory of *The Cat and the Blackbird*,[22] the "gardener" does not succeed in growing "moon beans" until he has despaired, given up, neglected to care for his garden after the eighteenth-century manner. The moon beans spring up at last wherever his tears fall, until the garden is singing in their light. Duncan shares with Bly and Ginsberg the prejudices against rationalism initiated by Blake, Whitman, and Lawrence. His attitude is somewhat more discriminating, however. In recent poetry he frequently uses the term "right reason" to distinguish the proper role of the Intellect—for which he has high respect—and its modern abuses. But even right reason must give way to the "syncopation" of the divine, to transcendent mystery. In his handling of Parmenides Dream ("A Shrine to Ameinias," *Bow*, p. 97) he seems to introduce an additional "gate" through which Parmenides must pass in his flight toward his vision of Holy Wisdom. There is only the one gate in Parmenides's own poem. The extra gate is one at which "Right Reason" must be cajoled into allowing Parmenides to pass on into realms beyond its ken and control.

The chief liability of the logical faculty is that it is in certain ways too "orderly" and therefore restricts the possibilities of discovery and growth. Paralleling Duncan's philosophy of "life-as-irregularity" is his epistemology of "knowledge-through-mistake." Thus we find him speaking of the necessity of breaking "orderly converse to address divine disorders" (*Letters*, ltr. ii), and claiming "I attempt the discontinuities of poetry. To interrupt all sure course of my inspiration" (Preface to *Letters*, ltr. iii). To Levertov he writes, "who works at his own word in all of our sentences might trick from even the ruts of once ritual the buts and mistakes that token the actual." His own desire is

> Step by
>   /to be idiot-awkward
>   step
>   to take care
>
> by the throat and throttle it.   (*Letters*, ltr. i)

Taking his cue from Freud, Duncan tries never to repudiate his poetic slips and inaccuracies but to face the error and seek to discover its meaning. He believes that the mistake often carries within it a higher truth (*Truth*, p. 63). In his statement on poetics in the Donald Allen anthology he writes: "After Freud, we are aware that unwittingly we achieve our form. It is, whatever our mastery, the inevitable use we make of the speech that betrays to ourselves and to our hunters (our readers) the spore of what we are becoming."[23]

In his organic poetic and philosophy, in his somewhat anarchic conception of order, in his bias for the spontaneity and joy of the dance, and in his epistemology of error, we see both the seeds and the flowers of Duncan's concern for *community* and *individual volition*. These are his preeminent values: he seeks and "will ever seek" the community of man, and believes community is possible only among persons acting freely as individuals. He is an avid communist—though surely not of the Marxist variety[24]—and a gentle anarchist who wears the black arm-band with some diffidence. Community implies unity in variety, and is impossible where persons are all alike or coerced into common conduct. That is not cosmos but chaos. If the poem must find its form by a haphazard freedom, so must society shape itself with a similar flexibility. Given this much insight into Duncan's values, it is not difficult to understand his hatred of modern warfare.

V

Duncan is not an avowed pacifist as such. Nonviolence was to him in the early years of the Vietnam War a new and fascinating idea. That is evident in the Preface to *Bending the Bow* and even more apparent in his private conversation concerning the experience of the Protest March on Washington. He himself would hesitate "to step on a snail," yet has never adopted nonviolence as a positive creed—and thinks it important to distinguish between the inability or disinclination to be violent, and the positive volition of true nonviolence.[25] In true nonviolence the individual volition is in a state of perpetual operation and renewal, since every moment is a decision to withhold violence (violence being a genus larger than physical force). Moreover, insofar as it is a voluntary action of individuals in concert, it involves true community. It is, furthermore, a demonstration of the perfect order of anarchy.

Nonviolence and pacifism appeal to Duncan, then, because of his temperament, but most of all because of their participation in volition and community. Where physical combat participated equally in these, he would perhaps not find it unacceptable. In "Passages 2" the Trojan War is seen in a favorable light because there each side and each man (save perhaps Achilles) fought

> . . . for the sake of
> the alliance,
> allegiance, the legion, that the
> vow that makes a nation
> one body not be broken. (*Bow*, p. 12)

But now that has become "a mêlée, / a medley of mistaken themes / grown dreadful and surmounting dread." If anything of that heroic time remains it is perhaps a perverted concern for "honor," a "mistaken theme perpetuated"

> so that Achilles may have his wrath
> and throw down
> the heroic Hektor who raised
> that reflection of the heroic
> in his shield . . . (*Bow*, p. 13)

There are here two different kinds of heroism—Hector's heroism of community, and Achilles's heroism of "honor." Given Duncan's values, one feels confident in judging against Achilles and in favor of Hector.* Community and compassion defeated by power and pride reflect the condition of the modern world.

---

* Convincing evidence may be found in the prose poem "Image of Hektor" in Duncan's *A Book of Resemblances* (New Haven: Henry Wenning, 1966), p. 89: "It is in falling, not falling in love but into death. As Troy fell into immortality. Had we fallen, been lost in his being lost, we had remained. So utterly destroyed that it draws the spirit out of all that survives into its immortal spirit."

Though there was once a deeper sense of mystery among men, Duncan laments the passing of no golden age, but sees community and love as still in the process of becoming, a nascent raying out into the wide gulfs that separate men. The universal poem is still in the early stages of its writing. The real "war" is that of love's and poetry's flame against the void and the cold, against the vast sea dividing the continents and persons and "just breaking at war with the light." This war must be pursued with the same honesty, freedom, and "planlessness" as is necessary in the writing of a good poem. We can hardly emphasize too much or too often the connection Duncan makes between the laws of the poem and all other activities. The proper poem is the paradigm, the universal signature of all action and being. Duncan's objection to modern war is that it is an atrocious poem written by bad poets *who have a plan.*

The motif of war as bad poetry is most audible in a poem that has nothing to do with Vietnam. Duncan wrote perhaps his best war poem in the early fifties during the Korean struggle. Complex and difficult enough, the lengthy "Essay at War" is nevertheless in some ways the clearest and most accessible of Duncan's works.[26] I would have to agree with Gilbert Sorrentino that "had Duncan focused his poetics on poems like 'The Venice Poem' and 'An Essay at War,' that is, continued to write in this luminous vein, a brilliant and single vision, I submit that he would have been accorded all the honors the literary establishment could afford. Perhaps not all the honors, but a meaty bone or two."[27] Avoiding the esoteric and mythological, and sticking to concrete image and symbol, this poem operates chiefly by elliptical juxtaposition suggesting necessary relationships between the conduct of war, the writing of a poem, the dying of an old man, the voluntary action of a comrade in battle, and the spread of love through the world. The essential themes of the Vietnam *Passages* of the sixties are here in some form, and provide a helpful way into the later war protest.

Early in "An Essay at War" we are offered the poetic of poem-as-dance, poem-as-Heraclitean-fire, poem-as-snake-constantly-changing-its-skin.

The design of a poem
    constantly
under reconstruction,
    changing, pusht forward;
alternations of sound, sensations;
    the mind dance
wherein thot shows its pattern:
    a proposition
    in movement.   (*Derivations*, p. 9)

Thought in the poem does not follow a pattern chosen before-
hand, obeys no academic formulas, has no absolute predestination.
The poem is evidently much like the dying old man in his last
days of cancer, like a "bombed house" or ravaged city, a pietà
absorbing grandeur in relation to his weakness and his draining
away. The man's life is a flame, a raying out that may remind the
reader of the quatrain in Shakespeare's Sonnet number 73:

In me thou seest the glowing of such fire
as on the ashes of his youth doth lie
as a deathbed whereon it must expire
consumed with that which it was nourished by.

"I am trying to let everything fall away" says the old man, and in
the detailed and unlovely picture of the bedridden man Duncan
finds a "Teacher! Your temper teaches."

The poem designed so.
To emit great snores
    or death's confusions.
A pressure.
            or a procession.
A dream.
            or a drain.   (*Derivation*, p. 13)

In the intense febrile energy of the dying man forced to live in
the present moment only, shorn of any programs and pretenses
for tomorrow, Duncan finds the symbol of the poem's unfolding
life. It is a manner of life obviously not well suited to military
success.

The design
not in the sense of a treachery or
   deception
but of a conception betrayd,
   without a plan,
   completed
in the all over thing heard;
   a hidden thing
reveald in its pulse and
   durations;
   a fire.
                         (*Derivations*, p. 9)

We must not miss here the important point that this is a poetic of *linguistic community*, a poetic of *harmonious linguistic anarchy*. Each word, each phrase, each line, each larger unit can act, in a sense, by its own "volition," its uniqueness unblunted in favor of any cause, the concerted effect of the poem resulting from the free participation of all parts, not bound together by a common teleology, but by a common delight. The interaction of words is multiple and uninhibited by anything other than the *character* of the participating figures. It is a community of words with no laws other than their own natures.

War necessarily operates under an entirely opposite poetic, and thus is anti-poetic not only by virtue of its unlovely *content*, but also by virtue of its blatantly anti-poetic *form*. Inasmuch as society and poetry have the same organic "signature," war is likewise anti-community not only in its brutal actions, but in its monolithic processes.

War demands that people act together in synchrony and symmetry, but it cannot rely on individual volition to accomplish this. The common arguments of rulers in wartime are echoed by Duncan:

What medley of voices, what free harmony,
can stand over against or answer
   single-minded tyranny?
Only a plan, a unanimous war, can win.
      An inspiration
not to be corrupted, not to be turnd.
                      (*Derivations*, p. 18)

The poem is just such a medley of voices and words, operating in a free harmony without a plan, standing against and in answer to the darkness. As poets, all of us "face uncertainties / the war, or the plan, mocks us."

Vietnam is the bad poem of "The Soldiers: Passages 26," written as badly as the one Chiang Kai-shek wrote against Mao's campaign for community/communism.

> Mao's own mountain of murdered men,
> the alliteration of ems like Viet Nam's
> burnd villages . . .   (*Bow*, p. 113)

President Johnson, perhaps because he is the "swollen head" of the nation, the faculty of control grown disproportionate, is the poetaster writing in the old inevitable forms.

> (Johnson now, no inspired poet but making it badly,
> amassing his own history in murder and sacrifice
>   without talent)
>   . . . irreplaceable irrevócable in whose name?
>   a hatred the maimd and bereft must hold
>   against the bloody verse America writes over Asia
>   (*Bow*, p. 113)

The bad poem is written *over* its matter and attempts to control and subjugate its parts; the good poem is the matter asserting its own freedom, breaking out of control—and the good poem in this instance is obviously "Asia" and the embattled Vietnamese. The line quoted from Whitman ("The United States themselves are essentially the greatest poem"), Duncan reads according to his own idea of poetry: "Then America, the secret union of all states of Man, / waits, hidden and challenging, in the hearts of the Viet Cong" (p. 113).

The United States was once a voluntary union of free states, but the only communities of volition today are the underground fraternities of the VC in Vietnam and the counter-culture in this country. Duncan shares in that confraternity, and his powerful sympathy with the VC is that they are a minority, underdogs, "gypsies." And, he reminds us (personal interview), poets are also gypsies, outcasts, persons whose "nation" can never be smaller than the total community of man. The effort of the VC against a larger ambience of power has the same general configuration as the struggles of a poet, especially of the poet of an irregularity.* Furthermore, that configuration parallels those of the God's eye opening in the darkness, the womb opening to admit light, the nucleus radiating outward toward the extremities, the seed lost in the heavy earth beginning to stir outward.

In Duncan's mind the Viet Cong know something of the great theme of war in contrast to the American troops:

> O you, who know nothing of the great theme of War,
> fighting because you have to, blindly, at no frontier
> of the Truth. (p. 114)

The VC fight as the Trojans did for the

> . . . alliance,
> allegiance, the legion, that the
> vow that makes a nation
> one body not be broken.

Soldiers on either side in the Korean War lacked this. There, according to "An Essay at War," the demand of Victory asked them

---

* Anyone who has felt the heavy hand of power or arbitrary authority can identify with the VC as Duncan does. Decrying the coercive structure of education, Duncan complains: "From the first grade through the eighth grade in compulsory education you have that, . . . and you have an absolutely ignorant school marm, rapping you over the knuckles because you wanted to do something, and wouldn't get it done exactly the way she did. So, some of my protest is . . . the black arm-band I discover I'm really wearing against such compulsion. The day when . . . the teacher . . . well, it's no great information if you want to know just how stubborn one is going to be: my handwriting which is admired now—it was a stubborn resistance to Pitman [Palmer?]. And a teacher stood and whacked me over the knuckles in a red rage because I would still not write with my whole arm because my father was an architect and I wanted to print as my father did. She was stronger than I was—as a matter of fact that's where I learned what the Vietnamese are. When you're whacked over the knuckles for not writing with your whole arm, you've got the message and not the one that the one who whacks you intends" (personal interview, 9 May 1969).

to give themselves to the plan, "join the army not to be turned, all volition given over to belief." The belief here is not vision, not love of community, but the idea of Victory

> ... moving
> not like the sea but
> as the fanatic mind moves, with a plan,
> shouting,
> inexorably forward.
> The plan is the war.   (*Derivations*, p. 17)

But as in any bad poem, a single line can sometimes break free of exact meter, the inexorable plan, and take on its own beauty. Though war is in general without volition or community, yet within it there are sometimes moments when individuals act freely and with brotherhood.

> So this ordinary G. I. stript to the waist
> carrying the wounded
> American soldier in his arms
> repeats in his hot Korean summer
> a pièta.
> He is like a nakedness of speech
> shedding its words; or
> an imaginary conclusion
> of acts or of words; without plan,
> a volunteer / having only a form in the mind
>
>   (*Derivations*, p. 21)

The "pièta" which he repeats is that not only of Christ but of the dying man and of the poem, both naked, without plan, with only a form in mind. Here, too, we sense the association of the poem with Eros on the rood of time, "Christ-crossd" always in behalf of the community of man. The poem dying so that it might give life.

The action of the G. I. is not part of the strategy laid out in command rooms full of maps with colored tacks. It is, in a sense, a disorder within the larger order. And it is in this flaw or gap that life *is*; as in the crystal pitcher the flaw is the beauty, and as in the poem that achieves "its more-than-language not in the form / but in the intrigue of lines, the shattering, / the inability"

(*Derivations*, p. 23). Anything that lacks this disequilibrium is not living or true. In the *Letters* we find the image of a map that lacks such an imperfection:

> How on the map spread on the table
> no mark shows the burning.
> It is unmarred, perfect, undependable.   (*Letters*, ltr. xii)

If it is perfect, it is dead, it is undependable. Life is a burning, a riot, a moving, and cannot be perfectly mapped or reduced to order. Life is an intrigue of lines with a certain "inability," a poem that, as Pound said of his own work, is "not so, not strictly so."

VI

In "Passages 26" Duncan indulges his fascination with the *Oxford English Dictionary* and the histories of words, as a means of revealing further evils of modern war.

> *Solidarius* : *sol*derd   this army having its sodality
> in the common life,   bearing the coin or paid in the coin
> *solidum*, gold emblem of the Sun
>   tho we fight underground
> from the heart's volition,   the body's inward sun,
>   the blood's natural
>   uprising against tyranny   ·
> And from the first it has been communism,   the true
> Poverty of the Spirituals   the heart desired;
>   I too removed therefrom by habit.
>   (*Bow*, pp. 113–114)

Soldiers and armies were once, at least for the purposes of the poem if not in reality, signs of community, of solidarity, of free union around a center from which the round coin of brotherhood came, in the image of the sun, symbol of natural authority and service supplying all things with vitality; and the fraternity *sol*dered together firmly by mutual benefit, every man a *sol*, a king. The only such community now is the "underground" movement against the war and the brutalities of modern life.

To recognize the importance of both the inward sun and the coin as an emblem of a center of light radiating out into a bounded circle (which it as center necessarily defines—there can be no center unless there is limit), one perhaps needs to be acquainted with Duncan's larger canon. The emblem is intricately involved with the question of the odd and even, the limited and unlimited, finite and irrational number, and is subtly influenced by Eleaticism, Pythagoreanism, and the mystical meanings of number itself. We should perhaps begin again with "An Essay at War" and its image of the poem as the heart, the hearth—remembering, too, that the "inward sun" of the later poem is a natural uprising of the heart. In "Essay"

> Even the subhuman Mousterian man left
>> ashes of fires.
> From the beginning we picture
>> the hearthlight
> in the room of the cave. Outside
>> the epoch of the greatest cold   (*Derivations*, p. 10)

And the primitive man also left ashes of another flame, symbolically parallel with the hearthfire, in the paintings and gravings where he

>> workt
>> the inaccessible rock-face
> and returnd from the deepest recesses of the mind
>> to the hearth
> to the place where we too are gatherd   (*Derivations*, p. 10)

"Essay" first describes the processes of poetry as those of fire, then associates the poem with the burning of the old man, and now with the hearth, and at last the fire is connected with Love. "It is the first named incarnation of Love. We burn with it. The fire of Hell. Pain. But it is also warmth. Demonic. But it is also light. The night is all about us. A darkness within which all known things exist" (*Derivations*, p. 11). The night is all about us. In the center is the heart, the hearth, the poem, the fire, Love, defining the circle within which the blackness may not flow. The darkness within which all known things exist reduces them to sameness, so that they are indistinguishable. The light defines, *disorders* the blackness into irregular shapes and recognizable objects. The *Logos*, the *Kosmos*. In this context the lines in the Preface to *Bending the Bow* gain their full dimension: "Life demands sight, and writes at the boundaries of light and dark, black upon white, then color in which the universe appears, chemical information in which Argus eyes of the poem strive. War now is a monstrosity in the hands of militarists who have taken no deep thought of the art of war and its nature" (p. v). Duncan's pervasive sense of the war of light and darkness is no doubt most influenced by his Zoroastrian readings, the battle of Ohmazd and Ahriman, but it is also medieval or pre-medieval. One is reminded of Hrothgar and Beowulf in the mead-hall in the circle of friends and light, surrounded by the unknown darkness and steaming fens.

VII

The image of light drawing lines into the darkness forms a figure corresponding to Parmenides's vision and consonant with the gnomonic diagrams of the Pythagoreans. Both Parmenides and Pythagoras figure importantly in specific poems and exert subtle influences on others.

Very briefly, the *Ent* of Parmenides is one, unchanging, indivisible, unifying principle, spherical because limited only by its self, extended in space but having its own bounds. In his "Way of Truth" Parmenides explains:

> For strong Necessity holds it firm within the bonds of the limit that keeps it back on every side, because it is not lawful that what is should be unlimited; for it is not in need—if it were, it would need all.
>
> But since there is a furthest limit, it is bounded on every side, like the bulk of a well-rounded sphere, from the centre equally balanced in every direction; for it needs must not be somewhat more here or somewhat less there.[28]

In "A Shrine to Ameinias" Duncan describes the *Ent* in these words:

> Truth, She told Parmenides, was a well-rounded ring,
> a circling without disturbance, seeming to move, but
> having an unwobbling pivot, an unmoved heart—$ατρεμης$
> is the Greek word: an untrembling center.
> Yes, it is there, at the heart of the work, and
> even in dreams, the world seems to encircle him,
> sure in him. —And you've to learn too,
> She promises, opinions in which there is no
> true belief at all, the accounts of mortal men
> (the word here is $βροτός$—$βρότος$, *the blood*
> *that has run from a wound*). Here, Truth trembles,
> and you will learn how all things that seem,
> as they pass thru all things, must take on
> semblance of Being. Immortal mortalities!
>
> (*Bow*, p. 99)

The "him" in the sixth and seventh lines is either and both Ameinias and Jess Collins, Duncan's loved companion, and also simply the pivot, the center or hearth, which later in the poem becomes love and at last is associated with the primal god of love, Eros. The center of love holds the circle of light steady, and within that *Ent* (One), the *Non-Ent* (Many) takes on its shadowy reality. Mirroring the hub of light in the One is the bleeding wound of the Many.

Duncan does not miss in Parmenides's poem the prefigured emblem of the *Ent* and *Non-Ent* in the whirling wheels of the chariot of thought. The exact center is a still point, "an unwobbling pivot."

> —the axle blazing in the socket—
> —the great wheels roaring round
> at each end, making
> the holes in the naves sing. (p. 97)

The third figure of the poem is the rings of the cosmos as known to man, differentiated into realms and colors:

> Iris in her chromatic scales
> out of Light / raises
> from teardrops her violet

and red   outer limits of our
    sight
        weeping,
  irradiate with self-defining
    steps of color into higher and lower
      realms set   (p. 97)

Thus light, Truth, Love again are the cohesive heart, like the
hearth of the "Essay at War." The love of Parmenides for Ameinias
is the unchanging reality behind the surface conflicts and agonies.
Despite the war, the *Ent* remains real, and gives order, meaning,
and beauty to the flux and the fire or dance.

The gnomonic diagrams were the basis of the "ten principles"
or polarities of Pythagoreanism.

Odd Number:	Even Number:
odd	even
limited	unlimited
one	many
right	left
male	female
resting	moving
straight	curving
light	darkness
good	evil
square	oblong

If we study these polarities we can see that the Pythagorean numbers contained what we could call "moral" values, and that, for
the Greeks at least, the "evens" got the worst of it.

The question of number, of limit, figures importantly in several poems. The Pythagorean *tetraktys* is associated in "Passages 6" with the Delta Δ and the life-door or vulva; and the gnomonic functions of the odd number seem to be involved with the idea of the hearth as a holding, unifying center. The odd-number gnomons of the diagram on the left differ from the even-number gnomons on the right in that each subsequent gnomon or level retains the constant ratio of the square, while the even-number gnomon is always changing the ratio of its sides. The odd numbers are not divisible by two, the odd unit always blocking the dividing line—"there is no way through or out of it." Moreover, according to Aristotle's explanation of the "ten principles," the odd numbers probably came to be thought of as "limited" because they had a beginning, a middle, and an end, whereas the even numbers have no "middle." (What has a middle necessarily has limits; what has no middle is necessarily boundless.) The odd number "one" was also unique in that it "ordered" the diagram in constant, unchanging gnomons. The first integer thus extended its influence throughout the number system, much as the hearth, the "inward sun," sometimes called the "household," binds together the community:

> household of the folk,
> commune of communes
> hidden seed in the hearts of men.   (*Bow*, p. 77)

The "unit" or "light" orders and defines, it *limits*, and thus fences out the chaos and the darkness at the peripheries. For the Greeks, *infinity* or the *unlimited* were negative concepts. *Kosmos* itself implied limits; and that bias against the infinite can be seen in Parmenides's dream of the *Ent* also: "it is not lawful that it should be unlimited; for it is not in need—if it were, it would need all." War lacks this central fire. It is without the unit or hearth, and thus is, despite its plan and its "order," nevertheless without Limit. The poet's mind quickly sees the correspondences between these abstract concepts and the endless body counts, endless rhetoric, endless durations of war.

In the Korean war poem, Duncan speaks for both himself and the soldiers:

> Ordered to stand—there being
> no order—
> we do not understand.   (*Derivations*, p. 17)

The several kinds of order here are instructive. In one reading of the lines, the first use of "ordered" means "coerced" rather than "put in order"; the second use means not "command," but proper ratios and relationships. The soldiers are coerced and thus there can be no genuine or legitimate pattern or order. The two are for Duncan apparently irreconcilable and mutually exclusive. Coercion and true order cannot coexist. "Coercion," we are told in "Passages 26," "is Ahriman," the Zoroastrian God of darkness. But the lines here twist like a snake, shed their skin, and metamorphose into another significant reading, and we see also that the soldiers are coerced and comply because both they and their commanders understand "reality" too fully, and do not know or recognize in it a mystery, a syncopation, a *shekinah* that is beyond understanding—they are ordered to stand because there is no order that they do not understand. But where one recognizes and reverences this higher dis-order, this odd number, light, hearth, unitive integer, then there is a real order beyond our usual orders and understandings. Where this true order exists Ahriman is confined outside the circle of its light. When he is admitted, the Light and Order necessarily give way, as we see in "Moira's Cathedral":

> A thousand men go into the dirt and flood to die
>   having nor name nor proportion
>   in their numbers. We
>
> lose count.   An army—
>   a single man rising
>   rememberd   falling back
>   —I do not know who he is—
>   —where he is—
>
>   cries out.

Is it $17 million a day, a
   million men finally to be laid down
   in wager?
      There is no Limit.
        The hydra breaks from his confines
            into Day's palaces   (*Bow*, p. 95)

The hydra that haunts a number of the poems here seems to be the hydra of Night and Darkness that exists outside of what would be the proper bounds. But because the unitive integer—love, hearth, fire—is lacking, the circle's circumference does not hold, and the hydra breaks in from its confines into the Day's palaces. The Limit is gone because the heart, the center, is missing. (A second irony is the motif of gambling—where no proper love or respect exists, there is no limit to the number of lives we are ready to wager.)

The Pythagorean concept of limit is important in "Moira's Cathedral," but secondary in importance to the idea of "imaginary number."

    "The imaginary numbers," wrote Gottfried Wilhem von Leibnitz in 1702, "are a wonderful flight of God's Spirit; they are almost an amphibian between being and not being."
    A field is "ordered" if the sizes of its
    elements can be compared.
  The sizes of its elements cannot
    be compared. For in the Eye of the Creator
        the trembling of a leaf
        in the roar of gun-fire,
           the fall of a tree,   strikes dismay.   (*Bow*, p. 95)

The Liebnitz epigraph and the first three lines of verse come directly from an article in *The Scientific American* where we are given a complex explanation of the axiomatic necessities behind a mathematical field.[29] All of the complexities of the article ultimately yield the simpler statement that "a field is a system (exemplified by the rational numbers) whose elements can be added, subtracted, multiplied and divided under the familiar rules of arithmetic." The war, with its body counts, bomb tonnages, and comparative firepowers, is frequently treated by those in charge as little more than a mathematical field, a system of ratios and arithmetic functions. One need not be a poet to realize that their analyses neglect important considerations. Interestingly, the spiritual truths that lie beyond the mathematical yardsticks of war have within the numbers systems a counterpart: imaginary number. Mathematicians deal most often in real numbers, but can imagine numbers at several levels of abstraction that indeed seem both to exist and not exist; numbers that contradict even the rules of their nonexistence and prove useful in complex computations. In them Duncan catches both an emotion and a glimpse of significance far beyond our usual cognizances, and senses that in the mind of God all things resonate with a uniqueness that defies man's calculations and manipulations.

VIII

The only order and limit that Duncan will accept are those that emanate from the heart and free volition of the individual. Not only must this hearth be free of external coercion, but must also be free from the exertions of self-will. Before community can flower under the "inward sun," there must first be a defeat, a giving-in of the ego. Though he sometimes speaks of it as "losing heart," the meaning is obviously different—in fact it means gaining heart (love) by losing heart (will). Just as Truth enters the poem through gaps and breaks in the author's inspiration, so love enters through chinks in the psychic armor. It is this faith that allows Duncan to be hopeful in the face of the world's present black crises. Out of winter comes spring; out of holocaust, a new respect for life. "An Essay" hopes that Korea will be for us like the burning home around which the family stands, united in a new way:

> seeing the sparks fly up from their losses
>   burning, brought together ...
>   only   Love left.   (*Derivations*, p. 11)

This perception allows him to say "you see, what I feel is needed at this point is a nadir, a breakdown, a failure of heart or of vision;

and then, all longing left will be hopeless." He believes that it is
in life as in the poem—at the point of extremity

> The thread
> breaks   ·   or the light
> breaks thru   (p. 13)

The attitude closely parallels Bly's "night in which we lose everything" and Levertov's strictures against the "vain will." It can
find hope in the fatigue, acedia, and despair growing out of Vietnam. If the thread of assumptions is tortured and strained enough,
perhaps it will break and a new possibility emerge. The "Essay"
asks that we give up the idea of Victory and, instead of sacrificing
our volition to the "plan," make a different denial: "Let us resolve /
the right surrender."

The above idea finds more vivid expression in "The Fire: Passages 13." Though the poem perhaps predates the rage against
Vietnam, it has a strong political content, and sees the American
spirit caught in a "forest fire" like that of Piero de Cosimo's painting
of similar name.

> From the wood we thought burning
> our animal spirits flee,   seeking refuge wherever,
>   as if in Eden,   in this   panic
>   lion and lamb lie down,   quail
> heed not the eagle in flight before the flames high
>   over head go.
> We see at last the man-faced roe and his
>   gentle mate;   the wild boar too
> turns a human face.   (*Bow*, p. 41)

The crisis has brought the animals together in a kind of new Eden.
In sharp contrast are the human faces of the Hieronymous Bosch
painting, twisted with the fanaticism of the religious wars. The
poet sees there the evidence of the Satanic:

> Eisenhower's idiot grin, Nixon's
> black jaw, the sly glare in Goldwater's eye, or
> the look of Stevenson lying in the U.N. that our
> Nation save face   ·

His face multiplies from the time of Roosevelt, Stalin,
    Churchill, Hitler, Mussolini; from the dream
    of Oppenheimer, Fermi, Teller, Vannevar Bush,
    brooding the nightmare formulae—to win the war!

                                                    (p. 43)

The counterposed faces of defeat (the humane animal faces) and
the faces of *Will* (the bestial human faces) dramatically expose
the qualities of each.

IX

"The Fire: Passages 13" involves the motif of the Satanic, a
theme that fascinates Duncan. Of himself and other poets Duncan
admits, "We're all apocalyptic, and you know, children of Milton
—you can draw the design. Both Denise [Levertov] and I have
very strong attachments to Bunyan, to Bunyan's Pilgrim's prophecy,
and I still see it [the war, the contemporary scene] as a spiritual
battle. It's very hard for me to humanize it" (personal interview).
Not only the interest in Bunyan, but the mythological proclivity
as well, causes Duncan to see and express the war in an abstract
and mythic dimension. There is in Duncan's work none of the
intense visceral experience of the war's suffering that we find in
Levertov, but instead a remoteness and grandeur like that in Milton's
battle on the plains of heaven. Duncan does not *experience* the
war but repeatedly attempts to place it in its large spiritual perspective. His protest and the war fall into the patterns of the
classic struggle between good and evil, light and darkness. Perhaps
it is already clear that it is not war itself that Duncan considers
evil, but rather its coercive implications in modern times. He
strongly disagrees with that cult of life that argues "war is death,
peace is life." "That's a great big lie—to me it is the coercion that
is the evil. Death isn't the evil at all, it is the shape of your life"
(personal interview). Evil is external power that can compel and
deny the inner law in every individual. Thus it is that in "Passages
26" coercion, habit, conscription, and blindness are named as
Ahriman, the god of darkness. The inner law moves man naturally

toward love and communion, but must be left wholly free and instantly flexible if it is to come into its own. Thus any outside power that inhibits its movement takes on the cosmic proportions of the Dragon, the Hydra, or Satan, looming over and constricting the flowering of the inner light. Duncan is obviously pleased to discover that the etymology of *evil* links it with "up" and "over," an association matching his own feeling about evil as any power that is above and over the individual volition. The Hydra of power over others will obviously have many heads in a society based on dominance-submission, hierarchy of control, and "terror and hatred of all communal things, of communion / of communism."

Both a weakness and a virtue of Duncan's protest is his ability to stand back and take the larger view. If one characteristic sets him apart from the other poets of this study it is the size of the scenes in his poems. Though seldom concretely realized or sensuously brought to life, they are recognizably of Titanic proportions —continents reared against one another, university power structures rising above the populace and decimating the countryside like Beowulf's Fire-worm. "The Multiversity: Passages 21" depicts the Hydra looming large over the students who demand "right reason." The image of Kerr and Chancellor Strong may be grossly unjust (Louis Simpson for example complains, "Now I find it impossible to conceive of Chancellor Strong as a dragon. I once had dinner with that gentleman, and not once did he breathe fire. I don't even think he smoked. Duncan's attempt to present Strong as a dragon makes me think only of Disneyland"),[30] but what is important is that it is rather vividly imagined in the Spenserian, Miltonic, Bunyanesque manner; and we get the feeling that these men, too, are victims of the Hydra, that they are being used by a larger force of evil:

> whose scales are men officized—ossified—conscience
>   no longer alive in them,
> the inner law silenced   (*Bow*, p. 70)

The worm is simply the structure of authority whose heads are the offices of power—"heads and armors of the worm office is."

And *office* itself negates the flexibility necessary to life, is itself the ossification or hardening of death.

As a Hydra to other nations, this country's general aspect is more nearly monocephalous than multicephalous. Johnson appears as the "swollen head of the nation" that is

> . . . a bloated thing,
> drawing from the underbelly of the nation
> such blood and dreams as swell the idiot psyche
> out of its courses into an elemental thing
> until his name stinks with burning meat and heapt honors
>
> (*Bow*, p. 81)

The "idiot psyche" here can also mean the unique individual spirit —as it does when Duncan speaks of wishing to "be idiot awkward" (idiocy/idiosyncracy). But the head and metabolism of the Hydra force the individual soul out of its natural course into an "elemental thing"—back to that out of which it was growing. As Duncan attests in person and in poetry, he believes love is evolving out of hatred, as imaged in the configurations we have discussed of the eye, womb, and heart opening out in the darkness. But under the Hydra, the evolution is stymied and even reversed.

The major motif of "Uprising," and of each poem where the Hydra appears, is power: the ravening eagle as the bird of men who would be masters; the all-American boy in the cockpit loosing napalm; the "Victory of American will over its victims." The Satanic force enters the heads of the Hydra, the persons of the men "officized," because the inner law in them has been allowed to atrophy, and they are empty. (Both Charles Olson and Denise Levertov have poems in which they pray to fill their space completely, "so that no devil may enter.") Duncan is not sure what to believe about the Satanic, and he understands the Buddhist and Christian idea that evil is a negative power and Satan cannot really exist (Evil is the absence or vacuum of Good). If Satan does not equal Emptiness, Emptiness is at least a condition of his entering. But the Satanic often manifests itself as a positive power, and appears as a living force in Duncan's poems. It is present not as metaphor alone but as a frighteningly literal perception on Duncan's part, of

> ... the very glint of Satan's eyes from the pit of the hell of
> America's unacknowledged, unrepented crimes that I saw in
> Goldwater's eyes
> now shines from the eyes of the President
> in the swollen head of the nation.   (*Bow*, pp. 82–83)

When Johnson announced his decision not to run for reelection, Duncan saw in his face "that thing that is left" when the spirit has gone out of a person, leaving him collapsed "like an empty sack." The demon enters from the first only because an emptiness is already there: "Really, what kind of a person gets to be used for that. A person like Nixon [too] is empty and has to be. . . . it's a bellows that has to be filled with something, and if it has to be filled it's for sure it's got to be with that thing. If we weren't in the war situation, by the way, Satan [would be] merely stupidity" (personal interview).

One very great value of Duncan's mythic imagination is that it frees him and can free his reader from hatred. Though "Uprising" seems to be a vicious attack on Johnson, it was not inspired by hatred; Duncan was relieved of the need to hate Johnson because he had sufficient imagination to see that it was the Hydra that moved the President. The first five lines of "Uprising" fail to communicate Duncan's intent, however, and perhaps deserve the bitter criticism that is sometimes leveled at the poem:

> Now Johnson would go up to join the great simulacra of men,
>   Hitler and Stalin, to work his fame
>   with planes roaring out from Guam over Asia,
> All America become a sea of toiling men
>   stirrd at his will   (*Bow*, p. 81)

Robert Pack finds these lines "clumsy pretentious language, dull rhythms, glib phrasing, and accusation that dulls any meaningful distinction regarding the causes and complexities of human evil."[31] The mythic mode does, of course, deal not with fine distinctions but with large truths. Nevertheless, Duncan fails to make clear his real intention—to communicate his sense that Johnson was like Hitler in being *used* by the military and other vested interests to serve their purposes. Though Johnson was no doubt a very different man from Hitler, the evil of which he was the figurehead is not dissimilar. All hatred and all evil, Duncan believes, grow out of *a failure of the imagination to put together a condition in which love can function.* Duncan feels that even "pity could intrude for an LBJ if you're looking across history and you are no longer a victim or in a tight box" (personal interview). But one must first be able to distinguish between the public and private person, between the man and his evil effects. Perhaps if the general consciousness began to deal as Duncan does with good and evil as cosmic forces rather than in terms of "righteous" or "criminal" persons, much suffering could be eliminated.

X

Beyond the coercive elements of militarism, there is the evil of war's milieu. The tragedy that informs the first half of "Passages 26" is that the ambience of war makes spirituality nearly impossible.

> From the body-remains of the bull Hadhayans
>   the food!   the immortality of the people!
> "No-man's land in which everything moving
> —from Saigon's viewpoint—was 'hostile' "
> They've to take their souls in the war
>   as the followers of Orpheus   take soul in the poem
>   the wood to take fire from that dirty flame!
>   in the slaughter of man's hope
>   distil the divine potion,   forbidden hallucinogen
>   that stirs sight of the hidden
>   order of orders!   (*Bow*, p. 112)

In the ritual slaughter and eating of the flesh and blood of the sacrificial bull, the people of the cult of Mithra gained perfection of both body and soul and thus immortality. In contrast, the ritual of slaughter in Vietnam destroys not only the victim but the soul of those enacting the rites. One mentality sees all things as sacred; the other sees all things indiscriminately as matter for annihilation.

The fire of war and the fire of poetry appear together here as they did in "Essay":

Let
even our troops in Hell who have
hell-fire return from their flame-throwers
thru flame to the fire that burns them.
It is Love. It is a hearth.
It is a lantern to read war by.   (*Derivations*, p. 11)

In the Vietnam poem, the Orphic flame is one that animates and enlivens all things, as Orpheus's song made the stones and trees to dance. The flame of war not only deadens the wood (dance versus defoliation) but slaughters man's hope and makes the distillation of the divine potion impossible. Here again that divine potion is, I believe, the forbidden hallucinogen of love, which not only stirs sight of the order or orders, but is itself the first of orders (the integer that orders the gnomons). In numerous poems Duncan offers the reminder: "first She created Eros."

The forbidden hallucinogen (*Bow*, p. 117) is Truth; but Truth, Love, Beauty, and Inner Law are all One, and form the nucleus of the community radiating out of free volition. And the imagination of Love is the integer that makes all things orderly:

Chaos / and the divine measures and orders
     so wedded are
we have but to imagine
     ourselves the Lover
     and the Beloved appears   (*Bow*, p. 121)

E. E. Cummings once gave it more homely expression: "unless you love someone nothing makes any sense." The Beloved is Eros and exists in both that which loves and that which is loved. Since man is both *in* and *of* the Kosmos he is himself in a sense both Lover and Beloved, and creates both, especially as imaginative man and poet:

> Pegasos / that great horse Poetry, Rider
>   we ride, who make up
>   the truth of What Is   (*Bow*, p. 122)

In spite of the ugly situations of the sixties, there has been much in recent years to cause a man with Duncan's philosophy to take heart. The present may be full of conflict, but it is not moribund with complacency and self-congratulation. There may be a dirty war in Asia, but there is also a more glorious war being waged again—Perseus hacks at the Medusa's head and Bellerophon rides the untamed Pegasus against the Chimaera. To the poet's eye men seem to be awakening like Pegasus from the horrible chaos of the Medusa's blood and feeling again the influence of Zeus,

> the pressure of whose tides
> upon the shores of life is like a horse raging,
>   thunderous hooves, striking
>   flashes of light from unbright matter.
>   (*Bow*, p. 129)

Duncan's optimism achieves its most vivid expression in "Earth's Winter Song" in the triple parallels of the birth of Christ, the anti-war movement, and Earth's inner life in winter. The Annunciation occurs now again

> In the dark and utter destitution of winter
> the face of the girl is a fresh moon
> radiant with the Truth she loves,   (*Bow*, p. 93)

even as "the old dragon" carries on his deadly destructions and Herod's hatred and the slaughter of innocents goes on. Driven inward by the cold of "Winter," the Underground of the individual and the Underground of society become "the sublime Crèche" where the Logos is born again.

> ... the new
> lord of the true life, of Love   ·
>
> we remember, was always born,
> as now, in a time of despair,
> having no place there at the Inn,
> hunted down by Herod's law,
> fleeing by night, secreted in Egypt.   (*Bow*, p. 94)

In this hopeful song of "the green spring-tide / of individual volition for the communal good, / the Christ-promise of brotherhood,"
Duncan achieves the coherent vivid expression that is all too rare
in his work.

XI

Duncan's virtues as poet are also his shortcomings—the mythic
and cosmic perspective allows him to transcend narrowness and
hatred, but fails to communicate vividly to any sizable audience.
His style leaves him vulnerable to such gross misunderstandings
as the following:

> Complete with footnotes and an allusive richness breathing
> life into the dust, Duncan is truly an academic poet. His lines
> are the hard-earned result of an intensive classical education of
> the traditional mode . . . . Attacks on President Johnson com-
> paring him to Hitler and Stalin rub shoulders with quotations
> from Victor Hugo and Jacob Sessler . . . . Duncan uses the in-
> sane rantings against Johnson to show the hollowness of such
> modern academic "protest" poetry. And they are insane, scream-
> ing, pointless, absurd. How rich and true then does his woven
> texture of the past appear, cool, intelligent, with the curves of mar-
> ble in every line. How brilliantly he has shown the lie of his
> angry contemporaries in the classic calm of the inquiring poetic
> mind.[32]

Though there can hardly be any excuse for such a gross misreading,
Duncan must be held partly to blame. Though in some of the war
poems he gives signs of a new, less abstruse mode, the metamorphosis promised in the following lines does not materialize:

> I put aside
> whatever I once served of the poet, master
> of enchanting words and magics,
> not to disown the old mysteries, sweet
> muthos   our mouth's telling   ·
> and I will still tell the beads, in the fearsome
> street I see glimpses of   I will pray again

to those great columns of moon's light,
"Mothering angels, hold my sight steady
and I will look this time as you bid me to see
the dirty papers, moneys, laws, orders
and corpses of people and people-shit."

(*Bow*, p. 77)

That is, it does not materialize if it was to be, as Laurence Lieberman
suggests it in fact is, a shift comparable in magnitude to Yeats's
1914 metamorphosis in *Responsibilities*.[33] We have seen such an
alteration in Levertov and less dramatically in Bly, but Duncan's
angle of vision was earlier changed by his own personal crises, as
was Ginsberg's, and the war occasions no shift in perspective.
Bending the Bow does represent something of a shift in *attention*,
however. The poet does not disown the old mysteries or put off
"A Coat"; the "master of enchanting words and magics" is only
set aside a moment while his same old Truths are shown to be
profoundly exemplified in the modern crisis. The war is really a
kind of "distraction," a time-out from his devotion to this other
poetry, and an energetic attempt to correct a bad line that mars
the cosmic Poem.

Duncan's dedication as scholar, poet, and priest of community
are praiseworthy indeed, but there is too often in his work, as in
his credo, an inevitable shortcoming, a breaking of inspiration, an
"inability" that this reader must regret. Perhaps we are to learn
from his failures and our dissatisfactions. Though he leaves us un-
satisfied, we cannot avoid admiring in him "the gaunt irregular
giantism of the spiritual man."

In summary: Duncan believes that paradise is a matter of the
here and now in the community and free volition of man; that the
City of God is hidden in the cities of man; that love is evolving
naturally out of hatred like a God's eye opening in darkness, but
needs a total freedom in which it may grow; and that not death
but coercion and loss of community are the real evils of war.
Duncan's outrage, then, is not merely against this war in particular,
and yet not indiscriminately against all war in general. But it is
unlikely that any modern war can ever again meet the conditions
of community and free volition that would justify it—and so

Duncan's reservations are in a way academic. Nevertheless, they are exactly the reservations we should have expected him to make. A poet of Duncan's mythological mind could hardly be expected to relinquish from his cosmology all possibilities of heroic combat against the monsters of evil. It is only that in an increasingly sophisticated world both St. George and the dragon must inevitably play out their drama under new forms. The "irreal"—that level of spiritual reality one step beyond our commonplace awareness—has new weapons: the actual hallucinogens that expand consciousness, the new music, and the new morality, the new spirit of poverty and anti-materialism, and the new adventures in nonviolence. Duncan's own protest against coercion and lovelessness grows directly and spontaneously from his poetics and biography and is but one manifestation of a truly different kind of consciousness, either a very old or a very new spirituality.

6 OTHER POEMS AND POETS AGAINST THE WAR

Away with themes of war! away with War itself!
Hence from my shuddering sight, to never more return, that
*   show of blacken'd, mutilated corpses!*
That hell unpent, and raid of blood, fit for wild tigers or for
*   lop-tongued wolves . . .*
                    Whitman, "Song of the Exposition"

Themes developed by Ginsberg, Levertov, Bly, and Duncan often figure prominently in the work of other contemporary poets. To be sure, there was in the sixties an abundance of "protest" poems in which, as in the poetry of World War I, "the poetry is in the pity"—poems which are not so political or revolutionary as those of the poets above. Though this more traditional poetry is often the work of older poets (a number of war poems appearing in the Vietnam anthologies are in fact aroused reminiscences and delayed reactions to World War II), younger poets, too, have produced many poems of simple compassion, pathos, and humanistic concern; or have written verses imaginatively identifying with the Vietnamese or American soldier, mother, bride, peasant, or orphan. But throughout the anthologies and little magazines, against the background of such poetry there sounds the insistent note of the changing perceptions and concerns we have explored in the work of the four poets above.

Themes and images surfacing again and again in the war-wounded poetry of recent years indicate that many poets share awarenesses and deep feelings about: (1) the crisis of language itself; (2) the desacralization of reason, order, intellect, and number; (3) the sanctity of the physical (and an awareness of war as perverse sexuality); (4) the imbalance of masculine/feminine impulses (and a desire to turn again to primitive mysteries and feminine vitalities); (5) the understanding of anarchy as order; (6) the association of life with water and sea; (7) the spiritual and psychological blight of the war; and (8) the portentous possibilities toward future catastrophe or utopia. The most pervasive of these concerns, and the one to which most time must be given here, is the crucial problem of language itself.

I

In the beginning was the Word,
And the Word was with God,
And the Word was God.   Gospel of St. John

I must translate it differently
If I am truly illumined by the spirit.
It is written: In the beginning was the Mind

. . . .

It should read: In the beginning was the Power

. . . .

Something warns me, I see in a flash what I need
And write: In the beginning was the Deed!
                    Goethe, *Faust*, translated by Louis MacNeice

Speech is the twin of my vision . . .
                                        Whitman

In the beginning, at the wellsprings of language, when language was magical and mysterious, primitive man found the word to be indeed Mind, Power, and Deed. And there is today still in the word some of that magic and joy that the poet would resurrect and blow into life again. But alongside man's joy in language there is, and undoubtedly always has been, a concomitant frustration with the impotence of language to create and preserve meaning from unmeaning, truth from untruth. The frustration can grow into misology or hatred of language when language becomes too powerful in the service of falsehood, too powerless in the service of truth. Though rightly the word should be the twin to vision just as the Word is twin to the Father, poets have always found words a precarious and scarcely sufficient medium for their insights; thus any abuse of language is a threat to an essential and already fragile medium of understanding and expression. Poets have, therefore, learned to be protective of the power of words, and have come to see abuses of language as abuses of poets and poetry themselves.

At least part of the poet's antagonism against war no doubt grows from the awareness that war (the ultimate insensibility and untruth) is itself an abuse of language (the ultimate vehicle of sensibility and truth), or at least the inevitable occasion for its abuse. War demands that language's careful loyalty to truth be prostituted to the service of obfuscation and unreality. Language can lead to right action, or be used to color actions as right; and in time of war it is the latter that almost inescapably prevails. The historical relationship between war and the decay of language is documented as far back as the Peloponnesian War. Thucydides understood that language "fits men's actions," and that when man's actions are noble, his language will be noble; when ignoble, his language will be ignoble, for it will be abused and falsified to make his actions seem both noble and necessary: "War, which takes away the easy supply of daily wants, is a stern teacher and degrades men's character, dragging them down to the level of their circumstances. The ordinary meanings of words were changed to fit men's actions. Reckless aggression was now regarded as the courage of a loyal ally, prudent consideration as cowardice, moderation as a disguise for weakness, ability to view a question from all sides as inability to act."[1] Closely related realizations prompt Falstaff's comments on "honor" (*Henry IV, Part I*, Scene 1) and Ernest Hemingway's famous attack on the abstractions of war in *A Farewell to Arms*.*

---

* "Can honor set a leg? No. Or an arm? No. Or take away the grief of a wound? No. Honor hath no skill in surgery, then? No. What is honor? A word. What is in that word honor? What is that honor? Air. A trim

Anger at the misuse of language to manipulate and obscure is likewise a primary force behind John Dos Passos's "Newsreels" in *U.S.A.*, and an important theme in the poetry of E. E. Cummings and W. H. Auden on the world wars.

But despair about language becomes extreme in the poetry against the Vietnam War. Many poets, like Allen Ginsberg in *Wichita Vortex Sutra*, have been "almost in tears to know / how to speak the right language" at a time when "almost all our language has been taxed by war."

The confluence of communications technology, transportation, increased education, and the propaganda demands of wartime have at this point in history created a veritable floodtide of language. Timothy Leary complains "now in the twentieth century, we are bombarded by words, thousands of words an hour, so that what I've just said is only another tattoo of syllables bouncing off your ears."[2] The poet Jonathan Williams speaks of "ear-pollution," and Paul Blackburn sadly recognizes that poets "have the most meager means of communication in a land overrun with communications."[3] Charles Reich in *The Greening of America* tells us that "The

---

reckoning! Who hath it? He that died o' Wednesday. Doth he feel it? No. Doth he hear it? No. 'Tis insensible, then? Yea, to the dead. But will it not live with the living? No. Why? Detraction will not suffer it. Therefore I'll none of it. Honor is a mere scutcheon. And so ends my catechism" (Falstaff, *Henry IV, Part I*, Scene I).

"I was always embarrassed by the words sacred, glorious, and sacrifice and the expression in vain. We had heard them, sometimes standing in the rain almost out of earshot, so that only the shouted words came through, and had read them, on proclamations that were slapped up by billposters over other proclamations, now for a long time, and I had seen nothing sacred, and the things that were glorious had no glory and the sacrifices were like the stockyards at Chicago if nothing was done with the meat except to bury it. There were many words that you could not stand to hear and finally only the names of places had dignity. Certain numbers were the same way and certain dates and these with the names of the places were all you could say and have them mean anything. Abstract words such as glory, honor, courage, or hallow were obscene beside the concrete names of villages, the numbers of roads, the names of rivers, the numbers of regiments and the dates" (*A Farewell to Arms* [New York: Scribner's, 1957], p. 191).

dominant means of communication in our society—words—has been so abused, distorted and pre-empted that at present it does not seem adequate for people of the new consciousness."[4]

One of the poets who spoke most lucidly about the language problem in the sixties was the late Thomas Merton. His lengthy *Cables to the Ace: or Famous Liturgies of Misunderstanding* is rich with references to the state of the language, and his subsequent essay, "War and the Crisis of Language," further develops the awareness.[5] In a time when we have become totally immersed in language, Merton suggested, there is no longer any need to say anything, nor any need to listen. Listening is as obsolete as silence, and the "better informed" have begun to declare war on language.[6]

Though Elizabeth Bartlett is not specifically one of those Merton has in mind, her "Silent Vigil in Vietnam" captures the language fatigue, despair, and general acedia that has spiraled out of the war. Spoken by a South Vietnamese *persona*, but with the heart of an American who has heard too many newscasts and press conferences, her poem is an exhausted plea for silence: "words cannot speak / for us or to us / words are nothing." "Words cannot bleed" and have become too widely estranged from reality.

> They can come down
> from their high places
> and wipe their mouths
>
> They can leave the conference tables
> and go home now
> Let them go home in silence
> it is too late now for words
> words are not peace[7]

The fabric or, better yet, the *crust* of language has in modern times become so heavy and profuse that it forms a reality of its own, quite cut off from actuality and experience. The war has been a prime impetus in the creation of this ersatz linguistic world. When world opinion surveys revealed that "attitudes toward the United States are at a fifty-year low point, with many foreigners considering it 'a violent, lawless, overbearing, even a sick society,' "[8] the government's response was predictably linguistic: a House subcommittee called for "a thorough, systematic reappraisal of the entire information policy of the U.S. government." When the survey indicated that "U.S. actions in [Vietnam] are strongly, at times passionately, disliked," the report concluded that "overseas opinion surveys indicate widespread misunderstanding and confusion about our purpose in Vietnam."[9] The circularity of logic here bears out Merton's belief that the language of war is essentially a language of tautology. He shows that, like the language of Madison Avenue —which, stripped of its rhetoric, claims only that "Arpége has Arpége"—the language of war is typified by the final logic of the perfect circle. Hitler wept over the ruins of Warsaw, "How wicked these people must have been to make me do this to them"; and a U.S. major in Vietnam argues that "it became necessary to destroy the town in order to save it." "One of the most curious things about the war in Vietnam," concluded Merton, "is that it is being *fought to vindicate the assumptions upon which it is being fought.*"[10]

Tautological and circular in structure, the language of the political-military establishment is also Latinate and abstract, verb-poor and noun-heavy. "Escalation," "pacification," "Vietnamization," "liberation," "saturation," and "defoliation" intersperse "kill-ratios" and "free-fire zones." When troops reoccupied the abandoned base at Khe Sanh and massed along the northwest border of Laos for an apparently imminent deep strike there, the peace negotiators in Paris sent "word" to the American people that "an invasion of Laos would not necessarily be an expansion of the war." Later, when South Vietnamese troops retreated from Laos in so much panic and disorder that U.S. air strikes were necessary to destroy the weaponry they left behind, we were given "word" that these troops were engaged in "mobile maneuvering." Distinctions between indiscriminate bombing of specific areas in North Vietnam and retaliatory saturation bombing of North Vietnam after the enemy has struck in the South are billed as "limited duration protective reaction strikes" and "spontaneous protective reaction strikes," respectively. (In relaying these official explanations to his viewers, CBS newsman Walter Cronkite concluded, "If I may be permitted a personal comment, 'Oh.'") By parodying and echoing this military and media language in their poetry—"Charlie," "Lazy Dog," "adhesion" (an admirable quality of napalm)—poets point to the tragic desensitization of language. Of the Angry Arts Week speeches and readings, Curtis Harnack wrote, "Now the poets were not saying *listen to me*; they were saying *listen to them*."[11]

Allen Ginsberg's vision of the "black magic power of language" engulfing the country is, regrettably, all too accurate. Poets especially are increasingly disturbed by the apparent assumption in America that "saying so" does "make it so," that the language and rhetoric of an event is the same as the event itself, and that reality can be manipulated simply by manipulating the language. This strange and primitive faith in the magic power of language manifests itself on another level, for example, in the public's irrational fear of taboo words. There are apparently words capable of making a situation right or wrong because rightness or wrongness is a linguistic property of words themselves. A peripheral but illustrative incident was reported several years ago by the underground newspaper *International Times*. Four girls, wearing sweatshirts bearing single letters that could be arranged to spell an obscenity, walked side by side for blocks without incident in all the possible configurations but one, but were immediately arrested for indecency and disturbing the peace when they moved abreast of one another in the feared and taboo order. Thus too, apparently, a book is obscene or acceptable because it has good or bad words, people are good or bad according to good or bad labels that can be attached to them, and the war is good and reasonable so long as we take care to speak of it with the right words.

But, of course, language is not reality. It is the way we come at reality. The language of Zen carries a wise caution against the error that mankind makes over and over again in nearly every area of his experience. The warning is almost universal in its applications, but especially appropriate here: "The finger is very useful for pointing at the moon, but one must take care not to mistake the finger for the moon." But over and over again man loses the light, the life, the vision, and wrongheadedly worships its shell, its symbol, its institution or form. Language is very useful for pointing to present and potential realities, both *What is* and *What ought to be*, but it is not reality itself. It is physical symbol used to draw for and from physical reality its metaphysical and moral-spiritual quality, in short, its meaning. And that meaning is not changed merely by changing the language. The world is not less immoral because we get rid of dirty words, and war is not less obscene because we "language" it in antiseptic abstract nouns.*

Yet, despite its many primitive aspects, the modern attitude toward language is far from the shamanistic view of language that is essentially religious and a tribute to the magical and mysterious in nature and self. There is nothing spiritual about the language of war, and tautology is not to be confused with mystical and paradoxical wisdom even though one may hear frightfully blasphemous echoes of "unless a man die, he shall not live" in the now classic "it became necessary to destroy the town in order to save it."

That incorrigible shaman the poet, with his finer sensitivity to both language and experience, is not easily taken in by the clumsy use of his own medium. His eternal concern has always been to make language approach reality, discover, approximate, and express it with magic and power. He senses acutely when language is used to camouflage rather than reveal, deaden rather than vivify. The revulsion of American poets at the over-abundance and incomparable abuse of language was strong even in the early Vietnam years, and grew steadily during the war. The conflict between the world of language and the tragic world of the war-experience becomes a dominant focus of the poetry. Louis Simpson's "The American Dream" strikes at the nightmarish unreality of the language that floods in upon the poet:

Every day I wake far away
From my life, in a foreign country.
These people are speaking a strange language.

---

* In another context Neil Postman and Charles Weingartner have also noted our modern propensity for nouns over verbs: "It is as if nouns battle verbs for dominance as our seminal metaphors. The nouns mostly win. Or *have* won, up to now. Marshall McLuhan implies that the dominance of the noun metaphor is, to a considerable extent, a function of an ABCED-minded, alphabetic-writing, and print-oriented culture" (*Teaching as a Subversive Activity* [New York: Dell, 1969], p. 85).

It is strange to me
And strange, I think, even to themselves.[12]

Poems against the war are littered with images and phrases drawn from daily television and newspaper language rituals. Television is an especially pervasive specter: perhaps never before has a body of poetry been so clearly affected by what amounts in one sense to a "domestic detail"—the presence of a TV set in every American living room. Body-counts and kill-ratios are hopelessly entangled in the poems with baseball scores, just as they were in the evening news roundups; and the poetry's frequent association of carnage and death with food, barbecuing, and all kinds of culinary details surely gets some of its impetus from the conjunction of evening news and evening meal in thousands of American homes.

Vern Rutsala's "News" does not, except for the title, mention the news, and yet the "glow" he speaks of seems not really the city neon but the television screen:

> **Our**
> candlelit meals,
> flecks of gold
> in the wine,
> feed on that glow;
> our easy talk
> in warm rooms
> draws heat
> from that fire;[13]

The neon glow is "white," and the poem speaks of "tensions / siphoned off / by pictures / of burned houses." Even if the poet has in mind the whole neon aura of our culture and not only the television specifically, most readers will identify the juxtaposition of war and food with the American habit of consuming the news with dinner. The tube does literally light the meal, and the horrors of war seem to have little effect on the appetite. In fact, the poets imply, the war, which is food and nourishment for the economy, has in a sense also become a kind of psychic food for the American public:

they grow young
on it. They like
it. It tastes
good to them.
They like it.
They like it.
They like it.
They like it.

(Rutsala, "News")

"Burning the News," by Lewis Turco, details imaginatively the physical burning of the violence-full newspaper whose ashes then float away over houses where the news rests over armchairs, or where "pages turn like gray wings." The fire "eating the news" makes for excellent irony and comment:

The child who drowned
is burned. Asia is in flames.
As he signs his great
bill, a minister of state chars

(*Calendar*, Jan. 15)

The news is good for burning, ought to be burned, and is itself a burning that consumes itself and all of us.

The number of poems directly or indirectly affected by the news media makes clear that McLuhan is at least partially right in asserting that "the medium is the message." And the "message" is *too much message*. It is the abundance of the content rather than the technical nature of the medium that is responsible for the problem; it is not the tactile quality of the mosaic of dots on the TV for instance, but the multiplicity of messages made possible by television itself. At the root of the poet's anguish is his awareness of how accustomed and calloused we have become to the daily tides of language and horror that the media bring into our lives. They see us as a people growing beyond shock or surprise, learning to experience the most grotesque events and sights as acceptable commonplaces, and finding nothing beyond our tolerances.

The reaction of poets to the news media and to the corruption of language cannot be easily or usefully separated. Both the technology and the debased language are frequently seen as symptoms of a civilization and a progress that is artificial and spiritless, quantitative rather than qualitative. The "war on language" that Merton tells us the "better informed" have declared is intimately bound up with the larger revolt against the scientific, technologically oriented, analytical mind; for it is the language of objectivity and reason (in its atrophied form) that inundates us, and not a language of poetry, spirituality, or primitive innocence. The Vietnam War greatly accelerated the poetic revolt growing since the fifties against this orientation and this language because the war greatly accelerated the flood of such language upon the poetic consciousness. There had already been a surfeit of it, but now it surrounded an issue that made it impossible to ignore, and impinged upon the poet's sensibility in a new way. Poets were already chafing against the inroads of "objectivity" into poetic theory that were clear in Eliot's idea of poet as catalyst and in the New Critics' compulsion to dissect poems as cadavers (even the metaphors here naturally gravitate toward those of science). But now the effects of this disposition in poetry and in the culture at large seemed no longer mistakable. Thus the critical dispositions of Eliot and John Crowe Ransom have been generally anathema to the writers against Vietnam whose views of language and art have seemed much closer to those of Tolstoy (that convenient whipping-boy of the New Criticism). Tolstoy believed art was not good art unless it in some way brought men closer together in a communion of understanding, generosity, and enhanced spirituality. The anger of poets and writers indicates they believe language is not good language unless it does the same. Language is itself an art, and the individual word was itself originally a poem. The recent replacement of poetic interest in irony, paradox, tension, and texture with an interest in understanding, freedom, vision, and community suggests that poets see not only language and art but perhaps all things as being at their best when they unite men in a common bond of tolerance and affection. Language at its best is antagonistic to war; at its worst, the servant and mouthpiece of war, the justification of all that is antagonistic to harmony and community.

Thomas Merton managed to compress his sense of the cause and effect of the language problem in a remarkable shorthand of twisted allusion—"I am doubted, therefore I am"—implicating Descartes in the pervasive modern metaphysic of suspicion and unreliability of language. Of such language and such learning, he cries with Caliban: "You taught me language and my profit on't / Is, I know how to curse. The red plague rid you / For learning me your language" (*Cables*, p. 4). Attitudes flowing out of the "myth of objective consciousness" lead indeed to an emotionless, value-neutral, amoral, abstract language, good for cursing, judging, differentiating, analyzing, defining, and manipulating objects, ideas, and men. They lead to the death of language, to the death of the spirit that poetic language struggles to vivify and illuminate. And nowhere has the charnel stench of dying, rotting language hung heavier than over the language of this war, its verbal muscles all unstrung, heavy with nouns, bloated with abstraction, and swarmed over with polysyllables.

Damage to the poetic powers of language has been occasioned not only by the war but by the very proliferation of words in thousands of papers, journals, panels, discussions, classrooms, lectures, phones, tapes, films, billboards, posters, radios, and televisions. Talk has become cheap and careless. Words that have been used carelessly lose their power even when used carefully; they pick up ragged connotations that cloud attempts at precise expression. Current language seems more and more unable to penetrate into the Thou-World of Martin Buber, the inner-world of Jacob Boehme, or the larger spiritual world beyond the ego or the limited self and word of "things." If the world of spirit has always been in danger of deteriorating or becoming submerged in the world of objects, art has always had the power to revitalize it. The tree, the market, the neighbor might fall out of the vital Thou, and into the mechanical and meaningless, but language was electric and snapping with life that restored the vision and the living presence, the personality of the world. It could, in Shelley's words, capture the visitations of divinity in man and awaken in the hearts of others a kindred spirit that would otherwise remain forever latent and unborn.

Instead of functioning creatively, current language seems more often to function destructively, and poets frequently associate it and the media with negative and hysterical images.

> The wind turns cold and the summer goes out,
> The disgusting newspaper waits on the floor.
> The lines of our grief go off into winter.   (Tony Towle)[14]

>   Nearby,
> a yellow news paper rack. I can read
> the headline. It says:
> TROOP CUTBACK HINTED. Above the fold
> there is a photograph of a blond in a swimming suit
> astride an enormous turtle.
> A newspaper left on the table behind me
> blows up. Giant paper heart
> attacks my chair.   (Stan Rice)[15]

> This meeting has gone on with small interruptions
> for eleven years and part of another.
> I classify the speakers in small bags.
> The words come out in paragraphs shaped by use.
> The words stain the room like dirty water.
> We all have scars   (Marge Piercy)[16]

In general the tone of the poets about the future of language is not optimistic, and they despair of its present effectiveness.

> Swept along with war
> the total machines
> in all their rhetoric
> have through echoes
> and violent language
> stolen the rhyme
> of word sculpture

> in the war tower office
> the possibility exists
> the process is in control
> those who oppose
> are struck puny and disassembled

>   (Gene Bloom)[17]

To set against that great carbuncle
of the world this inefficient edge,
words. Baudelaire was a conservative.
Rimbaud was less proficient in his politics
than Romney is. Setting the cold edge of that
pitiless art against the filth.   (Gil Sorrentino)[18]

Words are heavy, heavy.
I carry them back and forth in my skirt.
They pile up in front of the chairs.
Words are bricks that seal the doors and windows.
Words are shutters on the eyes
and lead gloves on the hands.
The air is a solid block.
We cannot move.   (Marge Piercy)[19]

Yet, for all of their hopelessness, poets have tried to speak loudly
and at the same time maintain the integrity of both art and language. Though there has been far too much undisciplined and un-
formed rhetoric passing for poetry in recent years, there has been
within the anti-war movement a spirit at least recognizably related
to Walter Lowenfels's energetic portrait of "The Permanent Revolutionary" who

Liberates framed-up words
    from death cells in dictionaries;
frees grammar
    from hangmen in the Establishment;
marries rhythms
    to echoes in the streets
always one poem ahead
    waving—Man, over here
is it—the real thing![20]

Poets against the war have had to fight against not only the
destruction of life but against the destruction of mankind's *life*,
his spirituality, vision, imagination, and love—in short, his *language*
—for it is through language that man discovers, deepens, communicates, and preserves this *life*, this divinity, and its inconstant visita-

tions. So in a very important sense, poets have been fighting three wars—the war to save human life, humane life, and language. But perhaps we would more accurately speak of fighting a war on three fronts, for indeed it is but one and the same war.

II

Logic and sermons never convince,
The damp of the night drives deeper into my soul

Whitman

Part of the adulteration of language is that it is controlled, used, and manipulated instead of followed and listened to as Charles Olson and Robert Duncan have argued it must be. The current prejudice against the manipulating faculty, reason—already seen in Ginsberg, Bly, and Duncan, and inchoate in Levertov—is strongly echoed in the work of other poets. It surfaces both as occasional comment and as the major theme of individual poems. Sometimes it results in inane utterances; sometimes it finds a temperate voice, like Duncan's lucid 1952 lines:

the empty altars, rendered
by reason
ready for the intellect
—that spider—
obsessed by design, unknowing.[21]

The stance is often coupled with a Rousseauistic primitivism, and sometimes—as in the *Revolutionary Letters* of Diane Di Prima —with a considerable naïveté. It incorporates criticism of all that is numerical and rigidly ordered, and frequently derogates the educational emphases of American culture. W. R. Moses's brief untitled poem is exemplary:

Everyone knows
The marks of pastoral with its petals falling—
Cold rock, cold air, cold grass;
The fish rebellious: the stringer empty . . . .
The cold child with a cold coming on
Knew them. But warmed himself

With a phantasy of order: a warmed room,
and pages neat with numbers: the arithmetic
learned in his months at school.
The wild river was welcome to its wild fish.
But warm pages neat with controlled numbers ...
That was a long, long time ago.
Who controls what? The world smothers in numbers.
Will it not be spring by the river
And the buds swelling?

(*Calendar*, March 25)

In the child driven by insecurity to the solace and certainty of
a "phantasy of order: a warm room, and pages neat with numbers,"
Moses offers a microcosmic history of Western intellectualized man.
But that shift to cerebration and orderly rationality was a long,
long time ago (500 B.C.? 1687?); now the world is smothered in
order and numbers, inundated with analysis, and the heart yearns
to return to some simple relationship with the wellsprings of life,
with the buds swelling by the unchecked river of nature, emotion,
and imagination.

Some poems associate the stifling anti-life law-and-order insistence of American culture with our insistence on grammatical
orders and regimented learning. For Doug Blazek the association
is so strong that his poem imagines "the sheriff teaches us grammar
and civics / in school."[22] Thanasis Maskaleris dramatizes both the
disease and the desired conversion in his "incantation . . . in the
images of reason and of Dostoevsky and of Dance":

I

In an immense geometric classroom
I would spend three long months
with eager youth digging *The Republic*—
adventuring up the world-making-spirals of Reason,
feasting in the gleaming courtyards of the mind ...
gulping even Ayn Rand's kings as a Lucullan side dish.

II

In a dark cellar, without wine and such soothing drugs,
I would go on to stretch their proud cocksure minds to their
    undoing—

smash them against the wall!—
slowly reading every word of *Notes from Underground,*
watching the bull's horn rend the stony flesh . . .
to turn them into Lucifers of spite!

III

Then I would read them a poem of Sappho
or Anakreon or ee cummings ("o sweet spontaneous earth . . .")
read it against the primordial dialectic deadlock
and turn youth loose upon the moon fields
to make love until the slow-coming dawn
explodes them into humanity.[23]

The conversion moves through three stages, from worship of reason; through Dostoevskian overdose, hyper-consciousness, and alienation; and into the ecstatic and impassioned celebration of the senses and the imagination. The geometric classroom, the neat spirals, the rectangular sun-flooded courtyards are replaced by the dark subterranean cave so that the horn of passion might break through the stony flesh and prepare it for awe, acceptance, and union, and for the orgiastic physical and spiritual potency of the human in the fields of the moon. This psychological metamorphosis moves from possession and self-control to abandonment and submission, to loss of self to energy forces larger than the ego and the rational mind.

Praiseworthy as it may be, the desire to move back toward some darker, deeper, more legitimate emotional life sometimes leads poets into frightening or silly utterances. Diane Di Prima, one of the most militant of the revolutionaries of consciousness, is disconcertingly ready to recognize violence as a part of that emotionality:

avoid the folk
who find Bonnie and Clyde too violent
who see the blood but not the energy form . . .[24]

(Unlovely shades of D. H. Lawrence! In fleeing from the conscious analytical mind toward a wisdom of the blood, there is always the dangerous tendency to revere the darkest and most violent forces of blood-lust.) Di Prima apparently does not feel the egregious contradiction in condemning American violence and repression while instructing her "brothers and sisters" to seek out "those who can tell you / how to make molotov cocktails, flame-throwers / bombs whatever" (*Letters*, ltr. 7); or in the same breath that encourages violence, urging them to pray, meditate, make love, and turn on to the insights of Eastern religions:

> but don't get uptight: the guns
> will not win this one, they are
> an incidental part of the action
> which we better damn well be good at,
> what will win
> is mantras, the sustenance we give each other
> this energy we plug into   (*Letters*, ltr. 7)

Surely it is doubtful that Di Prima really understands the spirit of the religions she touts; surely it is doubtful that the "energy we plug into" is understood with anything like the depth with which Duncan and Olson have understood it.

It is also apparent that some poets who want to escape the exaggerated forces of "mind" do not seek to transcend it and use it as a window on the world of spirit as Blake did, but instead would return to a more primitive and instinctual existence. Thus we find Michael McClure shouting "I AM A MAMMAL" and diagnosing our problem as "bodies gone mad with the forgotten memories that we are creatures."[25] Di Prima, too, believes that "forward is back":

> How far back
> are we willing to go? that seems to be
> the question. The more we give up
> the more we will be blessed, the more
> we give up, the further back we go   (*Letters*, ltr. 33)

One of the first steps on the way back, it seems, is to throw away the school system as it now operates, the symptomatic culmination of the mind-set and world orientation of the West that puts the child "cut off in a plaster box, encased / in a larger cement box called 'school' dealing with paper." How, Di Prima asks with incredulous indignation, can such a child ever "know to trap a rabbit, build a raft, / to navigate by stars?" (*Letters*, ltr. 22). The pastoral dream implicit in these last words is somewhat less than realistic.

Anti-rational tendencies grow primarily out of the extremities of the present time, but they also have important literary models in Walt Whitman, Blake, and Lawrence. The protestors most often invoke Walt Whitman. To be sure, Whitman could say, "I believe in the flesh and the appetites" and claim "the scent of these armpits aroma finer than prayer," but he never groveled in the senses for the sake of mammalian unconsciousness or at the expense of mind. He believed in the flesh and the appetites because "Seeing, hearing, feeling, are miracles, and each part and tag of me is a miracle." His sense of awe at the magnificent, miraculous, whole self, not merely at the animal he was, saved him from many of the inanities of his followers. And it was not "mind" but ossified and imposed ideas that he disdained: his own head, he knew, was "more than churches, bibles, and all the creeds." Similarly, Whitman's seeming prejudice against books and schooling was in fact only a desire that men learn to trust their own experience: "You shall no longer take things at second or third hand, nor look through the eyes of the dead, nor feed on the spectres in books / . . . . . You shall listen to all sides and filter them from your self."

If the stances of current poets exaggerate the Whitmanesque position, it is perhaps because the evils today are more exaggerated: we have come more and more in widely literate and "educated" culture to value the icons and ideas of the past (wherever they insure material or superficial order) or the ideas of the future (wherever they insure greater power, security, progress) to the neglect of the living and potentially ecstatic present moment and present self. Whether we must go backwards or forwards to a moonlit pastoral age to escape the manacles of mind, it seems a consensus among poets that the present age is "too much i' the sun," and that the lopsided balance of power between reason and imagination, sun and moon, thought and emotion, must somehow be corrected:

These days the sunlight almost seems total.
A few men, trees, stand between heaven and earth.

In the light of their shadows we others are/reading, still,
messages the dead have stopped sending,
these days of almost fatal sunlight.

(Henry Braun, "These Days," Calendar, Aug. 26)[26]

III

Welcome is every organ and attribute of me, and of any
man hearty and clean,
Not an inch or a particle of an inch is vile and
none shall be less familiar than the rest.

Whitman

Many poems of protest assert or imply that the Vietnam War
and modern wars in general grow out of the same rationalistic fear
of experience and emotion that represses sexuality, fences in People's Park, passes drug laws, and pushes censorship. Consequently,
the war enters poems that are ostensibly about quite different kinds
of repression and control. Sometimes, no doubt, it is merely thrown
in now and again as a "kicker" to show that the poet is on the right
side and "they" (his persecutors) are on the wrong side. Sometimes the mention of Vietnam can lend weight to what is otherwise
flimsy verbal diarrhea, self-gratulation, and paranoic self-pity. The
poet may or may not have any genuine feeling for those who
suffer from the war. D. A. Levy's poem of his troubles with the
Cleveland police is perhaps an example. He is afraid to leave his
house because of

... the rumor of my
death sentence by the county
Gestapo—My greatest crime of
course, is being poor
thank allah i am not black, with my
loud mouth i would have been
dead years ago; the war
in Vietnam continued and my siamese
cat wrestled with his shadow[27]

Though Levy is here more concerned with himself than with peace
or "humanity," the poem nevertheless tells us something about the

relationship of the war to other causes of dissent. Poems primarily concerned with the drug scene, oppression from "narks," and abuses of personal freedoms draw in Vietnam implicitly and suggest that "the war is here" or "the war is a state of mind." (Poets confronting a large and powerful establishment understandably feel an identity with the puny and embattled VC. And poets who might otherwise not endorse the drug culture are by nature persons who would keep "hands off" the choices and lives of others; and thus they, too, identify with the harried users and the Viet Cong. As Robert Duncan has said, the poet is and always has been, by necessity, a kind of Viet Cong.)[28]

All freedoms have been in demand, but for many protestors sexual freedom has been one of the stronger obsessions. It is understandable, then, that these poets should frequently compare the obscenity of war with the sex-related "obscenities" that the establishment fears, and come to see war as the inevitable expression of the establishment's repressed and perverted sexuality. The juxtaposition of orgy and combat we find in Ginsberg's poetry may at first seem facile, but it becomes more convincing when encountered again and again in work by other poets. One or two examples will illustrate.

George Dowden, an American expatriate in London, reacted poemically* to the confiscation of artist Jim Dine's collages and paintings (from a showing at the Robert Fraser Gallery) because the art works "incorporated sexual organs." The poem, though inspired against censorship, quickly becomes primarily an anti-war poem. Dine's "obscenities" are contrasted with those of "the also visual reality 'The War Game,'" which shows "no sexual organs, fortunately, only human brain-wasted black-burnt charred limb-dangling skin-blistered and bubbling poisoned bone catatonic." Dowden feigns surprise that the "still rousing election-year slogan" "protect our children!" is not concerned with "that ENDGAME war" but with "smut." He sees the year 1966 as "a sad anti-love-missile-missile luxury of sexjoy repression" and rejects not Jim Dine's art but the "Death-dealer's obscene newspaper / blue television surrogate sex violence" and the "hypocrisy that fires guns

---

* "Poemic"—my neologism for poems that are more polemic than poetic.

for orgasm, fearing orgasm (O, but why fear to fail orgasm? we have all been so hurt in our sexes, and sex fades so nature-ally in all creatures the same in time—I say let the soft-cocked feel guiltless at last, and be praised for what they CAN do requiring no victims!)."[29]

The rest of Dowden's poem builds around the argument that there can be no crime where there is no victim, that sex is more openly and suggestively exploited by advertising than by the artist, and that living young bodies are everywhere "sexier far than Jim's pictures." Though the poem has little to offer as poetry, it does reach the reader convincingly, and does so most forcefully in its essential comparisons of language and images of sex and war: "And arrest all soldiers and Bomb-makers: 'QUITE liable to damage the mental health of children and young persons' (sayeth the psychiatrist)."

RobertOh Faber's poem "Past the News Stand Up," in *Poets for Peace: Poems from the Fast,* makes similar comparisons, but does so in more poetically compressed images suggesting the monolithic-metallic-phallic buildings of Bly's poems and Ginsberg's *Howl.* The poem builds in energy, pace, and compactness toward its crisis:

> . . . there was a sound like drowning air condition
> to rain child death by Johnson's Barbecue Sauce his
> Texas Hots bursting American Metal Climax Building
> hates life hates life cells up over what goes up
> must come his Texas hots spurting down burning flesh
> bursting fire flesh fire flesh barbecue bursting
> spurting down fire on flesh-roast flesh roast today
> when you come up from the ground you see
> the signs American metal climax building . . .[30]

The bursting napalm and the spurting fire of war are here insinuated as the perverse orgasm of a harsh and metallic masculinity. At the same time, as in Duncan's poems, napalm and fire are associated with Texas barbecues and the inordinate gratifications of other perverted, exorbitant appetites.

IV

The Female equally with the Male I sing
Of Life immense in passion, pulse, and power

Whitman

Juxtapositions of sex, flesh, and life against war, fire, and death appear in numerous poems, often with the imagery moving further away from Ginsberg and Freud and closer to Bly and Jung. For example, images that associate the feminine with the wet, the fleshy, and the flexible, show up interestingly in Art Berger's "The American Male Is Beginning to Smell a Lot Like a Female (from a full page New York *Times* ad)." Ironically, and predictably, the American male's turning to perfumes has not made him more feminine in the Jungian sense but is on the contrary another twisted attempt to move even further from the flesh and the "feminine." (The world of Madison Avenue immediately recognizes this as a chance to sell cologne that smells tough and "masculine.") Berger, with the eyes and nose of a poet, is able to see and smell that in fact

> The American male is beginning to smell
> like   -death
>   by misplaced sprays of lead
>   from Texas towers
>   at low noon
> that might have been virtue
> if rained from a whirlyhawk
> over Mekong
> Death is a dirty word but so is
> underarm dew and as far as
> pubic sweat or clouds of crotch
> forget it man
> Dead fish tales rot
> in a black sun
> of the supermarket of America
> U-2—bay of pigs—Santo Domingo
> Tonkin Gulf and Hanoi   (*Fast*, p. 6)

These grouped images eloquently suggest the relationship between the smells of life and the smells of death, and imply that if we are afraid of the former ("the scent of these arm-pits aroma finer than prayer!"), we will inevitably surround ourselves with the latter. Though the smell of fish, sex, and sweat may be offensive, they are the smells of life, and if we deny, fear, or kill them, they will be replaced by the even greater stench of death—the smell not of fish but of dead fish; not of healthy sexuality or fish swimming in clean, life-supporting water, but of repressed and deflected sexuality, of fish (fish tails/tales—the events and their covering lies) rotting in the cold sun of America's supermarket anti-life values.

A number of other poems consciously or unconsciously work in related images. In Bert Lee's "Photograph: Mother and Father: 1930," in *The Writing on the Wall*, a specific and perhaps autobiographical situation takes on wide registrations in the American experience: "I have a wrought-iron father / And a mother pale as the work of a lampshade." The contrast of the powerful, hard, dominant masculine against the faded and fragile feminine continues:

Now my father keeps to himself and union meetings
And dresses as I think a mayor might dress
He sees the world as a billiard-table green
Where people meet and rebound
With the petty click of pool balls.
My mother keeps to herself and, humming,
Dresses with a sense of faded gingham.
She muses how youth once filled the light
Like the shadow of a failing moth.[31]

It little matters whether the poet has Jung in mind (there is other evidence to suggest he does); what does matter is that he is imaginatively experiencing the problem according to the archetypal patterns.

Vic Contoski's "War Poem" effectively pairs generals, congressmen, mathematicians, and the vampirish ghost of Thomas Jefferson against dark women, unfaithful wives, enemy dead, small things that move in the underbrush, and "a young virgin from Omaha, Nebraska" whose breasts "full as the moon, move slowly / as a night patrol through strange territory." The two sides, pathetically and hopelessly estranged, slowly destroy one another. In "the country beautiful as a girl's body / that proved too powerful for her dreams," Jefferson's ghost sucks the virginal blood, and "an evil old lady lies awake / hoping her only son will die."[32]

Stan Steiner's "But the Africans Walked at Night" (*Wall*, p. 123) begins by contrasting the early American spirit (tough, efficient, deadly) and the African spirit (mythic, magical, mysterious) —the double cultural heritage of the American Negro:

.. of graves of the peach trees
of Kit Carson,
      the father,
of death.
But, the Africans walked at night
succoring the Earth Mother ...

Like the Indians that fell before the onslaught of the willful and practical white man, the Africans, too, are co-opted and destroyed by Western values and a perverted Christianity:

... governmental
beasts
    to eat
tribal fables
mouthed by TV
tubes full of
Last Suppers
of Cheeseburgers
But, the Africans walked at night
black as Christs
shrouded
in whiteskinned
business suits of cellophane and aluminum foil
under the moon
of the coyote.

Instead of succoring the Earth Mother, their night nature becomes more and more contaminated—they walk "through the dark light / to uranium women / in unlit hogans," to "wickiups with beauty-rest beds," and eventually to "State / departmentalized guides who dreamt of reddest sex / frozen in ice cream cones of blackest secrets."

They walk through "four hundred miles of years of death" to become, like the Indians with which the poem constantly associates them, victims of the war and of the desert of American history.

The Indians and Africans of Steiner's poem share a primitive vitality and spirituality diametrically opposed to the death-in-life, materially oriented, no-nonsense mind of white Anglo-Saxon Protestant America. It is this emotionality and natural vigor that Norman Mailer covets for the white man in his essay on "The White Negro." But Mailer notwithstanding, American history has been a history of hatred of the Negro and Indian; and poets see in this hatred a fear of life and of the essentially shamanistic religious disposition that is also shared, in their own way, by the equally dark-haired and dark-eyed Orientals. Robert Bly brilliantly concretizes our complex and multifarious anxiety about this volatile life-force as fear and hatred of black hair itself. His "Hatred of Men with Black Hair" is not the shallow rhetorical piece it sometimes seems but is carefully built around the doubly powerful central synecdoche of darkness and hair, both marvelous symbols boasting a long literary tradition involving the black goddess Hagia Sophia, the story of Samson, the *Song of Songs*, the dark lady and femme fatale, and carrying through the work of Yeats and Lawrence.

V

From this hour I ordain myself loos'd of limits and
imaginary lines,
Going where I list, my own master total and absolute.
Whitman

It is no doubt only a coincidence that the flag of anarchy is also black, but it is an appropriate coincidence, for the fear of anarchy is a fear of the dark, uncontrolled forces of life that it would set free. An insistent motif of the protest poetry is the call to anarchy, the law of the moment, and the inner law of individual volition. The alternative (and that which becomes the polar force in the poems) is a strong and rigid central government, antagonistic to change, imposing a life-constricting control over all things.

The renascence of religious sensibility and the "rebirth of wonder" and love ("Aphrodite to grow live arms") are linked by poets to their own "war" to "make the world safe for anarchy." Art forms and the creative process itself have been since the fifties seeking this same freedom of anarchy, as can be felt in Ferlinghetti's early "I Am Waiting" (*Wall*, p. 4) where he is "perpetually waiting / for the fleeing lovers on the Grecian Urn to catch each other up at last / and embrace." Certainly the art of the fifties and sixties seeks to tap and release energy instead of ordering and preserving experience in static tension; it seeks to be experience itself, and that experience is to be ecstatic and passionate.

For some people the black flag, black hair, and the open art forms are all seen as frightening forces of chaos, as emotionality and passion unleashed from control of reason and judgment. But for more and more poets, as it is for Paul Goodman, the black flag is a sign of a higher order, not of chaos but of antagonism against the artificial imposition of law that should be organic in the sanity of free individuals and the societies they comprise:

And if the merry day shall come
again the black flag is my country's spirit,
lovingly my wife will take it home
and cut it up to make pants or a shirt.[33]

The disorder of anarchy feared by so many is in the poet's eye only and always a counterforce, and falls out of existence when it has no inflexible order to oppose. In that sense it is not a destructive order but a force for life and natural flexibility asking that things be allowed to grow as they will according to their developing nature. It is in this spirit that Robert Duncan wears the black armband of the anarchist—as a believer in consummate discipline and order, but an order of "individual volition." This, too, inevitably moves toward a simpler life and a denial of complex systems.

Flexibility and freedom. Tuli Kupferberg's "Would You Believe" (*Wall*, p. 13) shows how far we have come since Amy Lowell's "Patterns."

Break the patterns! Shatter the images! Down icons!
Tune In, Turn On, Drop Out!

Fake games! Your games are fake, boring.
Man was made to change. No single thing abides.

Kupferberg may not be a great poet, but he is infected by the same
intense spirit that animated many poets in the sixties—the desire
to return to the freedom of the sea, the Great Mother, the living
water.

VI

You sea! I resign myself to you also—I guess what you
   mean,
I behold from the beach your crooked inviting fingers.

Whitman

"All poems," claims Walter Lowenfels, "are one evidence that
we know to be more than rocks. Our whole history is a living
protest against geology" (*Wall*, Preface). If that is true, then poetry
is indeed the instrument of life, a vital vehicle of wisdom, The Way.
The Book of the Tao asks:

What is more fluid, more yielding than water?
Yet back it comes again, wearing down the rigid strength
Which cannot yield to withstand it.
So it is that the strong are overcome by the weak,
The haughty by the humble.
This we know
But never learn   (Witter Bynner's translation)

The form of poetry has, of course, itself sometimes forgotten to
remain fluid and yielding, and has been itself sometimes a rigid
strength—but this is not so of most recent poetry. And as the form
of poetry has become more open and flexible, so has its world-view
or "content."

Especially noteworthy in the protest poetry is the abundance
of sea and water images. Even the poetry of the, by comparison,
conservative Robert Lowell reveals a longing to return to the sea,
if not as a means of escaping the horror of the present (cf. Plato's
rotting blob of sea-flesh, p. 147), then at least as a way of redis-

covering a more legitimate integrity and vitality. Lowell's "For the Union Dead 'Reliquunt Omnia Servare Rem Publicam'" begins with the saddened perception of loss:

> The old South Boston Aquarium stands
> in a Sahara of snow now. Its broken windows are boarded.
> The bronze weathervane cod has lost half its scales
> The airy tanks are dry.[34]

In place of the Aquarium that once fascinated him as a child, there is only a vacant building, dry tanks, and a desert of white, lifeless, frozen water. Paralleling these images of death and dryness is the poet's awareness that the heroism, integrity, and genuine life of the Union Negro dead have also passed away, and that the commemorative monument is an embarrassing accusation of the sterility that now surrounds it. Lowell is careful to associate the statue of the black Colonel Shaw with the sea and the water: "Their monument sticks like a fishbone / in the city's throat." There can be no similar monuments for recent wars, either for Vietnam or the Second World War.

> There are no statues of the last war here
> on Boylston Street, a commercial photograph
> shows Hiroshima boiling
> over a Mosler Safe, the "Rock of Ages"
> that survived the blast.

The genius of this poetry makes it easy to understand why Lowell is generally regarded as the best poet of his time. What remains of the Second World War is a calloused and blind commercial exploitation of the deadly horror of Hiroshima, and a blasphemous prostitution of the "Rock of Ages" to titillate modern man's sterile lusting after security. The ironies compressed in these few lines deserve more discussion than they can be given here—suffice it to say only that there can be no safety in an atomic age, and that Lowell understands the Rock of Ages to be precisely opposite in nature to the lifeless, closed, hoarding, adamant Mosler Safe. The Rock of Ages is indeed more closely akin to the sea itself. But all that was once alive and associated with water has been replaced by the mechanical and artificial, that which is dry or repels water.

The Aquarium is gone. Everywhere,
giant finned cars nose forward like fish;
a savage servility
slides by on grease.

In the poem Lowell offered for Lowenfels's *Where Is Vietnam?*,
he pictures himself swimming "like a minnow behind my studio
window" in a world full of "the chafe and jar of nuclear war" in
which "the state is a diver under a glass bell," and where "we are
like a lot of wild / spiders crying together, / but without tears."[35]
The reader can readily understand and share Lowell's confession in
"The Union Dead": "I often sigh still / for the dark downward and
vegetating kingdom / of the fish and reptile . . . ."

The fish has long been an archetypal symbol of life, and figures
in many recent poems, some of which have already been discussed.
The poet finds in the fish an apt symbol of his own consciousness,
and in the anguish of modern culture is likely to feel,

I am a fish swimming in mined waters
I am a fish in water that has been torpedoed
I am a fish in a volcanic ocean.

Oh, the detritus, the confusion, the noise, the floating anger.[36]

Diane Wakoski, from whose work these lines are taken, also seems
to lament her "development" beyond this flexible form toward
strength and hardness:

The pain of sharks eating at my ridged, aching back.
Each vertebra a bullet. A lump of scar tissue.
A strength earned by sharks biting and making me
bleed.
        I could not stand up
                    I grew new bones
I am a tower of ugly strength, this body
only the sharks have enjoyed.   (p. 17)

Marge Piercy builds a remarkable poem, "In Praise of Salt and
Water," around the contrast between man and dolphin as two species who took differing evolutionary routes. Her feeling is that
the road not taken by man has proven to be the superior route,

and we are like fish struggling to maintain life in a waterless terrain. Those who struggle for power and dominance, however, do all that is possible to destroy the last possibility of this primitive and sea-associated vitality; they devote all their energies to "HELP STOP WETNESS." In this cry of the "arid ad in the subway" Piercy finds the perfect symbol for the modern condition wherein the "great contrary project is to dry up the world." In the face of this project the poet takes comfort in "the looseness of [her] flesh and the salty damp of [her] thighs" and ponders the tie between "wetness" and "life":

> Wet is what flows and seeps and comes again:
> ocean we carry in us
> where we spawned
> to nourish life among alien rocks.
> Even the trees cup sap that rises and falls.
> Wet and sloppy the mutual joy
> of stirring bodies together
> warm as breast milk.
> We are wet jokes and wet dreams.
> A scalpel slits us open
> like a busted bag of groceries
> and out we ooze.
> Noses drip. Armpits weep.
> Man is born from a small salt pond.
> Yet immersed in our own element we drown.
>
> (*Hard Loving*, p. 75)

It is essentially the "fear of drowning" in anarchic tides and the absence of structure that inspires the drive to "stop wetness" and any kind of flexible and undisciplined spontaneous life. But the dolphins, who "help one another" while rupicoline man "among rocks and cement fears man worse than the cyclone," prove the superiority of wetness as a medium of life. The "sea of mankind" must somehow again learn "to rise and roll" and become "part of one wave and each other." The time of decision has arrived. We have so successfully promoted the campaign to dry up the world that we must now reverse our direction or come to the final dryness and death.

In this time we shall fail into ashes,
fail into metal and dry bones and paper,
or break through into a sea of shared abundance
where man shall join man
in salty joy, in flowing trust.
We must be healed at last to our soft bodies
and our hard planet
to make live and conscious history in common.   (pp. 76–77)

VII

And I will make a song for the ears of the President, full of
weapons with menacing points,
And behind the weapons countless dissatisfied faces . . .
Whitman

The spiritual blight of the war in Vietnam is the most important of many forces that have made clear the necessity of a change in direction away from harshness and power. Piercy writes, in "Community":

Loving feels lonely in a violent world,
irrelevant to people burning like last year's weeds
with bellies distended, with fish throats agape
and flesh melting down to glue.
We can no longer shut out the screaming
that leaks through the ventilation system,
the small bits of bone in the processed bread.

(Hard Loving, p. 17)

The same soul sickness we have discussed in the poems of Ginsberg, Levertov, and Bly finds expression here and in the work of many other poets. The theme is especially pervasive in the poems Levertov selected for the 1968 War Resisters League's *Peace Calendar*. Gary Snyder's "In the House of the Rising Sun" carries the characteristic tone:

did I drink some filthy poison?
will I ever learn to love?
Did I really have to kill my sick, sick cat.

(Calendar, Feb. 26)

Given Levertov's distaste for raw, quivering autobiography, Snyder's last line is perhaps the most questionable line in the volume, but it succeeds as few others could in expressing the extremity and pervasiveness of this malaise of spirit.

The most pared and disciplined statement of the dilemma is Creeley's admirably controlled "Flowers," quoted in full here:

> *"No knowledge rightly understood*
> *can deprive us of the mirth of flowers"*
> *—Edward Dahlberg*

No thing less than one thing,
or more—

no sun
but sun—

or water
but wetness found—

what truth is it
that makes men so miserable?

Days we die
are particular—

This life cannot be lived
apart from what it must forgive.   (*Calendar*, June 10)

If poems such as this, or Creeley's "For No Clear Reason," or Galway Kinnell's "How Many Nights" can be called war poems—and in many cases they deserve to be since they are prompted by this war and life in its shadow—then some of the finest war poetry was written in the sixties. It is not uncommon to hear people speak of the shrill and hysterical tone of the poetry against the war, but there is much poetry that is political only in the best sense—it advocates no particular ideology or system but searchingly investigates the possibilities of spirit in a moment when a horrible war taints all our actions. Even Robert Bly, who has perhaps drawn most fire for his politicizing, furnishes perceptions of real value when he focuses on the dangers to the spirit. Though "Driving through Minnesota," like many of his Vietnam poems, seems to speak *at* rather than *with* the reader, we recognize the truth of his reactions to the war's atrocities:

> These instants become crystals,
> Particles
> The grass cannot dissolve. Our own gaiety
> Will end up
> In Asia, and in your cup you will look down
> And see
> Black Starfighters.[37]

Galway Kinnell has rarely spoken of the war directly except in "The Vapor Trail Reflected in the Frog Pond." But he does not admit to a wide difference between political and other poetry and believes that his "The Bear" is as political as the "Vapor Trail." "The Bear," too long to discuss here, obeys the same law as the brief "How Many Nights," which Kinnell submitted to Levertov for the Peace Calendar.[38] "How Many Nights" speaks not of the war but of the terrors of personhood, the spiritual and psychological struggles, loneliness, and fear that come into man's life from many sources, only one of which may be the dark burden of war. It is a simple poem that hints of nights spent in terror wrestling with various angels, and of the peace of nature in a morning walk. But the morning is no easy panacea, and the night has had its effect. Man is different for his sufferings, knows things that he did not know before: "and above me / a wild crow crying *'yaw yaw yaw'* / from a branch nothing cried from ever in my life" (*Calendar*, Jan. 1). This, it seems to me, is the truest kind of poetry, in that it evokes, hints, offers one the feeling of its truth without any need to state it. Given only the context of a peace anthology, it becomes powerfully political and anti-war, not because it centers on the problem but because it sets the problem humming in its universal registrations.

It is to be noted that Kinnell's poem is set as the first poem of the *Calendar* and strikes the "horizon note" for the volume, for if volumes and collections of poetry possess a "home key" as Levertov suggests individual poems should, then it is this chord—the effect of the war on the poet and the spirit—that recurs throughout the collection and gives it its special tonality. As in Levertov's own poetry, the war has caused in the poems of many other poets a voice to cry "from a branch that nothing cried from ever before."

It is not alone in Levertov's selection of poems that this blight and hysteria surface, but in other anthologies and journals as well. In *Poets for Peace: Poems from the Fast* one finds examples like the following. Sam Abrams's "Song for Some Sad Kid" expresses well the contamination of the war horror, its dehumanizing and bestializing forces, and the poet's sense of helplessness:

> i can
> say nothing
> understandable
>
> growl or whine
> the fur is on the backs of my hands
> as i type these lines.   (*Fast*, p. 1)

Other poets imagine war-related scenes in grotesque and Kafkaesque images. Allen Katzman's "Ode to the East Wind" (*Fast*, p. 39) sees legs walking and marching after the soldiers have shed packs and rifles and their bodies have dissolved. How then should one react when contronted with such sights? "What do you say to a leg? How / do you greet it? If you come upon a leg walking / in a field, should you act surprised?"

In "The Story Is Not to be Told, The Story Is to be Eaten Alive," Donald Katzman imagines "A million people or more rose from the empty holes, / Each ripping his right arm off / And shaping them into rifles" (*Fast*, p. 40). Shalom Sperber's poem of similarly bizarre title, "There's a Hole in His Head, Can't You See," deals in images wherein "Earless Van Goghs / Embrace / Leaveless trees / Waiting / For the bombing to stop" (*Fast*, p. 72).

Walter Lowenfels's *Where Is Vietnam?* anthology is similarly cankered with dark sores:

> I drag my shadow
> as if it were a sack
> full of discarded bodies
>
> . . . .

and on my spinal road,
the boy who crawls
farther and farther
from his legs   (Morton Marcus, p. 85)

David Ignatow asks "how come nobody is being bombed today"
and complains bitterly against

whoever started this peace
without advising me
through a news leak
at which I could have voiced a protest,
running my whole family off a cliff.[39]

Images of mutilation like those we have seen in Bly's poems
and in some of the above grow out of an extreme frustration and
impotence. The individual intensely feels his helplessness, and yet
feels his existence is untenable without some kind of act. The only
act open to the imagination is self-annihilation and mutilation. Ross
Feld's "War in Winter," in his *Winter Poems* published by Shortstop
Press in 1966, captures the realization and reaction:

"This has never happened before.
This has never happened before in America.
This has never happened before in America
                    where it's not supposed to
happen in the first place."
And I understand what he's saying,
                    that much the overcoat
exposes.
Winter time—yes, I know
            that IT'S never happened before,
whether in America or not.
Incredible   cold against my cheek,
to really come into anything
without a wound. Incredible
that when he finishes his short speech
he will tear himself
                    apart, limb from
            limb, screaming,

each rip, the coldest
frustration.

VIII

The sky o'erarches here, we feel the undulating deck
beneath our feet,
The boundless vista and the horizon far and dim are all
here

Whitman

The protest of the sixties, when it is not enervated by hopelessness, is energized with urgency, with the awareness that the
situation has swollen toward a decisive moment wherein men must
now "fail into ashes, fail into metal," or grow quickly into attitudes
and relationships of trust and openness toward the world and one
another. No doubt many of the grotesque and hysterical images
of mutilation grow as much from fear of the impending event as
from guilt and helplessness.

I have never seen suffering, Guernica,
  Jews, the black dream, but now
    rumblings. Omens of death. In the
      streetstalls, the titles,
        revolution impending,
          death, the high
            frenzy the tone
              takes and no
                one to
                  brake it.[40]

The ominous portent of disaster is "strong very strong now /
the hour of the locust!" and calls up visions of biblical plagues as
well as contemporary political cataclysms.[41] Either the negative
forces of darkness or the positive "dark" forces of life must necessarily overwhelm the cold, pale, impersonal men of the West.

The dark and alien watch,
Winging to their cities,
The pale men with worried faces,

The men from the West:
That ruled, but now propose treaties;
That smile, but need time.
Flesh moves in huge landslides,
Overwhelming the Ambassadors
Even as they extend their hands.[42]

The seemingly inevitable end of the peculiar *Weltanschauung* of Western man is frequently cheered and welcomed, sometimes with almost vitriolic energy born of anger and disgust. Aaron Kramer's message "to a dark skinned people" is that they "are the latest on a list of shame" that shadows him. He calls on them to purge him of this "dark inheritance" that has been growing

since first the European cast his glance
westward, and gave his greed a lofty name.
Cloven the footprint of his proud advance;
rabid the torch that fouled the nights with flame;
the soil was rich enough before he came,
but with the flesh of tribes he fed his plants.
Roll him aside! Aye, send him reeling home,
and let his hot mouth know for once the taste
of ruin!

("Year of Shame," *Fast*, p. 44)

That our direction and our doom is perhaps irreversible is recognized in a number of poems. American and Western culture in general is impelled along the path of its long determined trajectory, and is, in that sense, as enslaved by its past as a bullet is. But a more common metaphor in the poems is of a beast that has grown outsized and no longer controllable; and sometimes we are envisioned as being caught up in its belly. "We must name the giant in whose belly we are chained," argues one poet; and another realizes that "we are carried in the belly / of what we have become / toward the shambles of our triumph."[43]

In Yeats's system of interpenetrating gyres, when one emphasis (objectivity-rationality-action or subjectivity-imagination-contemplation) has reached its extreme development, then "the center cannot hold" and the direction must reverse or the system self-destructs.

In a poem prefaced with an appropriate epigraph from Diane Wakoski ("the wind is loose, / insane, / devouring the flowers"), Michael Rossman describes the pregnancy of the present crisis in terms reminiscent of Yeats: "and so violence / hangs like a three winged hawk in the flawed air of this season / and the young prepare."[44]

Perhaps the best "poem of portent" is William Stafford's "Report of an Unappointed Committee."* Stafford captures here the gut-twitching suspense and expectancy as well as the uncertainty and ambivalency about what is building behind the scenes, and makes the reader feel the power and awesomeness of whatever it is that is about to spring, lurch, or flood upon the world.

---

* Like Lowell, William Stafford protests the war energetically but rarely mentions it directly in his poems. Nevertheless, the war is an admitted force in such poems as "At the Bomb Testing Site," "Watching the Jet Planes Dive," "During the Evening News," and "Report to Crazy Horse." Interestingly enough, Stafford claims a protest element in many poems: "even poems like 'B.C.' or 'On a Church Lawn,' which do not seem to be protest poems but which to me are witnessings for a way of life that implies the anti-war stance. Maybe what I am drifting toward saying is that many fairly quiet, off-the-target poems are motivated and guided by impulses that to me are the very central elements in what real, effective protest could be. Some protest is an image of what is protested against, but a *change* requires something *other*." If one studies the tiny "B.C." he sees how wide Stafford's sense of the *"other"* is. Any poem that elevates truth, beauty, spirit, is in such an understanding a protest against war.

Though Stafford is sometimes associated with "pacifism," he prefers to describe his stance less rigidly: "for a long time I have found myself often disagreeing with those around me, but the nature of my daily experience is mild, and my feelings toward individuals [or issues] is not—I believe—doctrinaire." He is similarly diffident about the value and effect of his own and others' protest poetry: "It is a temptation to feel that one's insights are much needed in the world. Both intellectually and in terms of feeling, I shy away from presuming such a quality, for any individual. I think we must check each other, seek help and guidance and insight all around us. A poet participates in the human enterprise. He has no special knowledge or virtue. When something he says or writes appeals to us, we are ourselves qualified to judge and hence participate in the essentials of the poem or statement. Audience and poet share feelings and insights; they do not occupy give on the one side and receive on the other roles.

"I do protest, though!" (Personal letter, 31 Jan. 1972).

The uncounted are counting
   and the unseen are looking around.
In a room of northernmost light
   a sculptor is waiting.
In some university a strict experiment
   has indicated a need for
   more strict experiments.
A wild confusion of order is clawing through
   a broken system of our most reliable wires.
In the farthest province a comet
   has flamed in the gaze of
   an unofficial watcher.
In the back country a random rain drop
   has broken a dam.
And a new river is out feeling for a valley
   somewhere under our world.   (*Calendar*, Jan. 1969)

    Sixties poets are uncertain about whether the future leads to utopia or perdition, but they do possess the necessary imagination to presume a possible world without war. Such a world cannot, of course, be anything like the prosperous world envisioned by the New Deal or the Great Society, nor much like the land of Cockaigne that has always lurked behind the mists of the American dream. A society without the blight of war and the multitudinous minor evils that culminate in war will perhaps necessarily be a much simpler world, and one shaped in a very real way by the agrarian, pastoral, communal, religious, and artistic impulses of today's poets and young people. If the details of that world are difficult or impossible for these poets to depict convincingly, it is not a cause for astonishment or chagrin: all past literary attempts at such descriptions have failed with a reassuring consistency. The important fact is that poets now have a new attitude toward human possibility, and a faith that men can or could create a peaceful, anarchic, orderly, spiritual, and ecstatic community. It matters little if most scenarios of the "new world" are ludicrous or "unrealistic" by usual standards —and it is well to remember that the new world will have freed itself from just such standards and will be itself the contradiction of them.

Most poets are satisfied with suggesting that an alternative world is a magnificent possibility, but some—mostly the epigones of Ginsberg—are intrepid enough to try to paint its portrait. Michael McClure, for example, sees man on the verge of necessary change. Our present hysteria and madness result from our having come to the last extremity of our tolerance—"our bodies are mad with the forgotten memories that we are creatures." Healing and salvation will come when we remember "we are mammals," and with that seemingly regressive realization will also supposedly come an apotheosis toward the sacrificial and sacramental. In McClure's new world the only killing will be like that in Buddhist myths where Buddha's love for the hungry, emaciated lion causes him to lie down with a smile before its slavering jaws:

> (Now it is worst when man is at the edge,
>   he may be freed of his
>   carnivore past—and is on the verge
> of becoming a singer and glorious creature
>   borne free through the universe.
>   Soon no lamb or man
>   may be eaten
>   save
>   with the smile of sacrifice!)[45]

In his most ambitious anti-war poem, *After the Cries of the Birds*, Lawrence Ferlinghetti describes his "visionary" society of rock music, drugs, Eastern religion, and unapologetic sensuousness:

> I see the "future of the world"
>   in a new visionary society
>   now only dimly recognizable
>   in folk-rock ballrooms
>   free-form dancers in ecstatic clothing
>   their hearts their gurus
>   every man his own myth[46]

The depiction is not much enlarged or improved in sophistication by Ferlinghetti's second try later in the poem:

I see the lyric future of the world
  on the beaches of Big Sur
    gurus at Jack's Flats
nude swart maidens swimming
    in pools of sunlight
    Kali on the beach
   guitarists with one earring
lovely birds in long dresses and Indian headbands
                     What does this have to do with Lenin?
     Plenty!

There are more modest and more effective evocations of the utopian future, even sometimes by poets who are characteristically more reckless with their rhetoric. In contrast to much of Di Prima's work are the quiet and pleasing rhythms of these lyrics:

We return with the sea, the tides
we return as often as leaves, as numerous
as grass, gentle, insistent, we remember
the way,
our babes toddle barefoot thru the cities of the universe.

                                         (*Letters*, ltr. 4)

Fortunately most poets do not attempt to communicate more than their insistence that a new man is possible, or they wisely restrict themselves to glimpses of small and intimate scenes: Gary Snyder teaching his sons not about the American dream but about Chief Joseph, the bison, Ishi, fir trees, "the Buddha, their own naked bodies, / swimming and dancing and singing / instead";[47] or Paul Goodman carrying his obsolete black flag home to become pants or shirt worn in freedom and peace.

7 AGAINST CONCLUDINGS

Poets to come! orators, singers, musicians to come!
Not to-day is to justify me and answer what I am for,
But you, a new brood, native, athletic, continental, greater
    than before known,
Arouse! for you must justify me.

I myself but write one or two indicative words for the
    future,
I but advance a moment only to wheel and hurry back in
    the darkness.

Whitman, "Song of Myself"

I

All of the poems of the preceding chapters have their common issue in war and its physical and spiritual causes and effects: whether they investigate the individual or the national psyche, the torn flesh or the Gross National Product, the sexual mores or the educational systems, their common reference is at last that particular kind of anti-life violence leading to or resulting from war. But the poetry against Vietnam and related social evils does not (like the poetry of World War I) seek to expose the ugliness and horror of war, nor (like the poetry of World War II) to make sense of war or discover a compensating order or value in it, but rather to attack the systems and mentality behind war, to explore painfully what

247

we have become, and to prophesy the catastrophic or beatific directions of the future.

Walter Lowenfels, in his anthology of Vietnam protest, has written that it is not war in general but this particular war that the poets find intolerable: "Few of the contributors are pacifists, many are veterans . . . . It is this particular war that has aroused them."[1] Though there is an element of truth in this, it passes over the important differences in the poetry of Vietnam and earlier wars, and assumes that the antagonism against this war grows almost solely from the different nature of the war rather than from a possible difference in the sensibilities of poets and thinking people in 1917, 1942, and 1967. Surely it is questionable, even presumptuous, to suppose one's own age has "advanced" in morality and responsibility over past ages, but there can be no doubt that our ideas and perceptions have changed. Colonialism is in disrepute around the world, and our own culture suffers less from xenophobia and at least somewhat less from hallucinatory paranoia about "Communism." As a people we are better educated and more painfully aware of the clandestine machinations behind the idealistic linguistic camouflage of war. Granting that the Vietnam War is a disreputable one, it may well be becoming harder and harder, perhaps even impossible—because of our new perceptions—to find a reputable one.

The anti-war poetry of the last several years does, in fact, offer not so much a specific indictment of this war as it does a profound sense of involvement and humanitarian concern, a turning away from militarism and the system of values that goes with it, and a growing conviction that there are no words or abstractions that can justify the inhumanity of warfare in a modern world. The protest also seems to be inextricably related to the new directions of poetic theory, and to the chafing against totems and forms of all kinds, social or poetic. Both the content and form of current poetry reveal an intense drive for freedom, a freedom that allows the person and the poem *to become* and *to be* what each is.

Allen Ginsberg insists on allowing his poetry its own freedom, whatever it may prove *to be*, just as he has learned to allow his own life to be what it is. To coerce his poetry, or meddle with his "transcript of consciousness" so that it measures up to some pre-formed idea of what it should be, would be as much a failure and falsification as his early attempt to similarly coerce and shape his life.

Denise Levertov, the most orderly of the four major poets in this study until the heat of the war melted or fragmented her poetic forms, nevertheless from the beginning realized that her work and her life were truest when they went like the dog in the Mexican sunlight, trotting crookedly "haphazard, every step an arrival."[2] In *Relearning the Alphabet* the forms and contents of her poetry move more and more away from the older solidity and order, until in *To Stay Alive* one suspects that the irregularity itself is a necessity "to stay alive."

Robert Bly's preference for the deep image and for the un-conscious over the conscious mind likewise demands an abandon-ment of control, a relinquishment of conscious direction, so that the images of truth can swim to the surface and make their own shapes. Bly rejects the eyesight of the world with its "on the other hand" objectivity and judiciousness; finds that mystery and vision live in the uncontrolled and uncontrollable; and is thrilled that (as he translates a poem of Kabir) "between the conscious and the un-conscious the mind has put up a swing" so that we might occa-sionally catch glimpses of the divine.[3]

Robert Duncan reverences the individual volition of both his life and his language, and allows his poems to unfold themselves freely as linguistic communities. His primary concern is not, as with poets of previous decades, with product—the product will be right if the process is intense and free enough. Duncan believes "Poetry not to be a literary achievement or an affect of gentility (tho gentleness has its part in the real) and particularly not to be a commodity of cultured taste, but to be a process of the Process that is the culture of tillage of souls that there might be and is a spiritual reality."[4] And the life that is in poetry is not different from the life of his own organism: "what I am is only an instance of a series of me that moves thru time precisely because it continually dies away from itself in being born into itself. This is what it means to be mortal: to wax and wane, to have genius in the moment and to perish therein, to come into being and pass out of being in order to be at all.[5]

In these four poets, though each approach is unique, the common element is the desire for fluidity, spontaneity, and immediacy of form. That desire is shared in one degree or another by most of the poets who have spoken against the war and the rigidities, orders, and abstractions of our culture. Both form and content, both process and image, unite in rebellion against the war and the forces of death; and the images of the wet earth, the water, and the sea beckon the poem, the soul, and the culture alike.

The new poetry and new directions have been made possible by a variety of developments, not the least of which is a new way of seeing man and history. Our general sense of history, especially as it is manifest in our life-style and poetry, has shifted from one of cyclical change in a basically unchanging universe to one of evolutionary change in a growing and unfolding universe. Perhaps the "growing" and "unfolding" need not mean "progress" in the sense of movement to something better, but it must surely imply progress in the sense that a plant or an infant *progresses* from inchoate form toward maturity and fullness of form.

It remains for other disciplines to explain how and why this shift has occurred, but for students of literature to realize that the shift is having and will have profound effects on the contents, forms, and functions of literature. In a universe of fixed essences it is important to *con-form*, to *form* one's art and life *with* fixed forms and ideal values, and to be ready to do violence to one's own expression and voice or to one's fellow man to see that the proper shapes, systems, and orders are respected. But in a universe where fixed forms and ideal values are seen primarily as arbitrary and ossified impediments checking the vital flow and variegated oscillations of unfolding life, art changes its function from that of ordering and preserving experience in static and perfect form to promoting living experience and clearing away the roadblocks and stiffened conventions that inhibit or contain it. Instead of laboring to bring its materials and audience "into line," such art seeks to throw them "out of line"; instead of seeking the "ideal order," it seeks to escape any order in favor of a perpetual variation of orders.

In one way or another such impulses lie at the center of the poetics of each of the four major poets and many others of this study.

If man does have a *future*—not just a recycling of the past made necessary because man's nature does not change—then art seems indeed to take on new importance, and poets may with some justification indulge their idealistic and apocalyptic souls. If we have not been "through it all before";* if the universe and man are going somewhere; if conventional ways of seeing and relating to the world are only narrow and arbitrary accumulations of slow time and not insuperable God-given natural laws; if the universe is *becoming* rather than *being*—if these are the case, then the unfolding of life and art must be given freedom and not bound in by the conventions that grow out of our need to dominate and control. If human nature is not the static human nature of the Old Testament and Thomas Hobbes—the law of tooth and claw precariously subdued by social forms, law, and order—but is instead an open and fertile force unfolding toward vision and spirit, then we have less to fear from our own bodies and deepest impulses, and less to fear from the disorder and flux of life. Instead of knowing once and for all what the universe is and spending our psychic energies trying to conform ourselves to it, we can turn our eyes and

---

* The new attitude is echoed in Tim Hall's "Come Here, My Friends," in Walter Lowenfels, ed., *The Writing on the Wall* (Garden City: Doubleday, 1969):

"It is not true that our lives and troubles have
    been performed before
and everything to do has already been done.
Who has lived my life before?
Who has lived ours?
Produce him, bankers, leaders, fathers!
Show him to us" (p. 84).

So long as we assume that there is nothing new under the sun, then certainly there can never be a world without war. Harva Urpo says it concisely and well: "If we regard war as being inevitably implied by human character, we shall never be rid of it. To create the kingdom of eternal peace we must free ourselves of the illusion that strife is eternal." See "War and Human Nature," in Robert Ginsberg, ed., *The Critique of War* (Chicago: Henry Regnery, 1969), p. 46.

senses in awe at the sights and sounds of its and our own unfolding. Poetry in the sixties took to itself not only the task of praising and exploring these becomings but also of speaking out against the forces that would impede them.

Poets and poetry take upon themselves larger ultimate concerns and allegiances because their field of awareness has become larger —because isolated personal experience is being overlaid by the multifarious and unlimited experience of the world. In a very important sense poets now *know* more than ever before. As awarenesses have expanded to new contents and perspectives, poetics have likewise opened to new language, manners, and forms. Whether or not we think that it "is good for poetry" we must recognize in poetry a new social consciousness larger than the Vietnam issue and inseparable from the new poetics.

The statements of the more radical poets may sometimes be extreme, yet they indicate the way of the wind, and the way in which more traditional poets are also leaning. Kirby Congdon's "Manifesto" bids farewell to old ideas of poetry and to the poets who hold them:

> Good bye poets
> who think art is separated from politics,
> the law, the business and the big roast on Sunday,
> who think poetry an escape
> and poets spiritual fairies
> who make magic and beauty,
>
> . . . .
> And Hello poets
> who have seen us sink
> in and out of these cheap sins
> and who still call
> over our own torments
> louder than our tantrums,
> for each man's nation
> in each man's war:
> "Independence!"[6]

"Each man's nation" is for Congdon both smaller and larger than, but surely not the same as, national political boundaries. The poet's nation is his self, his country, his species, and the universe of his spirit, but most especially his poem. The older poetic can be seen as a denial of the poem's "Independence." Thanasis Maskaleris expresses vigorously how many contemporary poets experience the older demands on poetry:

> The Eliot artificers of culture
>> are choking poetry to death;
>> they are tying strings around our balls
>>> slowly . . . artfully,
>
> Poetry must again be the froth-flower of passion
>> the armed vanguard of the continuous revolution
>>> of the living.[7]

II

A number of books and articles in recent years have made the idea common that some kind of revolution is occurring in our society, yet there is little agreement about the nature of the revolution, or whether it is truly taking place or just barely failing to take place. How deep and how far reaching are the changes that are beginning to claw their way through the complex tangle of broken wires and values that were once but no longer are reliable and comforting? If we are to take our wisdom and eyesight from the collective wisdom and vision of our country's gift of poets—however variously shallow, exotic, traditional, visionary, or incomprehensible they individually may be—we are likely to be impressed that the revolution has been and is occurring, and that it is indeed a far-reaching and necessary one.

Close and expert prose analysis of our cultural milieu may indeed often seem more precise and valuable than the erratic flashes of insight or isolated grand visions of particular poems. But if poets and poetry are at all any of the things that we have over the centuries pleased ourselves with believing they are, then the recurrent themes and dispositions of a nation's poetic outpourings in any given period are perhaps the deepest and wisest statement that culture is able to make. It is easy to dismiss much of the poetry of recent years as "popular culture," as peripheral and borderline art if art at all. But we need to guard against selling ourselves short, against rejecting the works of our own time because they fail by standards that grow out of the partial visions and outdated wisdoms of a previous time. Whether the poetry of the sixties is "good" or "bad," it says what that decade had to say in the only way the decade had to say it.

What the poetry of the Vietnam War and the sixties says— though it cannot be said in fewer words than the poetry itself uses—is that life as we have known it is reaching the end of its tether and must change radically and rapidly or perish. It has no hope that the culture can continue in the same direction and perfect itself at last in a "technetronic society" or "meritocratic democracy"; it has no illusions that our problems will disappear when the present system works out its temporary kinks; it does not believe that the atrocities of Vietnam are in any way separable from our general values and directions; and it does not accept that life as we know it is the inevitable and only possible one for a flawed human nature. It calls for a revolutionary change of values in the individual and the collective man: what is needed is a startlingly new way of seeing, thinking, feeling, and being. The revolution this poetry calls for, in spite of its stridencies against external conditions, is internal and spiritual, and asks no less than a turning to the wisdom of the ages, to openness, praise, sympathy, compassion, celebration, ecstasy, community. It proposes no "program" and cares to promote none. It offers only its vision that life is more simple, surprising, and profound than the half-life man has generally mistaken for it; and explores the decimating or enlivening characteristics of the present and the possible future of man. It communicates its vision in a remarkable collage of images of hysteria, constriction, abrasion, paranoia, desert places, rocks, zeros, skyscrapers, beasts, cancers, sores, blemishes, shells, crusts, caves, rain, seeds, centers, blossoms, hearths, fires, flowing waters, and seas. It finds in our desire for certainty, stability, security; in our desire to remain in control, to possess, to manipulate, to dominate; in our desire for order, system, sameness, and permanence; in our desire to retain the past and determine the future—in these desires it sees a longing for death;

in these it sees a fear of life, a fear of perpetual change, fluidity, mystery, magic, sensation, vulnerability, sacrifice, beatitude.

But have poets not always taken such positions, expressed such ideas and used such images? Not really. Nor have they made their utterances in the shapes that they are now making them. Nor has poetry ever broken quite so free of traditional mannerisms to lead its own precarious and vulnerable but intense life. Perhaps the only definition of poetry that deserves to survive is that poetry is the best language that men at any given time are able to speak; or as Charles Olson puts it, poetry is what the poet "in his heat and that instant in its solidity yield."[8] An important factor in the solidity of any moment of the sixties was not merely the Vietnam War but a virulent iconoclasm (basing itself on discoveries made by Eliot, Pound, and Williams a generation before), a search for water among broken hopes and failed values, and a desperate struggle to reawaken a dangerously waning capacity for living deeply and spiritually.

A large part of the energy behind recent poetry and especially the protest of the sixties is directed to the effort to live more fully in the *now*, the *now* that moves as instants along the perpetual sequence of selves; to bring the consciousness back into the body and into the present, into the senses and the immediate; to draw it back from the abstract and out of time past and time future and *concentrate* it in space/time to the vanishing point deep at the center of self where life continually comes into being and passes out of being "in order to be at all." Paradoxically, as at least Bly, Levertov, Ginsberg, and Duncan variously understand and express, the way to go out to the world is to go in to the self. It would be wrong to claim that most contemporary poets are in command of a very large part of this mysterious understanding, or that all of them have even an intimation of it. Nevertheless, the sense of it is in the air and in the poetry, trying desperately to claw its way through the tangle of wires, breaking loose here and there in the streak of a comet, flooding now and again over the huge dam of conventional feeling and consciousness.

The poetry testifies that conventional consciousness has begun to crack and break apart like the snakeskin or cicada shell that constricts, and, if not broken, kills the life it once protected. The shell, it insists, must break up because it has become hardened and estranged from the vitality that once shaped it, and because it is a house in which all the growing that can be done has been done; and the organism, if it is to survive, must move on to a new phase of growth. Is man, then, going to break through the drying chrysalis of rational awareness into some new spiritual and visionary state? The poetry seems sometimes to hint of such a hope. Have things progressed so far that the whole of mankind must find the answer that individual men throughout time have had to find or perish? The poetry urges that it must. Even if it is true that all men cannot share deeply or even partially in this answer, the prophetic statement of the poetry of the fifties and sixties is that society must at least reverse itself in that direction. If spiritual man can never be the exclusive human modality, he must at least replace the ego-centered material man as the dominant. The latter has played his hand to the full, and time and space have called his bluff—he must give up his game or lose it all.

Poetry has always urged the deeper, larger life of man, but it has never done so with such a sense of urgency as it does today. If only a few men "caught on" to Blake in his own time, the tears and anguish along the "charter'd Thames" might go on unrelieved, but the planet would survive. The poet and visionary today no longer enjoys that confidence. He can no longer look only to himself or a select audience, but has become again an Isaiah or Jeremiah, calling on his people to awake.

NOTES

The first time a work is referred to, I have given full documentation in a note. Subsequent references are cited parenthetically in the text by short title and page number.

CHAPTER 1
POETRY, POLITICS, AND PAST WARS

1. A. A. Milne, *Peace with Honour* (New York: E. P. Dutton, 1934), p. 198.
2. A. E. Rodway, quoted by C. K. Stead in *The New Poetic* (London: Hutchinson & Co., 1964), p. 68.
3. *The Collected Poems of Rupert Brooke* (New York: Dodd, Mead & Co., 1946), p. 105.
4. Frank Foxcroft, ed., *War Verse* (New York: Crowell, 1918); George Herbert Clarke, ed., *A Treasury of War Poetry: British and American Poems of the World War 1914-1919* (Boston: Houghton Mifflin, 1919).
5. Bernard Bergonzi, "Before 1914: Writers and the Threat of War," *Critical Quarterly* 6 (1964):134.
6. *The War Poems of Siegfried Sassoon* (London: William Heineman, 1919), p. 41.
7. Wilfred Owen, *The Collected Poems of Wilfred Owen* (London: Chatto & Windus, 1964), p. 55.
8. Robert Graves, *Fairies and Fusiliers* (London: William Heineman, 1917), p. 33. Permission to reprint "A Dead Boche" was granted by the author and A. P. Watt & Son, London. From *Collected Poems 1914-1917*, by Robert Graves.
9. *The Poems of Robert Graves* (Garden City, N.Y.: Doubleday, 1958), p. 112. "Recalling War" was written in the late 1930s.
10. James A. Hart, *American Poetry of the First World War (1914 to 1920): A Survey and Checklist* (Ph.D. dissertation, Duke University, 1964), p. 2.
11. Florence E. Coates, "Their Vic-

tory Won," *Harper's Magazine,*
Dec. 1918, p. 77.

12. *The Complete Poems of Carl
Sandburg* (New York: Harcourt
Brace Jovanovich, 1970), p. 42.
"Wars" was first published in the
International Socialist Review in
1916.

13. Hart, p. 52.

14. Richard Fein, *Major American
Poetry of World War II: A
Critical Study* (Ph.D. dissertation, New York University,
1960), p. 4.

15. Ibid., p. 135.

16. Norman Cousins, "No Time for
Poetry," *Saturday Review of Literature,* 3 May 1941, p. 8.

17. David Daiches, "Poetry and the
War," *Poetry* 59 (1942):209–210.

18. Quoted by Fein, *Major American
Poetry,* p. 137.

19. Donald Stauffer's letter to Oscar
Williams, in Oscar Williams, ed.,
The War Poets (New York:
John Day Co., 1945), p. 15.

20. Karl Shapiro, *V-Letter and Other
Poems* (New York: Reynal and
Hitchcock, 1944), Preface.

21. Stephen H. Goode, *British War
Poetry of the Second World War*
(Ph.D. dissertation, University of
Pennsylvania, 1958).

22. Randall Jarrell, *The Complete
Poems* (New York: Farrar,
Straus & Giroux, 1969), p. 145.

23. John Ciardi, *As If: Poems New
& Selected* (New Brunswick,
N.J.: Rutgers University Press,
1955), p. 18.

24. Richard Fein, "Mary and Bellona: The War Poetry of Robert
Lowell," *Southern Review* 1
(1965):820–834.

25. Selden Rodman, "V-Letter to
Karl Shapiro in Australia," *The
Amazing Years* (New York:
Scribner's, 1947), p. 16.

26. James Schevill, *Tensions* (Berkeley: The Gillick Press, 1947),
pp. 20–21.

27. *The Complete Poems of Marianne Moore* (New York: The
Macmillan Co., 1967), p. 138.

28. Louis MacNeice, *Autumn Journal* (New York: Random House,
1940), p. 31.

29. *The Collected Poetry of W. H.
Auden* (New York: Random
House, 1945), p. 59.

30. *The Collected Poems of William
Butler Yeats* (New York: The
Macmillan Co., 1956), p. 153.

31. Hugh D. Ford, *A Poet's War:
British Poets and the Spanish
Civil War* (Philadelphia: University of Pennsylvania Press,
1965), pp. 17–26.

32. Allen Tate, *Reactionary Essays
on Poetry and Ideas* (New York:
Scribners, 1936), p. x.

33. Personal interview, Mar. 1969.

34. Barbara Gibbs and Francis Golffing, "The Public Voice: Remarks on Poetry Today," *Commentary,* July 1959, pp. 66–67.

35. Robert Bly, "The Collapse of
James Dickey," *Sixties* 9 (1967):
77.

36. Curtis Harnack, "Week of the
Angry Artist," *The Nation,* 20
Feb. 1967, pp. 245–248.

37. Peter Whigham, "Vietnam Peace
Poem," in The Community Council to End the War in Vietnam,

ed., *A Poetry Reading for Peace in Vietnam* (Santa Barbara: Unicorn Press, 1967), p. 10. Unicorn Press, which organized and sponsored the poetry reading, is now located in Greensboro, North Carolina 27402.
38. Cited by Denise Levertov in interview with James Finn in his *Protest: Pacifism and Politics* (New York: Random House, 1967), p. 471.
39. Ibid., p. 472.

40. Eric F. Goldman, "The White House and the Intellectuals," *Harper's Magazine*, Jan. 1969, p. 35.
41. Ibid., p. 43.
42. Kenneth Rexroth, "San Francisco Letter," *Evergreen Review* 1, no. 2 (1957):5.
43. Dave Rich, untitled poem, in Tove Neville, ed., *Poems Read in the Spirit of Peace and Gladness* (San Francisco: Peace & Gladness Co-op Press, 1966), p. 13.

CHAPTER 2
ALLEN GINSBERG: BREAKING OUT

1. John Ciardi, "Epitaph for the Dead Beats," *Saturday Review*, 6 Feb. 1960, p. 13.
2. Similarly phrased statements frequently occur in Ginsberg's interviews—in this instance an interview by the editors of *Mademoiselle*, Aug. 1969, p. 343.
3. All the poems of Allen Ginsberg's *The Empty Mirror* (New York: Totem, 1961) are pre-1952, the date of William Carlos Williams's Preface, but no publisher could be found until nearly ten years later.
4. Paul O'Neil, "The Only Rebellion Around," *Life*, 30 Nov. 1959, p. 126.
5. Ciardi, p. 12.
6. James Dickey, "From Babel to Byzantium," *Sewanee Review* 65 (1957):509.
7. Diana Trilling, "The Other Night at Columbia," *Partisan Review* 26 (Spring 1959):214–

230. See Robert Bly's parody, "The Other Night in Heaven," *The Fifties* 3 (1959):54–56.
8. Harold Rosenberg, "Six American Poets," *Commentary*, Oct. 1961, p. 349.
9. Printed in *Esquire*, Dec. 1965, pp. 151, 276, 278, 280.
10. Allen Ginsberg, *Reality Sandwiches* (San Francisco: City Lights, 1963), p. 9. Also printed with the letter to Cassaday in *Esquire*, Dec. 1965.
11. Quoted in Jane Kramer's *Allen Ginsberg in America* (New York: Random House, 1969), pp. 128–129.
12. Ibid., p. 40.
13. Amy Lowell, "The New Manner in Modern Poetry," *The New Republic*, 4 Mar. 1916, pp. 37, 40–41.
14. Jane Kramer, "Paterfamilias—I," *The New Yorker*, 17 Aug. 1968, p. 54.

15. Edmund Wilson, "Morose Ben Jonson," in Jonas A. Barish, ed., *Ben Jonson: A Collection of Critical Essays* (Englewood Cliffs: Prentice-Hall, 1963), pp. 60–74.

16. Kramer, "Paterfamilias—I," p. 60.

17. D. Jacobson, "America's Angry Young Men: How Rebellious Are the San Francisco Rebels?" *Commentary*, Dec. 1957, p. 477.

18. Allen Ginsberg, *Howl and Other Poems* (San Francisco: City Lights, 1956), p. 9.

19. Kramer, *Ginsberg in America*, pp. 119–120.

20. See Theodore Roszak's *The Making of a Counter Culture* (Garden City: Doubleday, 1969), pp. 205–238.

21. Allen Ginsberg, *Ankor Wat* (London: Fulcrum Press, [1968]), n. pag. Written in 1963. Except where otherwise noted, all quotations in section IV of this chapter are to *Ankor Wat*.

22. Allen Ginsberg, *Planet News* (San Francisco: City Lights, 1968), pp. 116–117.

23. Philip Whalen, "War Poem for Diane Di Prima," in Diane Di Prima, ed., *War Poems* (New York: The Poets Press, 1968), p. 86.

CHAPTER 3
DENISE LEVERTOV: PIERCING IN

1. Levertov's notes for a poetry seminar, quoted by Linda Welshimer Wagner, *Denise Levertov* (New York: Twayne, 1967), p. 140.

2. See Levertov's poem, "Claritas," *O Taste and See* (Norfolk: New Directions, 1964), p. 35; her comments in an interview with Walter Sutton, "A Conversation with Denise Levertov," *The Minnesota Review* 5 (1965):322–338; and the title poem of *Relearning the Alphabet* (New York: New Directions, 1970), p. 113.

3. The terms *phanopoeia, melopoeia,* and *logopoeia* are important and recurrent in Levertov's poetics, and she insists that poets ought to read Pound's *ABC of Reading* (where the terms are found) at least once a year.

4. Sutton, "Conversation," p. 329.

5. Denise Levertov, "Some Notes on Organic Form," *Poetry* 106 (1965):420.

6. Denise Levertov, "Advent 1966," *Relearning the Alphabet*, p. 4.

7. Denise Levertov, "Life at War," *The Sorrow Dance* (New York: New Directions, 1967), p. 79.

8. An extremely expressive paradox that appears in Zen and mystical writings, Pascal, Giordano Bruno, Alain de Lille, and the *Corpus Hermeticum*.

9. See Martin Buber's *I and Thou*, trans. Ronald Gregor Smith (Edinburgh: T. & T. Clark, [1957]) and James K. Lyon's, "Paul Celan and Martin Buber: Poetry as Dialogue," *PMLA* 86 (1971):110–120.

10. Denise Levertov, "An Argument," *The Floating Bear* 11 (1961), n. pag.

11. Ibid.

12. Denise Levertov, *With Eyes at the Back of Our Heads* (Norfolk: New Directions, 1960), p. 71.

13. Kenneth Rexroth, "The Poetry of Denise Levertov," *Poetry* 91 (1957):120.

14. See Ralph Mills, Jr., "Denise Levertov: Poetry of the Immediate," *Tri-Quarterly* 4, no. 2 (1962):31–37; reprinted in Edward Hungerford, ed., *Poets In Progress* (Chicago: Northwestern University Press, 1967), pp. 205–226.

15. Denise Levertov, *The Jacob's Ladder* (Norfolk: New Directions, 1960), p. 17.

16. Comments at a poetry reading at the University of Kansas, 2 Mar. 1967.

17. Denise Levertov, *The Double Image* (London: Cresset Press, 1946). Permission granted by Barrie & Jenkins, Publishers, London.

18. Denise Levertov, "H. D.: An Appreciation," *Poetry* 100 (1962): 183.

19. Reprinted as the second poem of *Relearning*, p. 4.

20. Sutton, "Conversation," p. 326.

21. Ideas that reach back to the *entelechy* of Aristotle, but are especially important to Buber and the *Hasidim*.

22. Denise Levertov, *Overland to the Islands* (Highlands, N.C.: Jargon Press, 1958), p. 2.

23. Robert Bly, *The Teeth-Mother Naked at Last* (San Francisco: City Lights, 1970), p. 16.

24. Foreword to Denise Levertov, ed., *Out of the War Shadow: The 1968 Peace Calendar* (New York: War Resisters League, 1967).

25. *The War Poems of Siegfried Sassoon* (London: William Heineman, 1919), p. 41.

26. Robert Bly, "Driving through Minnesota during the Hanoi Bombings," *The Light Around the Body* (New York: Harper & Row, 1967), p. 37.

27. Personal interview, 21 Apr. 1971.

28. Richard Howard, "Five Poets," *Poetry* 101 (1963):412–418.

CHAPTER 4
ROBERT BLY: WATERING THE ROCKS

1. Robert Bly, "The Work of James Wright," *The Sixties* 8 (1966): 77.

2. Cover blurb on back of Bly's *The Teeth-Mother Naked at Last* (San Francisco: City Lights, 1970).

3. Louis Simpson, "New Books of Poems," *Harper's Magazine*, Aug. 1968, p. 75.

4. Denise Levertov, in Walter Sutton, "A Conversation with Denise Levertov," *The Minnesota Review* 5 (1965):329.

5. Jonathan Williams, personal interview, 25 Feb. 1971.

6. Robert Bly, *The Fifties* 1 (1958): 39.

7. Ibid., p. 39.

8. Ibid., p. 38.

9. Robert Bly, "Some Thoughts on Lorca and René Char," *The Fifties* 3 (1959):8.

10. Robert Bly, "On Pablo Neruda," *The Nation*, 25 Mar. 1968, p. 414.

11. Robert Bly, *Silence in the Snowy Fields* (Middletown, Conn.: Wesleyan University Press, 1962).

12. Robert Bly, *The Light Around the Body* (New York: Harper & Row, 1967).

13. Robert Bly, "On Political Poetry," *The Nation*, 24 Apr. 1967, pp. 522–524.

14. Ibid., p. 522.

15. Martin Buber, *I and Thou*, trans. Ronald Gregor Smith (Edinburgh: T. & T. Clark, [1957]), p. 52.

16. See Robert Bly, "On Political Poetry," *The Nation*, 24 Apr. 1967, and Bly's Preface to *Forty Poems Touching on Recent American History* (Boston: Beacon Press, 1970), which he edited.

17. Comments at a poetry reading for The Resistance, 10 Apr. 1969, Lawrence, Kansas.

18. Robert Bly, "Crunk," *The Fifties* 2 (1959):11.

19. Louis Simpson, "The Inner Part," in Robert Bly and David Ray, eds., *A Poetry Reading Against the Vietnam War* (Madison, Minn.: The Sixties Press, 1966), p. 14.

20. Robert Bly, "Looking Backward," *Paris Review* 31 (1964): 107.

21. Especially such essays as "Thoughts on War and Death," in Sigmund Freud, *On War, Sex and Neurosis*, ed. Sander Katz (New York: Arts and Science Press, 1947).

22. Especially the lines on death in Part II. Personal interview with Duncan, 9 May 1969.

23. Robert Bly, "Lies," *The Nation*, 25 Mar. 1968, p. 417.

24. Michael Goldman, "Joyful in the Dark," *New York Times Book Review*, 18 Feb. 1968, pp. 10, 12; and Louis Simpson, "New Books of Poems," *Harper's Magazine*, Aug. 1968, pp. 73–77.

25. Louis Untermeyer, *Modern American Poetry* (New York: Harcourt, Brace & World, 1962), p. 288.

26. Robert Bly, "Murder as a Prudent Policy," Address before the National Book Award Committee, *Commonweal*, 22 Mar. 1968, p. 17.

27. "Locke," *Encyclopaedia Britannica*, eleventh edition, p. 850.

28. Henry Adams, *The Education of Henry Adams: An Autobiography* (New York: The Book League, 1928), p. 383.

29. Personal interview, 9 May 1969.

30. "National Book Awards," *The Nation*, 25 Mar. 1968, p. 414.

31. Wendell Berry, "Response to a War," *The Nation*, 24 Apr. 1967, pp. 527–528.

CHAPTER 5
ROBERT DUNCAN: IRREGULAR FIRE—EROS AGAINST AHRIMAN

1. Robert Pack, "To Be Loved for Its Voice," rev. of *Bending the Bow, Saturday Review*, 24 Aug. 1968, pp. 39–40.
2. Jim Harrison, "Pure Poetry," rev. of *Bending the Bow, New York Times Book Review*, 29 Sept. 1968, p. 66.
3. Ibid., p. 67.
4. Paul Zweig, "Robert Duncan's World," *Poetry* 111 (1967–1968): 403.
5. Quoted by Rudolph L. Nelson, "Edge of the Transcendent: The Poetry of Levertov and Duncan," *Southwest Review* 54 (1969):196.
6. Ibid., p. 197.
7. Robert Duncan, *The Years as Catches: First Poems 1939–1946* (Berkeley: Oyez), 1966, p. i.
8. Robert Duncan, *The First Decade: Selected Poems 1940–1950* (London: Fulcrum Press, 1968).
9. The first "Berkeley Poem," in Robert Duncan, *Heavenly City Earthly City* (Berkeley: The Gillick Press, 1947), p. 11.
10. Robert Duncan, *The Truth and Life of Myth: An Essay in Essential Autobiography* (New York: House of Books, 1968), p. 28.
11. Robert Duncan, "A Poem Beginning with a Line by Pindar," *Opening of the Field* (New York: Grove Press, 1960), pp. 66–67.
12. Robert Duncan, "Such Is the Sickness of Many a Good Thing,"

Bending the Bow (New York: New Directions, 1968), p. 6.
13. Robert Duncan, *Epilogos* (Los Angeles: Black Sparrow Press, 1967), p. 3. Reprinted in *Bending the Bow*, p. 134.
14. *Letters by Robert Duncan: Poems mcmlii-mcmlvi*, Jargon 14 (Highlands, N.C.: Jonathan Williams, 1958), n. pag., ltr. xxi.
15. See W. K. C. Guthrie, *Orpheus and the Greek Religion* (London: Methuen & Co., 1935), pp. 75–85. This and other volumes are cited by Duncan at the end of *Bending the Bow*.
16. Personal interview, 9 May 1969.
17. Robert Duncan, *The Sweetness and Greatness of Dante's Divine Comedy* (San Francisco: Open Space, 1956), n. pag. A lecture delivered 27 Oct. 1965 at the Dominican College of San Rafael.
18. Nelson, "Edge of the Transcendent," pp. 188–202.
19. G. R. S. Mead, *Thrice-Greatest Hermes: Studies in Hellenistic Theosophy and Gnosis* (London: John M. Watkins, 1949), pp. 307 ff.
20. Robert Duncan, *As Testimony: The Poem and the Scene* (San Francisco: The White Rabbit Press, 1964), p. 9.
21. W. K. C. Guthrie, *The Greek Philosophers from Thales to Aristotle* (New York: The Philosophical Library, 1950), pp. 38–39 ff., and G. S. Kirk and J. E. Raven, *The Pre-Socratic Philoso-*

phers: A Critical History with a Selection of Texts (Cambridge: Cambridge University Press, 1957), pp. 217–231.

22. Robert Duncan, *The Cat and the Blackbird*, with pictures by Jess (San Francisco: The White Rabbit Press, 1967).

23. Robert Duncan, "Statement on Poetics," Donald M. Allen, ed., *The New American Poetry* (New York: Grove Press, 1960), p. 400.

24. My application of the term "communist" to Duncan excited Edward Dorn (personal interview, Spring 1969) to exclaim "Duncan's no Marxist!" And that Duncan is not a "Communist" of the "bogeyman" variety should, I think, not need to be explained here.

25. Personal interview, 9 May 1969.

26. In Robert Duncan, *Derivations: Selected Poems 1950–1956* (Lon-don: Fulcrum Press, 1968), pp. 9 ff.

27. Gilbert Sorrentino, "Black Mountaineering," *Poetry* 116 (1970): 114.

28. Kirk and Raven, *The Pre-Socratic Philosophers*, p. 276.

29. Philip J. Davis, "Number," *Scientific American*, Sept. 1964, pp. 51–59.

30. Louis Simpson, "New Books of Poems," rev. of *Bending the Bow, Harper's Magazine*, Aug. 1968, pp. 73–77.

31. Robert Pack, "To Be Loved for Its Voice," *Saturday Review*, 24 Aug. 1968, p. 39.

32. Anonymous rev. of *Bending the Bow, Virginia Quarterly Review* 44 (Summer 1968), as excerpted in *Book Review Digest*.

33. Laurence Lieberman, "Critic of the Month," *Poetry* 114 (1969): 43.

CHAPTER 6
OTHER POEMS AND POETS AGAINST THE WAR

1. Excerpted in Robert Bly and David Ray, eds., *A Poetry Reading against the Vietnam War* (Madison, Minn.: The Sixties Press, 1967), p. 32.

2. Timothy Leary, "American Education as an Addictive Process and Its Cure," in H. Jaffe and J. Tytell, eds., *The American Experience: A Radical Reader* (New York: Harper & Row, 1970), p. 191.

3. Paul Blackburn, "The International Word," *The Nation*, 21 Apr. 1962, p. 360.

4. Charles Reich, *The Greening of America* (New York: Bantam, 1971), p. 26.

5. Thomas Merton, "War and the Crisis of Language," in Robert Ginsberg, ed., *The Critique of War* (Chicago: Henry Regnery, 1969), pp. 99–119.

6. Thomas Merton, *Cables to the Ace* (New York: New Directions, 1968), p. 3.

7. Elizabeth Bartlett, "Silent Vigil in Vietnam," in The Community Council to End the War in Vietnam, ed., *A Poetry Reading for*

Peace in Vietnam (Santa Barbara, Cal.: Unicorn Press, 1967), pp. 6–7.

8. AP News Dispatch in *Lawrence* [Kansas] *Daily Journal World*, 23 Dec. 1968.

9. Ibid.

10. Merton, "War and the Crisis of Language," pp. 114–115.

11. Curtis Harnack, "Week of the Angry Artist," *The Nation*, 25 Feb. 1967, p. 245.

12. Louis Simpson, "The American Dream," *The Nation*, 30 May 1966, p. 653.

13. Vern Rutsala, "News," in Denise Levertov, ed., *Out of the War Shadow: The 1968 Peace Calendar* (New York: War Resisters League, 1967), May 6.

14. Tony Towle, "Barbarossa Elegy," in *Artists and Writers Protest against the War in Viet Nam: Poems* (New York: Profiles Press, 1967), n. pag.

15. Stan Rice, "Waiting in the Cafe," in Nick Harvey, ed., *Mark in Time: Portraits and Poetry/San Francisco* (San Francisco: Glide Publishers, 1971), p. 116.

16. Marge Piercy, "The Organizer's Bogeyman," *Hard Loving* (Middletown, Conn.: Wesleyan University Press, 1969), p. 65.

17. Gene Bloom, "Words for a War," in Gary Youree and others, eds., *Poets for Peace: Poems from the Fast* (New York: n. p., 1967), p. 8.

18. Gilbert Sorrentino, "A Look Askance," in *Artists and Writers Protest*, n. pag.

19. Piercy, "Walking into Love," *Hard Loving*, p. 13.

20. Walter Lowenfels, "What Is Revolutionary," in his *The Poetry of My Politics*, vol. 2 of *My Man Lives: The Autobiography of Walter Lowenfels* (Homestead, Fla.: Olivant Press, 1968), p. 55.

21. Robert Duncan, *Fragments of a Disordered Devotion* (San Francisco: Gnomon Press, 1966), first published as fifty multilithed copies for friends in 1952.

22. Doug Blazek, "Sermon at a Delinquent Sunday Church," *Home News* 3 (1970), p. 20.

23. Thanasis Maskaleris, "Illuminations from Underground," in Tove Neville, ed., *Poems Read in the Spirit of Peace and Gladness* (San Francisco: Peace & Gladness Co-op Press, 1966), p. 60.

24. Diane Di Prima, *Revolutionary Letters Etc* (San Francisco: City Lights Books, 1971), ltr. 6.

25. Michael McClure, "Poisoned Wheat," *Star* (New York: Grove Press, 1970), p. 87.

26. "These Days" was also printed in Henry Braun, *The Vergil Woods* (New York: Atheneum, 1968).

27. D. A. Levy, "Kibbutz in the Sky —Book Two," *Xtra pp from D. A. Levy Anthology* (n. p., n. d.), n. pag. The poem is signed "Cleveland, 1967."

28. Personal interview, 9 Mar. 1969.

29. George Dowden, "Filthy Pictures Seized in London," *Evergreen Review* 11, no. 49 (1967), pp. 28–30.

30. RobertOh Faber, "Past the News

Stand Up," in Gary Youree and others, ed., *Poets for Peace: Poems from the Fast* (New York: n. p., 1967), p. 23.

31. Bert Lee, "Photograph: Mother and Father: 1930," in Walter Lowenfels, ed., *The Writing on the Wall* (Garden City: Doubleday, 1969), p. 86.

32. Victor Contoski, "War Poem," *Hanging Loose* 5–6 (Winter 1968):9–10.

33. Paul Goodman, "Black Flag, April 15, 1967," *Homespun of Oatmeal Gray* (New York: Random House, 1970). This poem, with a few differences, appeared in *Calendar*, Apr. 15.

34. Robert Lowell, "For the Union Dead: 'Reliquunt Omnia Servare Rem Publicam,'" *Critical Quarterly Poetry Supplement Number 7: New Poems, 1966*, pp. 21–22.

35. Robert Lowell, "Fall 1961," in Walter Lowenfels, *Where Is Vietnam? American Poets Respond* (New York: Doubleday, 1967), p. 79. Though Robert Lowell has been active against the Vietnam War from the outset, Vietnam does not often enter directly into his poems. Explicit references to war more often look back to details of World War II.

36. Diane Wakoski, *Greed: Parts 5–7* (Los Angeles: Black Sparrow Press, 1971), p. 13.

37. Bly, *The Light Around the Body* (New York: Harper & Row, 1967), p. 37.

38. Personal interview, Mar. 1969. "How Many Nights" was also included in Galway Kinnell, *Body Rags* (Boston: Houghton Mifflin Co., 1968), p. 22.

39. David Ignatow, "All Quiet," in Lowenfels, *Where Is Vietnam?* This poem first appeared in the April 1966 issue of *Poetry* (Copyright 1966 by Modern Poetry Association, Chicago). This excerpt is used by permission of the Editor of *Poetry*.

40. Gail Dusenberry, "The Shadow," in Levertov, ed., *Calendar*, May 13.

41. George Dowden, *Flight from America* (London: Mandarin, 1965), p. 12.

42. William Burford, "The Ambassadors," in Levertov, ed., *Calendar*, Apr. 22. This poem has also been published in Burford's *A World* (Austin: University of Texas Press, 1962).

43. Piercy, *Hard Loving*, p. 61; and Wendell Berry, "Dark with Power," in Levertov, ed., *Calendar*, May 27.

44. Michael Rossman, "15 December 1967: A Taste on the Breath of the Wind," a broadside (Urbana, Ill.: The Depot Press, 1968).

45. McClure, "Poisoned Wheat," *Star*, p. 88.

46. Lawrence Ferlinghetti, *After the Cries of the Birds* (San Francisco: Dave Haselwood Books, 1967), n. pag.

47. Gary Snyder, "A Curse on the Men in Washington, Pentagon," in Diane Di Prima, ed., *War Poems* (New York: The Poet's Press, 1968), p. 78.

CHAPTER 7
AGAINST CONCLUDINGS

1. Preface to Walter Lowenfels, ed., *Where Is Vietnam? American Poets Respond* (New York: Doubleday, 1967), p. x.
2. Denise Levertov, title poem, *Overland to the Islands* (Highlands, N.C.: Jargon Press, 1958).
3. *The Fish in the Sea Is Not Thirsty: Kabir Versions by Robert Bly* (Northwood Narrows, N.H.: Lillabulero Press, Inc., 1971), poem 10.
4. Robert Duncan, "Notes from a Reading at the Poetry Center, San Francisco, March 1, 1959," *Floating Bear* 31 (1965), n. pag.
5. Ibid., n. pag.
6. Kirby Congdon, "Manifesto." A one-page flier without publisher or date (Kenneth Spencer Memorial Library Literary Ephemera Collection, Box 2, Item 3).
7. Thanasis Maskaleris, "A Note for a Manifesto," in Tove Neville, ed., *Poems in the Spirit of Peace and Gladness* (San Francisco: Peace & Gladness Co-op Press, 1966), p. 54.
8. Charles Olson, "Against Wisdom as Such," *Black Mountain Review* 1 (Spring 1954):36.

LIST OF WORKS CITED

Adams, Henry. *The Education of Henry Adams: An Autobiography.* New York: The Book League, 1928.

Andrews, Charles Rolland. "A Thematic Guide to Selected American Poetry about the Second World War." Ph.D. dissertation, Western Reserve University, 1967.

Artists and Writers Protest against the War in Viet Nam: Poems. New York: Profiles Press, 1967.

Bergonzi, Bernard. "Before 1914: Writers and the Threat of War." *Critical Quarterly* 6 (1964):126–134.

Berry, Wendell. "Response to a War." *The Nation,* 24 Apr. 1967, pp. 527–528.

Blackburn, Paul. "The International Word." *The Nation,* 21 Apr. 1962, pp. 357–360.

Blazek, Doug. "Sermon at a Delinquent Sunday Church." *Home News* 3 (1970):20.

Bly, Robert. "The Collapse of James Dickey." *The Sixties* 9 (1967): 70–79.

———. *The Fish in the Sea Is Not Thirsty: Kabir Versions by Robert Bly.* Northwood Narrows, N.H.: Lillabulero Press, 1971.

———, ed. *Forty Poems Touching on Recent American History.* Boston: Beacon Press, 1970.

———. "Lies." *The Nation,* 25 Mar. 1968, p. 417.

———. *The Light Around the Body.* New York: Harper & Row, 1967.

———. "Looking Backward." *Paris Review* 31 (1964):107.

———. "Murder as a Prudent Policy" (address before National Book Award Committee). *Commonweal,* 22 Mar. 1968, p. 17.

———. "On Pablo Neruda." *The Nation,* 25 Mar. 1966, pp. 414–418.

———. "On Political Poetry." *The Nation,* 24 Apr. 1967, pp. 522–524.

———, and David Ray, eds. *A Poetry Reading against the Vietnam War.* Madison, Minnesota: The Sixties Press, 1967.

———. *Silence in the Snowy Fields.* Middleton, Conn.: Wesleyan University Press, 1962.

———. "Some Thoughts on Lorca and René Char." *The Fifties* 3 (1959):7–9.

———. *The Teeth-Mother Naked at*

Last. San Francisco: City Lights, 1970.

Brown, William Richard. "American Soldier Poets of the Second World War." Ph.D. dissertation, University of Michigan, 1965.

Buber, Martin. *I and Thou,* trans. Ronald Gregor Smith. Edinburgh: T. & T. Clark, [1957].

Ciardi, John. "Epitaph for the Dead Beats." *Saturday Review,* 6 Feb. 1960, pp. 11–13.

Clarke, George Herbert, ed. *A Treasury of War Poetry: British and American Poems of the World War 1914–1919.* Second Series. Boston: Houghton Mifflin, 1919.

Coates, Florence E. "Their Victory Won." *Harper's Magazine,* Dec. 1918, p. 77.

Contoski, Victor. "War Poem." *Hanging Loose* 5–6 (Winter 1968): 9–10.

Cousins, Norman. "No Time for Poetry." *Saturday Review of Literature,* 3 May 1941, p. 8.

"Crunk." "The Work of James Wright." *The Sixties* 8 (1966): 52–78.

Daiches, David. "Poetry and the War." *Poetry* 59 (1942):209–210.

Davis, Philip J. "Number." *Scientific American,* Sept. 1964, pp. 51–59.

Dickey, James. "From Babel to Byzantium." *Sewanee Review* 65 (1957):508–530.

Di Prima, Diane. *Revolutionary Letters Etc.* San Francisco: City Lights, 1971.

———, ed. *War Poems.* New York City: The Poets Press Inc., 1968.

Dowden, George. "Filthy Pictures Seized in London." *Evergreen Review* 11, no. 49 (1967):28–30.

———. *Flight from America.* London: Mandarin Books Ltd., 1965.

Duncan, Robert. *As Testimony: The Poem and the Scene.* San Francisco: The White Rabbit Press, 1964.

———. *Bending the Bow.* New York: New Directions, 1968.

———. *A Book of Resemblances: Poems 1950–1953.* New Haven: Henry Wenning, 1966.

———. *The Cat and the Blackbird.* San Francisco: The White Rabbit Press, 1967.

———. *Derivations: Selected Poems 1950–1956.* London: Fulcrum Press, 1968.

———. *Epilogos.* Los Angeles: Black Sparrow Press, 1967.

———. *The First Decade: Selected Poems 1940–1950.* London: Fulcrum Press, 1968.

———. *Fragments of a Disordered Devotion.* San Francisco: Gnomon Press, 1966.

———. *Heavenly City, Earthly City.* Berkeley: The Gillick Press, 1947.

———. *Letters by Robert Duncan: Poems mcmliii–mcmlvi.* Jargon 14. Highlands, N.C.: Jonathan Williams, 1958.

———. *The Opening of the Field.* New York: Grove Press, 1960.

———. *Roots and Branches.* New York: Scribner's, 1964.

———. *The Sweetness and Greatness of Dante's Divine Comedy.* San Francisco: Open Space, 1965.

———. "Statement on Poetics." In *The New American Poetry,* ed.

Donald M. Allen, pp. 400–407. New York: Grove Press, 1960.

——. *The Truth and Life of Myth: An Essay in Essential Autobiography.* New York: House of Books, 1968.

——. *The Years as Catches: First Poems 1939–1946.* Berkeley: Oyez, 1966.

Fein, Richard. "Mary and Bellona: The War Poetry of Robert Lowell." *Southern Review* 1 (1965):820–834.

——. "Major American Poetry of World War II: A Critical Study." Ph.D. dissertation, New York University, 1960.

Feld, Ross. *Winter Poems.* N.p.: Academy Press, 1966.

Ferlinghetti, Lawrence. *After the Cries of the Birds.* San Francisco: Dave Haselwood Books, 1967.

Finn, James. *Protest: Pacifism and Politics.* New York: Random House, 1967.

Ford, Hugh D. *A Poet's War: British Poets and the Spanish Civil War.* Philadelphia: University of Pennsylvania Press, 1965.

Foxcroft, Frank, ed. *War Verse.* New York: Crowell, 1918.

Freud, Sigmund. *On War, Sex and Neurosis,* ed. Sander Katz. New York: Arts and Science Press, 1947.

Ginsberg, Allen. *Ankor Wat.* London: Fulcrum Press, [1968].

——. *The Empty Mirror.* New York: Totem, 1961.

——. *Howl and Other Poems.* San Francisco: City Lights, 1956.

——. "Letter to Neil Cassaday," 14 May 1953. Printed in *Esquire,* Dec. 1965, pp. 151, 276, 278, 280.

——. *Planet News.* San Francisco: City Lights, 1968.

——. *Reality Sandwiches.* San Francisco: City Lights, 1963.

Goldman, Eric F. "The White House and the Intellectuals." *Harper's Magazine,* Jan. 1969, pp. 31–45.

Goldman, Michael. "Joyful in the Dark." Review of *Light Around the Body,* by Robert Bly. *New York Times Book Review,* 18 Feb. 1968, pp. 10, 12.

Golffing, Francis, and Barbara Gibbs. "The Public Voice: Remarks on Poetry Today." *Commentary,* July 1959, pp. 63–69.

Goode, Stephen H. "British War Poetry of the Second World War." Ph.D. dissertation, University of Pennsylvania, 1958.

Goodman, Paul. *Homespun of Oatmeal Gray.* New York: Random House, Inc., 1970.

Graves, Robert. "*Playboy* Interview: Robert Graves, a Candid Conversation with the Venerable Poet, Author, Critic and Mythologist." *Playboy,* Dec. 1970, pp. 103–116.

——. *The Poems of Robert Graves.* Garden City: Doubleday, 1958.

——. *The White Goddess: A Historical Grammar of Poetic Myth.* New York: Vintage Books, 1959.

——. *Fairies and Fusiliers.* London: William Heineman, 1917.

Guthrie, W. K. C. *The Greek Philosophers from Thales to Aristotle.* New York: Philosophical Library, 1950.

——. *Orpheus and Greek Religion.* London: Methuen, 1935.

Harnack, Curtis. "Week of the

Angry Artist." *The Nation*, 20 Feb. 1967, pp. 245–248.

Harrison, Jim. "Pure Poetry." *New York Times Book Review*, 29 Sept. 1968, pp. 66–67.

Harrison, John R. *The Reactionaries: A Study of the Anti-Democratic Intelligentsia*. New York: Schocken Books, 1967.

Hart, James A. "American Poetry of the First World War (1914 to 1920): A Survey and Checklist." Ph.D. dissertation, Duke University, 1964.

Harvey, Nick, ed. *Mark in Time: Portraits and Poetry/San Francisco*. San Francisco: Glide Publishers, 1971.

Howard, Richard. "Five Poets." *Poetry* 101 (1963):412–418.

Jacobson, D. "America's Angry Young Men: How Rebellious Are the San Francisco Rebels?" *Commentary*, Dec. 1957, pp. 475–479.

Jarrell, Randall. *The Complete Poems*. New York: Farrar, Straus & Giroux, 1969.

Karl, Frederick R., and Marvin Magalaner. *Great Twentieth-Century English Novels*. New York: Noonday Press, 1959.

Kherdian, David. "Brother Antoninus." In *Six Poets of the San Francisco Renaissance*, pp. 131–151. Fresno: Giligia Press, 1965.

Kirk, G. S., and J. E. Raven. *The Pre-Socratic Philosophers: A Critical History with a Selection of Texts*. Cambridge: Cambridge University Press, 1957.

Kramer, Jane. *Allen Ginsberg in America*. New York: Random House, 1969.

———. "Paterfamilias—I." *The New Yorker*, 17 Aug. 1968, pp. 32–73.

———. "Paterfamilias—II." *The New Yorker*, 24 Aug. 1968, pp. 38–91.

Lawrence, David Herbert. *Studies in Classic American Literature*. New York: Viking, 1968.

Leary, Timothy. "American Education as an Addictive Process and Its Cure." In *The American Experience: A Radical Reader*, ed. Harold Jaffe and John Tytell, pp. 191–202. New York: Harper & Row, 1970.

Levertov, Denise. "An Argument." *Floating Bear* 11 (1961):n. pag.

———. *The Double Image*. London: Cresset Press, 1946.

———. "H. D.: An Appreciation." *Poetry* 100 (1962):182–186.

———. *The Jacob's Ladder*. Norfolk, Conn.: New Directions, 1961.

———. *O Taste and See*. Norfolk, Conn.: New Directions, 1964.

———. *Overland to the Islands*. Highlands, N.C.: Jargon Press, 1958.

———, ed. *Out of the War Shadow: The 1968 Peace Calendar*. New York: War Resisters League, 1967.

———. *Relearning the Alphabet*. New York: New Directions, 1970.

———. "Some Notes on Organic Form. *Poetry* 106 (1965):420–425.

———. *The Sorrow Dance*. New York: New Directions, 1966.

———. *To Stay Alive*. New York: New Directions, 1971.

———. *With Eyes at the Back of Our Heads*. Norfolk, Conn.: New Directions, 1960.

Levy, D. A. *Xtra pp from D. A. Levy Anthology*. N.p., n. pub., n.d.

Lieberman, Lawrence. "Critic of the Month: VII, a Confluence of Poets." *Poetry* 114 (1969):40–58.

Lowell, Amy. "The New Manner in Modern Poetry." *The New Republic*, 4 Mar. 1916, pp. 37, 40–41.

Lowell, Robert. "For the Union Dead: 'Reliquunt Omnia Servare Rem Publicam.'" In *Critical Quarterly Poetry Supplement Number 7: New Poems, 1966*, pp. 21–22.

Lowenfels, Walter. *The Poetry of My Politics*. Vol. 2 of *My Man Lives: The Autobiography of Walter Lowenfels*. Homestead, Fla.: Olivant Press, 1968.

———, ed. *Where Is Vietnam? American Poets Respond*. New York: Doubleday, 1967.

———, ed. *The Writing on the Wall*. Garden City: Doubleday, 1969.

Lyon, James K. "Paul Celan and Martin Buber: Poetry as Dialogue." *PMLA* 86 (1971):110–120.

Mailer, Norman. "The White Negro." In *The American Experience: A Radical Reader*, ed. Harold Jaffe and John Tytell, pp. 8–27. New York: Harper & Row, 1970.

McClure, Michael. *Star*. New York: Grove Press, 1970.

Mead, G. R. S. *Thrice-Greatest Hermes: Studies in Hellenistic Theosophy and Gnosis*. London: John M. Watkins, 1949.

Merton, Thomas. *Cables to the Ace*. New York: New Directions, 1968.

———. "War and the Crisis of Language." In *The Critique of War*, ed. Robert Ginsberg, pp. 99–119. Chicago: Henry Regnery, 1969.

Mills, Ralph, Jr. "Denise Levertov: The Poetry of the Immediate." In *Poets in Progress*, ed. Edward Hungerford, pp. 205–226. Chicago: Northwestern University Press, 1967.

———. "Denise Levertov: Poetry of the Immediate." *Tri-Quarterly* 4 (Winter 1962):31–37.

Milne, A. A. *Peace with Honour*. New York: E. P. Dutton, 1934.

"The National Book Awards." *The Nation*, 25 Mar. 1968, pp. 413–414.

Nelson, Rudolph L. "Edge of the Transcendent: The Poetry of Levertov and Duncan." *Southwest Review* 54 (1969):188–202.

Nemerov, Howard, ed. *Poets on Poetry*. New York: Basic Books, 1966.

Neville, Tove, ed. *Poems Read in the Spirit of Peace and Gladness*. San Francisco: Peace & Gladness Co-op Press, 1966.

Olson, Charles. "Against Wisdom as Such." *Black Mountain Review* 1, no. 1 (Spring 1954):35–39.

O'Neil, Paul. "The Only Rebellion Around." *Life*, 30 Nov. 1959, pp. 115 ff.

Pack, Robert. "To Be Loved for Its Voice." *Saturday Review*, 24 Aug. 1968, pp. 39–40.

Piercy, Marge. *Hard Loving*. Middletown, Conn.: Wesleyan University Press, 1970.

Plowman, Max. *An Introduction to the Study of Blake*. London: J. M. Dent & Sons, 1927.

A Poetry Reading for Peace in Viet-

nam. Santa Barbara: Community Council to End the War, 1967.

Postman, Neil, and Charles Weingartner. *Teaching as a Subversive Activity*. New York: Dell, 1969.

Reich, Charles, *The Greening of America*. New York: Bantam, 1971.

Rexroth, Kenneth. "The Poetry of Denise Levertov." *Poetry* 91 (1957):120–123.

———. "San Francisco Letter." *Evergreen Review* 1, no. 2 (1957): 5–14.

Rosenberg, Harold. "Six American Poets." *Commentary*, Oct. 1961, p. 349.

Rossman, Michael. *15 December 1967: A Taste on the Breath of the Wind*, a broadside. Urbana, Ill.: The Depot Press, 1968.

Roszak, Theodore. *The Making of a Counter Culture: Reflections on the Technocratic Society and Its Youthful Opposition*. Garden City: Doubleday, 1969.

Sandburg, Carl. *The Complete Poems of Carl Sandburg*. New York: Harcourt Brace Jovanovich, 1970.

Shapiro, Karl. *V-Letter and Other Poems*. New York: Reynal & Hitchcock, 1944.

Simpson, Louis. "American Dream." *The Nation*, 30 May 1966, p. 653.

———. "New Books of Poems." Rev. of *Bending the Bow*, by Robert Duncan. *Harper's Magazine*, Aug. 1968, pp. 73–77.

Sorrentino, Gilbert. "Black Mountaineering." Rev. of *The First*

Decade and *Roots and Branches*, by Robert Duncan. *Poetry* 116 (May, 1970):110–120.

Stead, C. K. *The New Poetic*. London: Hutchinson, 1964.

Sutton, Walter. "A Conversation with Denise Levertov." *The Minnesota Rev.*, 5 no. 3–4 (1965):322–338.

Tate, Allen. *Reactionary Essays on Poetry and Ideas*. New York: Scribner's, 1936.

Trilling, Diana. "The Other Night at Columbia." *Partisan Review* 26 (Spring 1959):214–230.

Untermeyer, Louis, ed. *Modern American Poetry*. New York: Harcourt, Brace & World, 1962.

Wagner, Linda Welshimer. *Denise Levertov*. New York: Twayne Publishers, 1967.

Wakoski, Diane. *Greed: Parts 5–7*. Los Angeles: Black Sparrow Press, 1971.

"We Talk to Allen Ginsberg." *Mademoiselle*, Aug. 1969, p. 343.

Williams, Oscar, ed. *The War Poets: An Anthology of the War Poetry of the 20th Century*. New York: John Day, 1945.

Wilson, Edmund. "Morose Ben Jonson." In *Ben Jonson: A Collection of Critical Essays,* ed. Jonas A. Barish. Englewood Cliffs: Prentice-Hall, 1963.

Youree, Gary, and others, eds. *Poets for Peace: Poems from the Fast*. [New York: n.p., 1967.]

Zweig, Paul. "Robert Duncan's World." *Poetry* 3 (1967–1968): 402–404.

INDEX